Jan Karon's

Mitford Cookbook & Kitchen Reader

Jan Karon's
Mitford Cookbook & Kitchen Reader

EDITED BY MARTHA McINTOSH

VIKING

VIKING
Published by the Penguin Group
Penguin Group (USA) Inc., 375 Hudson Street, New York, New York 10014, U.S.A.
Penguin Group (Canada), 10 Alcorn Avenue, Toronto, Ontario, Canada M4V 3B2 (a division of Pearson Penguin Canada Inc.) · Penguin Books Ltd, 80 Strand, London WC2R 0RL, England · Penguin Ireland, 25 St. Stephen's Green, Dublin 2, Ireland (a division of Penguin Books Ltd) · Penguin Books Australia Ltd, 250 Camberwell Road, Camberwell, Victoria 3124, Australia (a division of Pearson Australia Group Pty Ltd) · Penguin Books India Pvt Ltd, 11 Community Centre, Panchsheel Park, New Delhi—110 017, India · Penguin Group (NZ), Cnr Airborne and Rosedale Roads, Albany, Auckland, New Zealand (a division of Pearson Ne/w Zealand Ltd) · Penguin Books (South Africa) (Pty) Ltd, 24 Sturdee Avenue, Rosebank, Johannesburg 2196, South Africa

Penguin Books Ltd, Registered Offices: 80 Strand, London WC2R 0RL, England

First published in 2004 by Viking Penguin, a member of Penguin Group (USA) Inc.

1 3 5 7 9 10 8 6 4 2

Copyright © Jan Karon, 2004
Illustrations copyright © Penguin Group (USA) Inc., 2004
All rights reserved

Illustrations by Donna Kae Nelson

Portions of this book first appeared in *At Home in Mitford; A Light in the Window; These High, Green Hills; Out to Canaan; A New Song; A Common Life; In This Mountain;* and *Shepherds Abiding.* Copyright © Jan Karon, 1994, 1995, 1996, 1997, 1999, 2001, 2002, 2003. By permission of Viking Penguin, a division of Penguin Group (USA) Inc.

"The Right Ingredients" originally appeared in *Victoria* magazine.

Grateful acknowledgment is made for permission to reprint "I Sing a Song of the Saints of God" by Lesbia Scott from the book of the same title. Text © 1929 by Lesbia Scott. Used by permission of Morehouse Publishing, a Continuum imprint.

LIBRARY OF CONGRESS CATALOGING IN PUBLICATION DATA
Karon, Jan, date.
Jan Karon's Mitford cookbook & kitchen reader / edited by Martha McIntosh.
p. cm.
Includes index.
ISBN 0-670-03239-5
1. Cookery. 2. Cookery in literature. I. Title: Mitford cookbook & kitchen reader.
II. Title: Mitford cookbook and kitchen reader. III. McIntosh, Martha. IV. Title.
TX714.K3673 2004
641.5—dc22   2004051894

This book is printed on acid-free paper. ∞

Printed in the United States of America · Set in Centaur, Bellevue, and Filosofia
Art direction and design by Jaye Zimet

Dedicated to my faithful Mitford readers,

and to all who know that good food isn't just for bodily nourishment,

it's also for making memories, drawing families close, and sweetening friendships.

Here's your Mitford author, sandwiched between two great cooks:
my mother, Wanda Setzer, and my sister, Brenda Furman

*Looking over the manuscript of this book with my
literary editor and friend, Carolyn Carlson*

Introduction

They say that once you learn to ride a bicycle, you never forget how to do it. The same principle, I've discovered, does not apply to cooking. Indeed, I was once a pretty good cook, but my skills have fallen on hard times—and a roast chicken is absolutely the very best I currently can do.

Here's why.

Cooking takes time. It takes focus. It takes love. And that's what I pour, instead, into the work of creating and running an entire town named Mitford.

After a day of heaving and hauling several dozen obstinate, funny, cantankerous characters around in my head, I'm famished.

Thus, on most evenings you may find me standing at the sink, devouring such culinary delicacies as pepperoni left over from last week's pizza, or fried chicken from the gas station up the road. If I am blessed with the company of my sister, Brenda, we might have her luscious pork roast with mashed potatoes and gravy and a cake of golden-crusted cornbread, or if dear Darlene is here, we might have Mexican Chicken Bake, which I found posted on my website by Cajun Lady.

As you can see, I depend heavily upon someone else's cooking these days, which is one reason I invited cookbook editor Martha McIntosh to take over the job of creating and borrowing and generally rounding up and testing the recipes herein.

Martha came with stunning credentials, not the least of which is that she was born in Mississippi, just down the road from Father Tim, and is wise in the ways of all the things he loves. A classic Southern ambrosia? She grew up on it. A totally scrumptious chicken pie? She learned this secret at her grandmother's knee. Sweet ice tea, banana puddin', and crispy fried chicken? Piece of cake!

I went to Atlanta, where Martha lives, to make absolutely, positively certain that she could cook like Puny and Louella, and bake like Winnie and Esther. And she *can*!

In truth, there's not a Mitford cook who wouldn't applaud Martha's talents, just as her husband and children did as she went through the year-long testing of every single recipe in this book. To find out more about Martha McIntosh, see page 354.

I've also worked closely with Martha to give each ingredient the ring of authenticity. Would Louella fry her chicken in bacon fat, lard, or Crisco? Lard. (One doesn't easily get away from their raising.)

Would Lottie Greer use extra-virgin olive oil or vegetable oil? Vegetable oil. (She would use whatever is on the shelf of her brother's country store.)

And what about upscale ingredients like balsamic vinegar? Cynthia is one of the few Mitford cooks who use balsamic vinegar, as everyone else continues agreeably with the old-fashioned cider variety. Indeed, we've been picky, picky, picky about each and every ingredient and recipe, so that when you make one of our dishes, your family and friends can sit down to the real thing—and feel truly at home in Mitford.

Of course, this cookbook isn't just for cooking.

It's also for reading.

So, if you're not in the mood to create Puny's cornbread or Ray Cunningham's cole slaw or Edith Mallory's seductive crab casserole, curl up with our cookbook and read.

From *At Home in Mitford* to *Light From Heaven*, we've tried to include all the food scenes you'd like to revisit. You'll also find table blessings, Puny's Saving Graces, and a scrapbook of photographs of my family and me.

I hope you'll discover some fun in these pages. You might even ask one of the family to read aloud the passage in which your special Mitford dish makes its appearance. If your meal contains several recipes from our cookbook, that would allow for more readings and an even happier family time.

May God tenderly bless the cook who invests the love and energy to prepare these favorite Mitford dishes, and may His gracious favor rest upon each and every one with whom they are enjoyed.

Draw close. Hold hands. Life is short. God is good.

Yours faithfully,

Contents

A Light in the Window *excerpts, favorite recipes, helpful hints* 87

A Common Life *excerpts, favorite recipes, helpful hints* — 125

Jan Karon's
Mitford Cookbook
& Kitchen Reader

xvii

In This Mountain *excerpts, favorite recipes, helpful hints*

Shepherds Abiding *excerpts, favorite recipes, helpful hints*

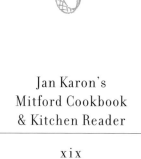

Jan Karon's
Mitford Cookbook
& Kitchen Reader

At Home in Mitford

On rare occasions, and for no special reason he could think of, he imagined he was sitting by the fire in the study, in the company of a companionable wife.

He would be reading, and she would be sitting across from him in a wing chair.

In this idyll, he could not see her face, but he knew it had a girlish sweetness, and she was always knitting. Knitting, he thought, was a comfort to the soul. It was regular. It was repetitious. And, in the end, it amounted to something.

In this dream, there was always a delectable surprise on the table next to his chair, and nearly always it was a piece of pie. In his bachelor's heart of hearts, he loved pie with an intensity that alarmed him. Yet, when he was offered seconds, he usually refused. "Wouldn't you like another piece of this nice coconut pie, Father?" he might be asked. "No, I don't believe I'd care for any more," he'd say. An outright lie!

In this imaginary fireside setting, he would not talk much, he thought. But now and then, he might speak of church matters, or read Blake or Wordsworth aloud, and try a sermon outline on his companion.

That would be a luxury far greater than any homemade sweet—to have someone listen to his outline and nod encouragement or, even, for heaven's sake, disagree.

—*At Home in Mitford*, Chapter One

Jan Karon's
Mitford Cookbook
& Kitchen Reader

Miss Sadie Baxter was the last surviving member of one of Mitford's oldest families.

At the age of eighty-six, she occupied the largest house in the village, with the most sweeping view. And she owned the most land, much of it given over to an aged but productive apple orchard. In fact, the village cooks said that the best pies weren't made of Granny Smiths, but of the firm, slightly tart Sadie Baxters, as they'd come to be called.

As far as anyone knew, Miss Sadie had never given away any of the money her father had earned in his lumber operation in the valley. But she dearly loved to give away apples—by the sack, by the peck, by the bushel.

—*At Home in Mitford*, Chapter Two

Baxter Apple Pie

½ cup	unsalted butter, melted, more for greasing the pan
½ recipe	*Pastry for a Double Crust Pie* (page 4) (Halve the recipe, or make the whole recipe and freeze half)
¾ cup	granulated sugar
¼ cup	brown sugar
¼ teaspoon	salt
1½ tablespoons	White Lily all-purpose flour
2 teaspoons	apple pie spice
2 large	eggs
5 medium	Winesap, Granny Smith, or Rome Beauty apples, peeled and chopped
	Vanilla ice cream, for serving

Preheat the oven to 375°F. Lightly butter a 9-inch pie pan. Roll out the pastry dough and fit it into the pan. Refrigerate while you're making the filling.

Use an electric mixer to combine the butter, granulated sugar, brown sugar, salt, flour, and apple pie spice. Add the eggs, one at a time, mixing well after each addition. Remove the bowl from the mixer and stir in the chopped apples.

Pour the filling in the prepared crust. Bake the pie for 30 to 35 minutes, or until the custard is set. Remove the pie from the oven to a cooling rack, and cool completely before serving.

Serve pie slices with a scoop of vanilla ice cream.

"Any Southerner worth his pie crust knows that White Lily is the only flour worth stocking in the larder."

—RICHARD DAVID STORY,
NEW YORK MAGAZINE

❖ *If you have trouble finding apple pie spice, substitute 1¼ teaspoon cinnamon, ¼ teaspoon nutmeg, and ½ teaspoon allspice.*

Pastry for a Double Crust Pie

2½ cups	White Lily all-purpose flour, more for rolling out the dough
1 teaspoon	salt
1 teaspoon	granulated sugar
½ cup	unsalted butter, chilled and cut into small pieces
½ cup	shortening, chilled and cut into small pieces
1 tablespoon	sour cream
4 to 5 tablespoons	ice water

Place the flour, salt, and sugar in the bowl of a food processor fitted with the steel blade and pulse to combine. Add the butter to the flour mixture and give the food processor 5 short pulses. Add the shortening and give it another 5 short pulses. Add the sour cream and give it 5 final short pulses. Turn the mixture into a large bowl.

Sprinkle 3 tablespoons of ice water over the mixture. Using a rubber spatula, press down on the dough until it sticks together. Add more ice water if needed, 1 tablespoon at a time. Divide the dough in half, shape each piece into a ball with your hands, and then flatten into a disk. Dust each half lightly with flour, wrap in plastic, and refrigerate at least 30 minutes before rolling out.

To roll out the dough, lightly flour a rolling pin and the countertop. Using 1 disk (half of the recipe), roll the dough into a circle that is 2 inches larger than the pie pan. Lightly flour the top of the rolled dough using a pastry brush. Fold the dough in half, then in half again. Place the folded dough in the prepared pan and unfold. Trim the excess dough to ½ inch and fold under around the edges. After shaping, chill the dough for at least 30 minutes before filling or baking.

❖ *When preparing your pie recipe, make sure you've allowed enough time for the dough to rest in the refrigerator for at least 30 minutes, and up to 8 hours, before rolling out to prevent the pastry from excessive shrinkage when baked. The pastry can also be made ahead and frozen for up to 2 months.*

❖ *If time is short, use a Pillsbury prepared pie crust for the pie crust recipe.*

"I gain ten pounds just reading a Mitford book!" someone writes to say.

Why is there so much food in the Mitford books?

First, food is a great way of communicating. When I write about Dooley loving fried baloney sandwiches, you can connect with that. When I write about Puny baking cornbread and Louella frying chicken, most of you can connect with that. (Hardly anyone, of course, connects with Percy Mosely's gizzard special in *In This Mountain*, but that's another story.)

Food is something we all understand; it's a common language. And it's one more way readers are encouraged to feel at home in Mitford.

There's a deeper reason, however, why food is endlessly referenced in the Mitford books.

When I began writing the series in 1990, I had stepped out on faith and left a successful writing career in advertising. In order to put food on the table, I freelanced in my old profession while trying to learn how to write a book.

Two things happened:

One, I found that I had absolutely nothing to say. And two, the economy went into a serious downturn, which meant that ad agencies weren't hiring freelancers; they were struggling to keep their own people busy.

So, (a) I had stepped out on faith to a new life of writing books, but discovered I knew nothing *at all* about writing books, (b) the money wasn't coming in, and (c) the bills were piling up.

Woman's dream turns to nightmare?

Yes and no. What happened during this long and anxious period is that God was drawing me closer to Himself, strengthening my faith, encouraging my trust.

We know that nothing grows on the high mountain peaks; fertility lies in the valleys.

After journeying with me through a very long valley, He brought me out with "something to say."

One night while lying in bed, the mental image of a priest walking down a village street came to me. In my imagination, I followed him as he walked. He went to a dog named Barnabas, and they went to a boy named Dooley.

That's when I got out of bed and went to my desk and started to write.

Who would want to write a book about a balding, overweight, sixty-something small-town priest? Not me! And would anybody actually *read* such a book? I knew only that I'd found something *I* would like to read. Thus, I wrote on.

And while the ideas were starting to flow, the money was most definitely *not.*

Indeed, my first novel is loaded with food references largely because my cupboards were bare, and I was writing hungry. No self-pity here, however. I could wear my size tens!

This is when I learned to make soup from chicken bones, which is explained on the next page. It has a sort of World War II spirit, which some of you will recognize from personal experience.

After you've enjoyed several meals from what was originally roasted chicken (see Cynthia's recipe on page 145), sauté some chopped onion in a little olive oil, add the remains of the chicken, bones and all (that's where much of the flavor still resides), pour in two or three cups of water, and start simmering. Add salt and pepper, a handful of rice or pasta, some left-over canned peas, a carrot if you have it, a few garlic cloves. As it simmers some more, it will begin to smell marvelous. You will feel happy. You will feel expectant. *You will feel rich!*

I learned a lot of other things about making "something out of nothing" as I wrote the first three books, including how to cut open a presumably empty toothpaste tube and find that *it isn't empty at all.* And trust me, in the absence of Chanel's costly Serum Extreme, Vaseline works just fine as a night cream.

What I learned mostly, however, is that God is faithful. He really does love us. And here's what some may have trouble believing:

He really does want the best for His children.

If you're on a painful journey through the valley, ask Him to walk through it with you. Make some chicken soup from chicken bones, and give thanks. And when you finally get to the mountain top, give thanks for the valley you've just been through. Because you will almost certainly go there again. And again, it will be hard.

But it will be good.

—Jan Karon

im, Hal here. I heard what's going on with the painting, and in case you're feeling sick and tired of the whole thing, I'd like to give you a prescription."

He didn't know how he felt about receiving medical care from a vet.

"Here it is: be ready at eight o'clock in the morning and I'll pick you and Barnabas up in the truck. We'll spend the day at Meadowgate, chasing rabbits and looking for woodchucks. For supper, Marge'll make a big chicken pie, and I'll bring you back in time to get your beauty sleep for church on Sunday."

If he had gotten a call to say he'd won the lottery, he couldn't have been happier. Thank heaven he'd worked all week on his sermon, thereby giving him the freedom of an entire Saturday.

He drank two full mugs of coffee, which was unusual, with cream, which was even more unusual, and, according to Emma, spent the rest of the morning "chattering like a magpie."

~

Meadowgate Farm was situated in one of the most beautiful valleys around Mitford. Just ten miles from the village, the land began to roll steeply, looking like the pictures he had seen of Scotland.

A flock of sheep grazed in one green pasture, across the fence from a herd of contented Guernseys. The white blossoms of wild bloodwort gleamed along the roadsides, and here and there the bank of an old farmplace was massed with creeping pink phlox.

You leadeth me beside still waters! he thought happily. You restoreth my soul!

It was a glorious morning, drenched with birdsong, and as they turned into the drive, a horde of farm dogs came bounding toward the red truck. There was Buckwheat, an English foxhound. Bowser, a chow. Baudelaire, a soulful dachshund. Bodacious, a Welsh corgi. And Bonemeal, a mixed-breed foundling who, as a puppy, had dug up the new tulip bulbs in order to eat the fertilizer.

The rector opened his door cautiously, and Barnabas dived into the barking throng. Was it possible his hearing could be permanently impaired? "Let 'em get acquainted," Hal said.

At the back door, Marge gave Father Tim a vigorous hug, which he returned with feeling.

"Tim! You've got your annual planting tan!"

"And you've got your perennial joie de vivre!"

In the center of the kitchen was a large pine table, bleached by age, with benches on either side. A Mason jar of early wildflowers sat in the center, along with a deep-dish apple pie, fresh from the oven. A dazzling beam of light fell through the windows that looked out to the stables.

Their guest stood transfixed. "A foretaste of heaven!" he said, feeling an instant freshness of spirit.

"Sit," said Marge, whose blonde hair was captured in a bandanna the color of her dress. "We'll start with freshly ground coffee and cinnamon stickies. Then, I've packed lunches, because I hear you guys are going tromping in the woods."

"'Til we drop," promised Hal, lighting his pipe. "Tim has some heavy-duty stress to contend with. Holy Week, two Easter services, a Vermeer, a new dog the size of a Buick, fourteen azaleas to get in the ground, and," he looked at Father Tim, "there must be something else."

"A bone spur in my left heel," he said, cheerfully.

Marge's Deep-Dish Apple Pie

2 tablespoons	unsalted butter, more for greasing the pan	½ cup	granulated sugar, more for sprinkling on top
1 recipe	*Pastry for a Double Crust Pie* (page 4)	¼ cup	White Lily all-purpose flour
		1 teaspoon	ground cinnamon
7 medium	Granny Smith apples, peeled and sliced	½ teaspoon	ground nutmeg
		¼ teaspoon	salt
1½ tablespoons	fresh lemon juice		Half-and-half, for brushing the crust
¾ cup	brown sugar		

Preheat the oven to 400°F. Lightly butter a 9-inch deep-dish pie plate. Roll out half of the pastry dough and fit it into the pan. Press a piece of aluminum foil directly on top of the dough (covering the bottom and sides of dough) and fill with pie weights or dried beans. Bake the bottom crust for 10 minutes. Remove the pie plate from the oven and remove the pie weights and foil.

Place the apples and lemon juice in a large bowl and mix well. In a smaller bowl, combine the brown sugar, granulated sugar, flour, cinnamon, nutmeg, and salt. Sprinkle over the apple mixture and toss to coat. Spoon the apple mixture into the prepared crust. Cut the butter into small pieces and place on top of the apples.

Roll the remaining dough out into a circle according to the directions on page 4. Place over the apple filling, crimping the outer edges with the bottom dough. Cut slits in the top crust to allow steam to escape. Brush the top crust with half-and-half and sprinkle with granulated sugar.

Bake the pie for 10 minutes at 400°F. Reduce the temperature to 350°F and bake for another 35 minutes, or until top crust is golden brown.

If the edges of the pie crust begin to brown too quickly, use a pie crust shield to prevent over-browning. Remove the pie from the oven to a cooling rack, and cool completely before serving.

At two-thirty, Marge rang the farm bell, and the men came at a trot across the early spring field with Barnabas, Bowser, and Buckwheat dashing ahead. The bell rang only for an emergency.

"Trissie Steven's pony. Caught in a barbed wire fence. Bleeding badly," Marge said in the telegraphic way she had of communicating urgent news to her husband.

"Want to come or stay, Tim? Your call."

"Oh, stay!" said Marge. "We haven't had a good visit in a hundred years. Besides, you've been talking man talk all day. Let's talk peonies and rose bushes, for heaven's sake."

His breathing was ragged from the trot across the field. "Well," he said, lamely, thinking of downing a glass of Marge's sweetened iced tea.

"I'm off," Hal said, kissing his wife on the cheek.

Marge cleared the remains of the pastry she'd rolled out for the pie, while the chicken simmered on the stove. "Sit down and talk to me while I finish up. The tea's in the pitcher, and fresh peppermint. A few shoots are already out; that tall grass by the garden shed kept it protected over the winter."

He poured the tea, got ice from the refrigerator, and sat down in the rocking chair that had belonged to Marge's father.

It was balm to his soul to sit in this beamed, high-ceilinged room, with its wonderful smells and golden, heart-of-pine floors. At Meadowgate Farm, he mused, nothing terribly dramatic ever seemed to happen. Life appeared to flow along sweetly, without many surprises or obstacles to overcome.

Marge sat down on the window seat, and tucked her hair into the bandanna. He thought she looked unusually bright, radiant.

"Did Hal tell you?"

"Tell me? Tell me what?"

Perhaps their Annie was getting engaged, he thought. Or maybe Hal had finally come across with their much-discussed vacation in France, to celebrate her fiftieth birthday.

"I'm pregnant," she said simply, wiping her hands on her apron.

—*At Home in Mitford*, Chapter Two

Marge's Sweet Tea with Peppermint

3   Lipton family-size teabags, tags removed
Handful   fresh mint
1 cup   granulated sugar
    Lemon slices

Place the teabags and mint in a pottery or glass pitcher and pour 2 cups cold water over them. Bring a kettle with 4 cups of water to a rolling boil. Pour into the pitcher and cover with a small plate. Let steep for 10 minutes. Remove the teabags and mint, add the sugar, and stir until dissolved. Add the lemons, and another 3 cups cold water. Serve over ice and garnish with a sprig of mint.

M̲iss Sadie arrived with Hal and Marge, who had fetched her down from Fernbank.

She carried a small shopping bag that contained several items for her rector's freezer: two Swanson's chicken pies, one package of Sara Lee fruit turnovers, and a box of Eggos. This was what Miss Sadie considered a proper hostess gift when the Baxter apples were not in season.

Marge was busy hugging one and all, including Miss Rose, who did not relish a hug.

Hal was talking with Hoppy and Uncle Billy about baseball, and Miss Sadie was chattering with Emma.

Why, it's a real celebration already, the rector thought happily, seeing two golden finches dart toward the feeder.

"Miss Sadie, your apple trees have been the prettiest I've ever seen," Marge said, taking a glass of mineral water from her host.

"Do you know carloads of people have driven by the orchards this year? They've been a regular tourist attraction! And somebody from over at Wesley stopped to ask if they could get married under the trees that back up to Church Hill."

"What did you say?"

"I said when do you think it might be, and she said she didn't know, he hadn't asked her yet!"

Their host brought in a tray of cheese and crackers. He refused to serve anything that had to be dipped. He thought dipping at parties was perilous, to say the very least. If you didn't drip dip on yourself, you were likely to drip it on someone else. He'd once had a long conversation with his new bishop, only to look down afterward and discover that his shirt front displayed a regular assortment of the stuff, including bacon and onion.

That he did not serve dip seemed especially convenient for Miss Rose, who took two of everything offered, eating one and putting the other in her dress pocket. Uncle Billy, on the other hand, took two of everything and ate both at once.

As he passed around the mushrooms in puff pastry, Miss Sadie was admiring Miss Rose's military decorations.

He had to admit that he'd never given a party quite like this.

"Uncle Billy, I'd sure like to hear a joke, if you've got one."

Uncle Billy grinned. "Did you hear the one about the sky divin' lessons?"

"I hope you didn't get this from Harry Nelson," said Emma, who didn't like Harry Nelson jokes, not even secondhand.

"Nossir. I got this joke off a feller at the Grill. He was drivin' through from Texas."

Everyone settled back happily, and Miss Rose gave Uncle Billy the go-ahead by jabbing him in the side with her elbow.

"Well, this feller he wanted to learn to sky dive, don't you know. And so he goes to this school and he takes all kind of trainin' and all, and one day comes the time he has to jump out of this airplane, and out he goes, like a ton of bricks, and he gets on down there a little ways and commences to pull th' cord and they don't nothin' happen, don't you know, and so he keeps on droppin' and he switches over and starts pullin' on his emergency cord, and they still don't nothin' happen, an' th' first thing you know, here comes this other feller, a shootin' up from the ground, and the feller goin' down says, 'Hey, Buddy, do you know anything about parachutes?' And the one a comin' up says, 'Nope, do you know anything about gas stoves?'"

Uncle Billy looked around proudly. He would have considered it an understatement to say that everyone roared with laughter.

"I've heard that bloomin' tale forty times," Miss Rose said, removing a slice of cheese from her pocket and having it with her coffee.

The Company Stew, which had simmered with the peel of an orange and a red onion stuck with cloves, was a rousing success. In fact, he was so delighted with the whole affair that he relented and let Barnabas into the study after dinner.

Marge helped serve coffee and triple-layer cake from the old highboy, as the scent of roses drifted through the open windows.

—*AT HOME IN MITFORD*, CHAPTER FOUR

Father Tim's Company Stew

8 strips	bacon, cut into 1-inch pieces	1 tablespoon	chopped fresh marjoram (or 1 teaspoon dried)
3 pounds	boneless lamb shoulder, cut into 2-inch cubes	1 tablespoon	chopped fresh thyme (or 1 teaspoon dried)
	Salt and freshly ground black pepper	1 strip	orange peel (about 3 inches long)
3 tablespoons	all-purpose flour	1 medium	whole onion, peeled and stuck with 8 whole cloves
1 cup	chopped onions		
3 cloves	garlic, minced	6 cups	beef stock
3 tablespoons	unsalted butter	½ pound	fresh button mushrooms, sliced
1¾ cups	red wine		
3 tablespoons	brandy		

Preheat oven to 350°F. Sauté bacon in a large skillet over medium heat, turning, until crisp. Move the cooked bacon to a Dutch oven, leaving the drippings in the skillet. Season the lamb with salt and pepper, toss the lamb in the flour, and brown on both sides in the bacon drippings. Transfer the lamb to the Dutch oven. Place the chopped onions and garlic in the skillet with the bacon drippings and 1 tablespoon of unsalted butter, and cook until soft, 8 to 10 minutes. Spoon into the Dutch oven. Stir the wine and brandy into the skillet and scrape up the browned bits. Pour the wine mixture into the Dutch oven along with the marjoram, thyme, and orange peel. Place the clove-studded onion in the Dutch oven. Pour the beef stock over everything, cover, and bake for 2½ hours, or until the meat is tender. Place the remaining 2 tablespoons of butter in a medium skillet over medium heat and sauté the mushrooms until soft, 5 to 6 minutes. Add the mushrooms to the stew during the last 30 minutes. Remove the studded onion and orange peel before serving.

❖ *This stew can also be made with beef stew meat instead of lamb.*

It was unusually cool for late June, and he savored his short walk to the office, noticing that he was feeling better than he had in years. He had dashed off a note to Walter after his morning prayers, quoting the encouraging message of Hebrews 4:16: "Let us, therefore, come boldly unto the throne of grace, that we may obtain mercy, and find grace to help in time of need."

Boldly! That was the great and powerful key. Preach boldly! Love boldly! Jog boldly! And most crucial of all, do not approach God whining or begging, but boldly— as a child of the King.

"I declare," Emma said as she made coffee, "you're skinny as a rail."

"That's what I hear," he said with obvious satisfaction.

"What do you mean?"

"They're not calling me 'that portly priest' anymore."

"I can fix that," she said, and opened her bottom desk drawer to reveal several Tupperware containers. The open drawer also contained a glorious fragrance that wafted upward and soon filled the small room.

"Pork roast with gravy, green beans, candied sweet potatoes, cole slaw, and yeast rolls."

"What in the world is this?"

"Lunch!" said Emma. "I figure if we eat early, it'll still be hot."

Just as his clothes were beginning to fit comfortably again, he saw temptation crowding in on every side. He could outrun Winnie Ivey, but in an office barely measuring ten by fourteen, it looked like it was going to be pork roast and gravy, and no turning back.

"Emma, you must not do this again."

"Well, I won't and you can count on it. You've been meek as any lamb to the slaughter, and I thought a square meal would be just what the doctor ordered."

"Not exactly," said her rector, who enjoyed it to the fullest, nonetheless.

After lunch, Emma went headfirst into the deep bottom drawer, looking for something. She came up with a large bone, wrapped in cellophane.

"For Barnabas," she said, much to his astonishment. That she had called his dog by name was a landmark event. And to have brought him a bone was nearly a miracle.

"I don't know why you're being so good to me," he said, cheerfully.

She glared at him and snapped, "I just told you, for Pete's sake. Weren't you listening?"

For at least two weeks, he'd noticed that her moods were as changeable as the weather.

"Emma, what is it?"

"What do you mean what is it? What is what?" she demanded, then burst into tears, and fled into the bathroom, slamming the door.

—*At Home in Mitford*, Chapter Five

Emma's Pork Roast

4 teaspoons	Morton's Nature's Seasons Seasoning Blend (or other seasoned salt)
2 tablespoons	all-purpose flour
2 tablespoons	dried thyme
1 (3 to 4 pound)	Boston butt pork roast
2 tablespoons	vegetable oil
4 cups	chicken or beef stock
¼ cup	red wine vinegar
2 medium	onions, peeled and quartered
1 cup	sliced button mushrooms
1½ pounds	new potatoes, quartered
1 cup	baby carrots

Mix together the seasoning blend, flour, and thyme and rub it all over the roast. Warm the oil in a large Dutch oven over medium-high heat. Place the roast in the pot and brown on all sides. Add the stock and vinegar, scraping the bottom of the Dutch oven to remove any browned bits. Add the onions and mushrooms and reduce the heat to a simmer. Cover and cook until the pork is almost tender, about 4 hours.

Add the potatoes and carrots, cover, and continue to cook until the vegetables are tender, at least 30 to 45 minutes more.

To serve, remove the roast from the Dutch oven, place on a large dish, and let sit, covered, for 10 minutes. Slice the meat and serve with vegetables and gravy.

"I never worry about diets. The only carrots that interest me are the number you get in diamonds."

—MAE WEST

Emma's Candied Sweet Potatoes

6 medium	sweet potatoes
¼ cup	unsalted butter, more for greasing the pan
½ cup	orange juice
½ cup	brown sugar
¼ teaspoon	salt

Place the sweet potatoes (with skins on) in a large pot over high heat with water to cover, bring to a boil, lower the heat and simmer until just tender when pierced with a fork. Drain the potatoes and remove their skins when cool enough to handle. While the sweet potatoes are boiling, preheat the oven to 400°F. Lightly butter a 9 x 13-inch baking dish. Slice the potatoes into 1-inch rounds and place in layers in the baking dish.

Combine the butter, orange juice, brown sugar, and salt in a small saucepan over medium heat. Cook, stirring occasionally, for 5 minutes, or until the butter is melted and the sugar dissolved. Pour over the potatoes, stir to evenly coat, and bake for 10 to 15 minutes, or until the juice mixture is bubbling.

Emma's Cole Slaw

4 to 5 cups (about 1 pound)	grated cabbage
2 teaspoons	salt, plus more to taste
1 cup	grated carrots
1 large	sweet onion, sliced into thin rings
1 cup	vegetable oil
1 cup	white vinegar
2 cloves	garlic, pressed through a garlic press
1 cup	granulated sugar
Dash	cayenne pepper
	Freshly ground black pepper

Combine the cabbage and the salt in a colander, cover with plastic wrap, and place a heavy plate on top. Set the colander over a large bowl and place in the refrigerator for at least 1 hour, or up to 4 hours, allowing the excess water to drain. Remove the cabbage from the refrigerator, pat to dry with paper towels, and place in a large bowl. Add the carrots and onions. In a smaller bowl, whisk together the oil, vinegar, garlic, sugar, and cayenne. Pour over the cabbage mixture, cover, and let sit for at least 2 hours. Before serving, adjust the seasonings with salt and pepper.

❖ Salting and draining the cabbage removes excess water and produces pickle-crisp cabbage.

Emma's Green Beans
with New Potatoes

2 pounds	fresh green beans, washed
2 ounces	salt pork
1 cup	chopped onions
12 to 14	small new potatoes, halved
2 teaspoons	salt, plus more to taste
	Freshly ground black pepper

Remove the ends and string the green beans. Combine the green beans, salt pork, onions, new potatoes, and the salt in a large saucepan. Add water to cover and bring to a boil over high heat. Reduce the heat, cover, and simmer for 45 minutes to 1 hour, or until the beans and potatoes are tender when pierced with a fork. Adjust the seasonings with salt and pepper before serving.

When he arrived home that afternoon at five-thirty, he found a steaming, but spotless, kitchen and a red-cheeked Puny.

"That bushel of tomatoes like to killed me!" she declared. "After I froze that big load of squash, I found some jars in your garage, sterilized 'em in your soup pot, and canned ever' one in th' bushel. Looky here," she said, proudly, pointing to fourteen Mason jars containing vermillion tomatoes.

"Puny," he exclaimed with joyful amazement, "this is a sight for sore eyes."

"Not only that, but I scrubbed your bathroom 'til it shines, and I want to tell you right now, Father, if I'm goin' to stay here—and I dearly need th' work—you're goin' to have to put your toilet seat up when you relieve yourself."

He felt his face burn. A little Emma, her employer thought, darkly. Now I've got one at the office and one at home, a matched set.

He could not, however, dismiss the joy of seeing fourteen jars of tomatoes lined up on his kitchen counter.

"It's difficult to think anything but pleasant thoughts while eating a homegrown tomato."

—Lewis Grizzard

Jan Karon's
Mitford Cookbook
& Kitchen Reader

❖ *Editor's note: Puny decided to try a new recipe with the abundance of tomatoes. She knew Father Tim would be able to eat the Gazpacho while following his diabetic diet.*

Puny's Gazpacho

3 medium	tomatoes, cored and seeded
3 medium	seedless cucumbers, peeled
2 medium	red bell peppers, cored and seeded
2 medium	yellow bell peppers, cored and seeded
1 bunch	green onions
3 large	cloves garlic
¾ cup	white wine vinegar
¾ cup	extra-virgin olive oil
1 (46-ounce) container	tomato juice
2 teaspoons	sea salt
1½ teaspoons	freshly ground black pepper
	Sour cream, for serving
	Chopped fresh chives, for garnish

In the bowl of a food processor fitted with the steel blade, coarsely chop the tomatoes, cucumbers, red peppers, yellow peppers, green onions, and garlic, one at a time. Do not over-process! After each vegetable is coarsely chopped, combine them in a large (non-metallic) bowl. Add the vinegar, oil, tomato juice, salt, and pepper. Chill well and adjust the seasonings before serving. To serve, ladle the soup into individual bowls and garnish with sour cream and chopped chives.

This soup is better if made the day ahead so the flavors are allowed to mellow.

"I'll scrub your floors and wash your drawers and put up your tomatoes and feed your dog, but I'll not scrape your shoes after you been stompin' around a farm."

—PUNY BRADSHAW

On Friday afternoon, he arrived at the rectory to find the house filled with ravishing aromas.

Baked chicken. Squash casserole. Steamed broccoli. Corn on the cob. And frozen yogurt topped with cooked Baxter apples. Oh, ye of little faith, why didst thou doubt? he quoted to himself.

"I know about that old diabetes stuff, my granpaw had it worse'n you," Puny told him with satisfaction. "An' not only can I cook for diabetes, I can cook for high blood pressure, heart trouble, nervous stomach, and constipation."

During the past twelve years, he had sometimes asked in a fit of frustration, "Lord, what have I done to deserve Emma Garrett?" Now, he found himself asking with a full heart, "Lord, what have I done to deserve Puny Bradshaw?"

—*At Home in Mitford*, Chapter Seven

Jan Karon's
Mitford Cookbook
& Kitchen Reader

Puny's Squash Casserole

3 tablespoons	unsalted butter, more for greasing the baking dish
8 medium	yellow squash, chopped
1 medium	onion, chopped
2 large	eggs, beaten
2 tablespoons	minced fresh parsley
1 cup	grated sharp cheddar cheese
1 teaspoon	salt
½ teaspoon	freshly ground black pepper
1 cup	crushed potato chips

Preheat the oven to 350°F. Lightly butter a 9 x 13-inch baking dish and set aside. Place the squash and onions in a large pot with a small amount of water over medium heat. Bring to a simmer and cook until tender, 8 to 10 minutes, then drain into a colander. Place in a large bowl and mash with a potato masher. Add the butter and stir until melted. In a separate bowl, combine the eggs, parsley, cheese, salt, and pepper and add to the vegetable mixture. Pour into the baking dish and bake for 20 minutes. Top with the crushed potato chips and bake an additional 10 minutes, or until the potato chips are browned.

"I wonder why th' Lord is always dishin' out preachers t' me."

—Puny Bradshaw

On Saturday morning, he visited the Oxford Antique Shop, carrying an apple pie in a basket.

"Little Red Riding Hood!" said Andrew Gregory, coming from the back of the store to greet him.

The rector held out the basket. "Homemade apple pie," he said, with some pride.

"'The best of all physicians is apple pie and cheese'!" exclaimed Andrew, quoting a nineteenth-century poet. "What an excellent treat, my friend. Thank you and come in." He took the basket, delighted as a child. "Why don't we just polish off the whole thing right now and you can carry your basket back?"

The two men laughed.

"I'm afraid I'll have to take my basket back in any case, as there's five more to be delivered in it."

A Sweet Bite

I live in the country, precisely thirty-five minutes from a good food store. If I need milk or bread or a pair of luscious lamb chops, I can just get over it—until Monday, when provisions are usually "laid in."

Thus, on this rainy Sunday in the first days of winter, I had to be creative. Coming home from church and hungry as a bear, I began to forage. Walnuts. Blue cheese. Cooked apples . . .

Aha, I heated the apples until they were fragrant and steaming. I toasted the walnuts in a speck of butter in a very hot skillet. I tossed the apples and walnuts together in a bowl and crumbled liberal amounts of blue cheese on top.

Let me assure you that you want to try this, and soon.

Serve as a side dish to pork roast, or as a dessert. (I love foraging.)

—Jan Karon

"I don't know how you find time to feed your sheep physically as well as spiritually."

"Andrew, Providence has blessed me with the finest house help a man could ever have. Puny Bradshaw is her name, and she not only baked a dozen pies yesterday, she canned fourteen quarts of tomatoes last week."

"Extraordinary!!"

—*At Home in Mitford,* Chapter Seven

Puny's Apple Pie

	Nonstick cooking spray for the pan	1 tablespoon	vanilla extract
½ recipe	*Pastry for a Double Crust Pie* (page 4) (Halve the recipe, or make the whole recipe and freeze half)	4 large	Granny Smith apples, peeled and sliced
		For the topping	
		¼ cup	unsalted butter, at room temperature
1 large	egg, lightly beaten	⅓ cup	White Lily all-purpose flour
¾ cup	granulated sugar	⅓ cup	granulated sugar
2 tablespoons	White Lily all-purpose flour	½ teaspoon	ground cinnamon
		¼ teaspoon	ground nutmeg
1 cup	sour cream	⅛ teaspoon	salt

Preheat the oven to 425°F. Coat a 9-inch pie pan with nonstick cooking spray. Roll out the pastry dough and fit it into the pie pan. Press a sheet of aluminum foil large enough to completely cover the dough on top of the crust and fill with pie weights or dried beans. Bake the crust for 8 to 10 minutes. Remove from the oven and remove the foil and pie weights. Set aside to cool slightly.

Place the egg, sugar, flour, sour cream, and vanilla in a medium bowl and mix well. Spread the apples out evenly in the prepared crust. Spoon the sour cream mixture evenly over the apples. Bake the pie at 425°F for 15 minutes, then remove from the oven and reduce the temperature to 350°F.

While the filling is baking, make the topping: Combine the butter, flour, sugar, cinnamon, nutmeg, and salt in a medium bowl. Using a pastry blender, mix the ingredients together until it resembles coarse crumbs. Sprinkle the crumb topping evenly over the pie, return to the oven, and bake for 30 minutes more, until the crumb topping is browned. Remove the pie from the oven to a cooling rack and cool completely before serving.

Peggy Newland's
Summer Squash Casserole

	Nonstick cooking spray for the casserole dish
6 ounces	herb-seasoned stuffing mix
¾ cup	unsalted butter, melted
2 pounds	yellow squash, sliced
1 medium	onion, chopped
1 cup	shredded carrots
1 can	cream of mushroom soup
1 cup	sour cream
¼ cup	chopped water chestnuts
1 teaspoon	salt
¾ teaspoon	freshly ground black pepper

Preheat the oven to 350°F. Coat a 2-quart casserole with nonstick cooking spray and set aside. In a small bowl, mix together the stuffing mix with ¼ cup of the butter and set aside. Warm a large sauté pan over medium heat. Add the squash, onions, carrots, and remaining ½ cup of the butter. Sauté until the squash is soft, 8 to 10 minutes. Add the soup, sour cream, water chestnuts, salt, and pepper and combine with squash mixture. Place half of the stuffing mix on the bottom of a 2-quart casserole. Place the squash mixture on top, then cover with the remaining stuffing. Bake, uncovered, for 25 to 30 minutes, or until browned on top.

On Monday, Emma was wreathed with smiles. "It worked."

"What worked?"

"Your prayer about me meetin' Harold's mother."

"Never let me say I told you so."

She sat down and put her lunch bag in the bottom desk drawer. "Dottie Newland is a peck of fun. Why, we had such a good time, I think Harold felt left out!"

"Tell me everything."

"We went to Dottie's house and Harold grilled steaks. She made potato salad and deviled eggs and tea and I brought green beans and a pound cake. I washed, Harold dried, and she put up. Guess what?"

"What's that?"

"She's six years older than me, not five."

"I'm glad to hear it."

—*At Home in Mitford*, Chapter Eight

Puny's Saving Grace #1

Puny Bradshaw Guthrie is one of the best housekeepers who ever drew breath. As you recall, she's not ashamed to get down on her hands and knees to scrub a kitchen floor, which drives Father Tim crazy. Thinking her above such lowly effort, he'd like to see her stand upright and do it with a long-handled mop. No way. This girl was raised to clean, and every Mitford reader in creation would give, as my grandmother said, "a war pension" to have Puny come to their house twice a week, if not every single day.

Of course, Puny doesn't get all that work done without a few tricks, which Father Tim calls "Puny's saving graces."

Here's one I'm especially fond of.

"Put four or five folded-up kitchen garbage bags on th' bottom of th' trash can under your sink. Then when you take out th' garbage, you'll have another bag waitin' on th' bottom, ready t' go." —Jan Karon

Emma's Pound Cake

	Nonstick cooking spray for the pan
3 cups	White Lily all-purpose flour, more for dusting the pan
1 cup	unsalted butter, at room temperature
½ cup	shortening, at room temperature
3 cups	granulated sugar
5	large eggs
½ teaspoon	baking powder
¼ teaspoon	salt
1 cup	milk
1 teaspoon	vanilla extract
1 teaspoon	almond extract

Set a rack in the middle of the oven and preheat the oven to 350°F. Coat a 10-inch tube pan with nonstick cooking spray, then dust with flour. Shake out excess flour and set aside. Cream the butter and shortening together in the bowl of an electric mixer. Add the sugar and beat on medium speed until the mixture is light and fluffy, at least 5 minutes. Add the eggs, one at a time, beating well after each addition. In a separate bowl, sift together the flour, baking powder, and salt. With the mixer on low, add a third of the flour mixture. Then add half of the milk, then the flour again, and continue until everything is mixed in, and ending with the flour mixture. Add the vanilla and almond extracts. Spoon into the pan and bake for 1 hour, or until a toothpick inserted in the center comes out clean. Cool in pan for 10 to 15 minutes, then unmold onto a wire rack. This cake freezes well.

"It's th' unblessed food that makes you fat."

—PUNY BRADSHAW

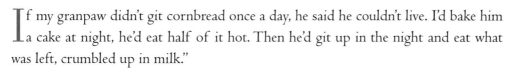

If my granpaw didn't git cornbread once a day, he said he couldn't live. I'd bake him a cake at night, he'd eat half of it hot. Then he'd git up in the night and eat what was left, crumbled up in milk."

"Really?"

"Stayed a string bean all his life, too. He said preachin' the word of God kept the fat wore off."

"It has never served me in that particular way, I regret to say."

—*AT HOME IN MITFORD*, CHAPTER TEN

Jan Karon's
Mitford Cookbook
& Kitchen Reader

Puny's Cornbread

¾ cup	vegetable oil
3 large	eggs, lightly beaten
1½ cups	canned creamed corn
1½ cups	sour cream
1 cup	self-rising cornmeal
½ cup	self-rising flour
¾ teaspoon	salt
½ teaspoon	baking powder
1 tablespoon	sugar

Preheat the oven to 425°F. Pour the oil into a 9-inch black iron skillet and place it in the oven to heat for 5 minutes. In a large bowl, mix together the eggs, creamed corn, and sour cream. In a separate bowl, mix together the cornmeal, flour, salt, baking powder, and sugar. Add the wet ingredients to the dry and mix well. Remove the skillet from the oven and stir in the hot oil to the batter. Immediately pour the batter into the skillet. Place the skillet back into the oven, turn the temperature down to 375°F, and bake for 35 to 40 minutes, or until the top of the cornbread is browned. Remove from the oven and immediately flip the cornbread out onto a plate to serve.

The Heart of the Home

Everybody knows it's true—we like to congregate in kitchens. What was once the hearth of the house has become the heart of the home. Legions of Mitford scenes take place in the kitchen, which is where, in At Home in Mitford, *we first meet Dooley Barlowe.*

[Puny] opened the back door for fresh air, and was startled to see a red-haired boy in ragged overalls standing on the step. From what she'd heard, this would be Russell Jacks's grandson. Barnabas barked joyfully and dashed to the door, yelping to get out. "Hush up and lay down! Philippians four-thirteen, f'r gosh sake!"

The boy looked intently at her through the screen.

Puny didn't know which was more noticeable, his blue eyes or his dirty feet.

"I was jis' goin' to knock," he announced. "Are we kin?"

"Not that I know of. What makes you ask?"

"Freckles same as mine."

"We couldn't be kin. You come from down th' mountain!"

"Blood travels," he said soberly.

"What can I do for you?"

"Granpaw told me to come an' git th' preacher."

"Father Tim's not here, he's at th' hospital."

"What's th' matter with 'im?"

"Nothin's th' matter with 'im. He goes an' calls on sick people an' makes 'em feel better."

He looked down at his feet and spoke in a low voice. "My mama's sick," he said.

"Why don't you come in and wait for him? He'll be here in a little bit." As she pushed open the screen door, Barnabas growled.

"Will 'at ol' dog bite?"

"Not unless he has to," Puny said, catching Barnabas by the collar. "Go set down on that stool."

He ran to the stool and tucked his feet on the top rung. "A dog like t' eat me up one time."

"Based on your overalls alone, this dog won't mess with you," she said with conviction.

"What's your name?"

"Puny."

"Why'd you git a name like 'at?"

"'Cause when I was born I was all sickly an' puny-like."

"How did you git over bein' puny?"

"Hard work, honey, that's how." She started paring the great mound of apples in the sink. "What's your name?"

"Dooley."

"Dooley? Don't you have a real name like Howard or Buddy or Jack or somethin'?"

"Dooley is a real name!" he said with feeling.

There was a long silence as Puny bent to her task.

"Did you ever try stump water?" Dooley asked.

"Stump water! Shoot, I tried everything, but nothin' ever worked."

"I hear if you lay face down in fresh cow dump, 'at works."

She turned around, still peeling the apple. "Did you try that?"

"Nope."

"Me neither, 'cause I heard you had to lay there awhile for it to take."

"Can I have one of them apples?"

"If you'll say 'May I,' you can have one."

"May I," said Dooley.

He quickly put it in his overalls pocket. "My uncle said if you wash y'r face with th' same rag you wash y'r feet with, that'll do it."

"I wouldn't try that, if I was you. Besides, I think we ought to be content with what th' good Lord gave us. I don't mess with my freckles no more, and I think you ought to stop wastin' your time, too."

He studied his feet, which he was swinging freely now, since Barnabas had fallen asleep. The kitchen was quiet. Birdsong drifted through the open window and a breeze puffed out the curtains.

Dooley decided to eat his apple. "What else you want t' talk about?"

"How old are you?"

"'Leven."

Puny peeled furiously. "I'm glad I ain't eleven."

"Why?"

"I didn't like bein' a kid. Somebody was always beatin' on you, pullin' your hair, chasin' you around th' house, throwin' mud on you. I wouldn't be your age for all th' tea in China, much less Japan."

"When I'm twelve, I'm goin' t' whip th' horse hockey out of somebody."

"You better not be usin' that kind of language in this house. Nossir, that won't go around here."

He ate his apple. "When's 'at preacher comin'? My granpaw said make it snappy."

"He'll git here when he gits here. What's th' matter with your mama?" Puny started slicing the peeled apples. The room was silent except for the slices dropping into the pot. "Well, cat got your tongue?"

"I ain't tellin' you nothin' about that."

"Why not?"

"Because it ain't none of your stupid business."

She turned and looked at him. His face had hardened, and he looked older, like a little old man perched on the stool.

"Let me tell you somethin', then, buster. Don't come in here in my kitchen with them dirty feet, and think you can go sassin' me. I'll pitch your little butt out on th' porch."

He slid off the stool and headed toward the door. "You ol' fat witch!"

She caught him on the back stoop. "Witch, is it? You know what witches do t' back-talkin' young 'uns?" She held him by his galluses and put her face close to his. "They boil 'em in that big ol' pot in yonder."

"Oh, yeah?"

"Yeah!" She bared her teeth at him ominously. "And then . . ."

"And then what?" asked Father Tim, walking into the yard.

"I was just about t' cook this young 'un alive," she said, "and you come and spoiled everything."

—*At Home in Mitford,* Chapter Seven

34

On the heels of the previous scene is Father Tim's visit to the little yellow house, which is newly occupied by Cynthia Coppersmith. She's invited him to dinner, and who knew (certainly your author didn't know at that time) they would wind up spending the rest of their lives together?

On Wednesday evening, he took a shower and dressed, and prepared to visit his new neighbor in her tiny house next door. Cynthia Coppersmith had done as promised and invited him to dinner. And the invitation, it seemed to him, was perfectly timed.

The last of his Rector's Meatloaf was gone, and good riddance. To his chagrin, he'd used more oatmeal than before, which resulted in the most unsavory concoction he'd tasted in years. But he had soldiered on and eaten the entire loaf over a period of several days. He was so ashamed of it, he had hidden it at the back of the refrigerator, where he hoped Puny wouldn't find it.

—*At Home in Mitford*, Chapter Ten

Rector's Meatloaf (Old Faithful)

	Nonstick cooking spray for the pan
2 tablespoons	vegetable oil
1½ cups	minced onion
¾ cup	minced green pepper
2 pounds	ground round
1 cup	uncooked rolled oats
2 large	eggs, beaten
1 (8-ounce) can	tomato sauce
2½ teaspoons	salt
1 teaspoon	freshly ground black pepper
¾ cup	ketchup

Preheat the oven to 350°F. Coat a loaf pan with nonstick cooking spray and set aside. Warm the oil in a small skillet over medium heat. Add the onions and green peppers and sauté until soft, 8 to 10 minutes. Place in a large bowl, add the ground round, oats, eggs, tomato sauce, salt, and pepper and mix well. Press the mixture into the loaf pan. Bake for 1 hour. Remove the meatloaf from the oven and pour the ketchup on top. Return to the oven and cook for another 15 minutes.

Every light in the small house glowed warmly through the heavy mist that lay upon the village.

"Pleasant!" he said, aloud. "A small house for a small person." He lifted the old brass knocker and rapped three times.

There was no answer to his knock, so he tried again.

Nothing.

Since callers occasionally had to go to the back door of the rectory to rouse him from his study, he thought the same might apply in this case. He stumbled around the side of the house, over broken flagstones, toward a light shining above the back door.

He knocked and waited. Not a sound.

He cautiously opened the door and peered into a minuscule but inviting kitchen.

A broiling pan sat on the stove, containing a blackened roast. Next to it, a pot had boiled over, and a tray of unbaked rolls sat disconsolately on the countertop. "Hello!" he called.

A white cat leaped onto the breakfast table, looked at him curiously, and began cleaning her paws. "Violet, I presume?" He had never been fond of cats.

He heard her coming down the stairs, then she appeared at the kitchen door, her eyes red from crying.

"I've done it again," she said, sniffing. "I can never get it right. I sat down at my drawing table for just one minute. One minute! An hour later, I looked up, and the rice had boiled over and the roast had burned, and well, there you have it."

"'Whatever your hand finds to do, do it with all your might'!" he quoted cheerfully from Ecclesiastes. "You must have been doing something you liked."

She sighed. "I was drawing moles."

Moles again! That explains it, thought her caller. "Look here," he said, "if you don't mind, let me experiment with this." He made a broad gesture toward the ruined dinner.

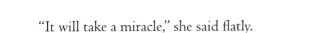

"It will take a miracle," she said flatly.

"I'd be very open to a good miracle. Where's your carving knife?"

He drew the sharp knife across the end of the roast, and a thick slice peeled away neatly. "Well, now! Just the way I like it. Overdone on the outside and rare in the middle." He carved a sliver and handed it to his hostess on the point of the blade. "See what you think."

Cynthia eyed it suspiciously, then did as he suggested. "Delicious!" she declared with feeling. "It *is* a miracle!"

He lifted the lid on the pot that had boiled over on the burner, and stirred the contents with a wooden spoon. "It's stuck on the bottom, but I think it's just right. Yes, indeed. Wild rice. A favorite!"

"You really are infernally kind," she said tartly.

"Not kind. Famished. I ran today and missed lunch entirely."

"Well," she said, the color coming back into her cheeks, "I did make a hot crab-meat casserole for the first course. That worked! And there are glazed onions with rosemary and honey that appear edible." She took two fragrant, steaming dishes out of the oven and set them on the counter.

"I hear you like a drop of sherry now and then," she said, and poured from a bottle with a distinguished label. She handed him a glass, and poured one for herself.

"You've prepared a grand feast!" exclaimed her guest.

"Cheers!" said his relieved hostess.

—*At Home in Mitford*, Chapter Ten

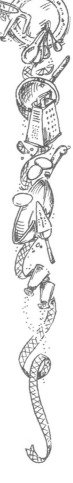

Jan Karon's
Mitford Cookbook
& Kitchen Reader

Cynthia's Glazed Rosemary Onions

	Nonstick cooking spray for the pan
8 medium	yellow onions, quartered
⅔ cup	honey
¼ cup	unsalted butter, melted
1½ teaspoons	chopped fresh rosemary (or ½ teaspoon dried)
½ teaspoon	salt
	Freshly ground black pepper

Preheat the oven to 350°F. Coat a large baking dish with nonstick cooking spray. Place the onions in the dish, being careful to leave the onion quarters intact. Pour the honey and butter over the onions and add the rosemary, salt, and pepper. Bake for 1 hour, until the onions are soft. Adjust the seasonings before serving.

As you see, kitchens can be full of drama, to say the least. I wonder what would have happened if Father Tim had arrived at Cynthia's house and everything had been in apple pie order. Would a courtship have ensued out of order and perfection? Maybe. Maybe not.

I seldom have a clue how my characters will handle a situation; in truth, I had no idea that Cynthia's dinner had gone amok until Father Tim opened the door and I saw the mess.

I remember the time I had some fairly important guests, and while heating the hors d'oeuvres, the oven caught fire. Do you think I hadn't cleaned my oven in a while? And so there I was, all dressed up, and on my hands and knees cleaning the blasted thing so I could finish heating the hors d'oeuvres. (I have no idea, by the way, why I'm confessing this.)

I always loved Father Tim's visits to Miss Sadie's big kitchen, and actually had Louella and Miss Sadie living in the kitchen once the Fernbank stairs became too much for them to climb. And, it was in the rectory kitchen that Father Tim read Miss Sadie's letter, written a short time before her death, which revealed she was leaving a million bucks to Dooley Barlowe.

Clearly, my books aren't only full of food, they're full of kitchen scenes. In fact, *In This Mountain* ends in the kitchen, where Father Tim is baking a couple of potatoes, as Mitford's serious drought comes suddenly, gloriously, to a close. (Much to their credit, he and Cynthia have just celebrated their seventh wedding anniversary by dashing out in the rain like maniacs.)

He set the dial to 450 and was popping the potatoes in the oven when the phone rang.

"Hello!"

"Hey, Dad!"

"Hey, son!"

"You won't believe this."

"Try me."

"No seriously, there's no way you could believe it."

Was it sheer unbounded joy he heard in his boy's voice? Whatever it was, he had never, ever heard it in Dooley's voice before. It was something like jubilation.

"You've won the lottery!"

Dooley cackled. "Yeah, right." A brief pause. "Lace called me back."

"No way."

"I was walking down the hall and the phone rang and I picked it up, like, 'Hello, Tau Kappa Epsilon,' and she said, 'Dooley?' Man."

"Man!" he echoed.

"She returned my call," Dooley said again, as if trying to fully comprehend the truth.

"Never say never." He was a temple of wisdom.

"It only took her a year and a half."

His grin was stretching clear around his head. "Oh, well, these are busy times." There was brief silence in which each sought to digest the miracle.

"Well, hey, look, Dad, I've got to go. Catch you later."

"Alligator," he whispered, hanging up.

He stood at the kitchen island, looking out to the rain that continued unabated. He'd completely forgotten to tell Dooley about Sammy. Later, he and Cynthia would call and tell him together.

"Timothy . . ."

His wife came into the room wearing her bathrobe and slippers. "You have tears in your eyes, what is it, sweetheart?"

"Life!" he said. "And love."

He drew her to him, feeling her damp hair against his shoulder. They would talk about the phone call over dinner. It would be a great treat.

Now, he held her close, wordless, rocking her gently in his arms.

Life and love. What wonderful blessings to have in our kitchens.

—Jan Karon

That evening before dinner, he built a fire. Dooley made popcorn, and Barnabas did his business at the hedge with great expediency. He was as glad as a child for the comfort of home, and rest, and peace.

For what he estimated to be the fourth or fifth time, he picked up the *Mitford Muse*, which by now was four days old, and tried to read Esther Cunningham's editorial on the July Festival of Roses. J.C. had done it again. "Festival of Ropes Will Transform Main Street," said the headline.

Dooley answered the ringing phone in the kitchen. "Rec'try. Yep, he's here, but he don't want t' talk t' nobody."

Dooley put his hand over the receiver and yelled, "It's y'r doctor!"

"Hang up," he said, and lifted the cordless by the sofa. "Got anything for exhaustion, sleeplessness, and general aggravation?" he asked.

"I was calling to ask you the same thing."

"The blind leading the blind. How are you, my friend?"

"This place is eating me alive. I've got to get out of here for a while, and the kitchen said they'd make me a plate. I wondered if I could bring it to your place. Dining out, it's called."

"Of course!" he said, trying to conceal the weariness in his voice.

"I'll bring you a plate, too."

"I don't know," said the rector, with some caution. "What do you . . . ah, think it might be?"

"God only knows."

"I've had that a few times. Bring it on, then. I need more surprises in my life."

"Yuck," said Dooley, "don't give me any of that stuff. I eat somethin' off granpaw's plate th' other day at th' hospital, an' it like t' gagged me."

"Thanks for reminding me."

"I'll jis' have me some popcorn, peanut butter an' jelly, an' fried baloney."

"Yuck," said the rector.

—*At Home in Mitford*, Chapter Thirteen

Jan Karon's
Mitford Cookbook
& Kitchen Reader

43

Dooley's Fried Baloney
Sandwich Supreme

1 tablespoon	butter
1 slice	baloney
1 teaspoon	mayonnaise
2 slices	white loaf bread

Warm half the butter in a small skillet and fry the baloney. Spread mayonnaise on the bread slices and place the baloney between the 2 slices. Add the remaining butter to the skillet and fry the sandwich on both sides until crispy brown.

Dooley's Second Favorite Sandwich—The Doozie

When Dooley first came to live at the rectory, his second favorite sandwich, though never mentioned in the books, was "The Doozie."

> White bread slice
> Smooth peanut butter
> Cheerios cereal

Spread a slice of white bread with a generous amount of smooth peanut butter. Sprinkle the peanut butter liberally with Cheerios. Fold the sandwich in half and jump on your bike and go.

Rodney passed a basket of ham biscuits his mother had sent. "Let's bless these ham biscuits, boys," he said, and launched into a prayer covering world hunger, food stamps, stray animals, firewood, the Baptist conference, Little Mitford Creek, Big Mitford Creek, the sick, the unsaved, an unwelcome forecast for more snow, the town council's decision on sidewalks for Lilac Road, the president, the Congress, the Senate, the House of Representatives, and the local fire and police departments.

"Amen!" said Homeless. "That ought t' last me 'til this time next year."

—*At Home in Mitford*, Chapter Eleven

Rodney's Mother's Ham Biscuits

½ cup	shortening, chilled, more for greasing the pan
3 cups	White Lily self-rising flour, more for rolling out the dough
1 teaspoon	salt
2 tablespoons	granulated sugar
½ teaspoon	baking soda
1½ cups	buttermilk, chilled
½ pound	baked ham, sliced thin

Preheat the oven to 475°F. Grease a baking sheet and set aside. Combine the flour, salt, sugar, and baking soda in a large bowl. Cut in the shortening with a pastry blender until the shortening is the size of small peas. Add the buttermilk and stir until just mixed.

Pat or roll out the dough onto a lightly floured surface into a ½-inch thick round. Cut out biscuits with a 2½- or 3-inch round cookie cutter and arrange on the baking sheet. Gently reshape leftover dough and cut again. Bake for 15 to 20 minutes or until brown on top.

Remove the hot biscuits from the oven, split them open, add ham to each biscuit, and serve right away.

The Year of the Other Christmas Tree

Speaking of writing hungry, as I did earlier, how about coming up with worthy Christmas gifts for loved ones when money is either short or altogether unavailable?

One year, when I thought I'd have nothing to give at Christmas, my attention was drawn to the lovely, very old apple tree standing in a grove of rhododendron near my cottage door.

This dear tree was having its best year ever. In truth, it appeared that a veritable horde of apples would soon be bouncing to my gate.

I rolled up my sleeves. I made a list of friends and family. Soon, I started peeling and cooking and freezing them in quart containers. Then, I sat down and wrote this poem, drew a border around it, hand-colored the border, and made a copy to accompany each quart container.

For your author, it was one of the best Christmases in a long time.

A Poem for My Apple Tree, Which Made This Christmas Gift for Thee

This year your blossoms flourished,
Making apples by the score.
They fell into the emerald grass
And rolled right to my door!

In August and September
They were falling one by one,
Then, a golden mid-October
Brought them earthward by the ton.

For weeks on end, the baskets filled,
The heavy sacks were loaded;
The barrow caught its happy share
And hardly could be toted.

I peeled for hours at the sink,
Thankful for my "farm"
That consisted of one apple tree,
But alas, no apple barn.

You gave me endless pies and sauce
And filled this busy dwelling
With fragrances that charmed the heart—
With delight beyond all telling.

Your ancient limbs are barren now,
The holly thrives instead;
Yet, your summer isn't over
Nor your comely spirit dead.

In this fruit I give at Christmas
To a special, much-loved friend
Are all the sun-kissed summer days
We hoped would never end.

And blended with the sugar
And stirred in with the spice
Are those autumn days so dazzling
No words could quite suffice.

Now I share this gift with you, my friend,
And ask that Christ may bless
Your Noel and your New Year
With deepest happiness.

P.S.
(Herewith, my neighbor's recipe for making tasty pie:
Just roll some biscuit dough real thin,
Fold in these apples, and fry!)

There is an exquisite and poignant hymn which, along with "Once in Royal David's City," I love to hear each year at Christmas. Forthwith, the early, anonymously written lyrics of "Jesus Christ the Apple Tree," from the collection of Joshua Smith of New Hampshire, 1784:

The tree of life my soul hath seen,
Laden with fruit and always green;
The trees of nature fruitless be
Compared with Christ the apple tree.

I'm weary with my former toil,
Here I will sit and rest awhile;
Under the shadow I will be,
Of Jesus Christ the apple tree.

His beauty doth all things excel;
By faith I know but ne'er can tell
The glory which I now can see
In Jesus Christ the apple tree.

This fruit doth make my soul to thrive.
It keeps my dying faith alive;
Which makes my soul in haste to be
With Jesus Christ the apple tree.

For happiness I long have sought,
And pleasure dearly I have bought;
I missed of all, but now I see
Tis found in Christ the apple tree.

—JAN KARON

The concert reading and musicale drew a packed house, and the choir had, in his opinion, reached a new pinnacle of praise. After the event at church, the choir proceeded out the church doors and along Main Street, caroling in the chill evening air, carrying lanterns. They made a glowing procession along the old street, stopping here and there in an open shop for hot cider and cookies.

The rector had the caroling choir finish up at the rectory, where he laid a fire in the study and spread out a feast that Puny had spent days preparing. Curried shrimp, honey-glazed ham, hot biscuits, cranberry salad, fried chicken, roasted potatoes with rosemary, and brandied fruit were set out in generous quantities.

The little group gathered around the roaring fire and, as the last carol of the evening, sang something they knew to be their rector's great favorite.

"In the bleak mid-winter," ran the first lines of Christina Rossetti's hymn, "icy wind made moan, earth as hard as iron, water like a stone . . ."

Then, the poignant last verse: "What shall I give him, poor as I am? If I were a shepherd, I would bring a lamb; if I were a wise man, I would do my part; yet what can I give him . . . I give my heart."

That's the key! he thought, as they pulled on heavy coats and gloves, mufflers and boots. Then, with much laughter and warm hugs, they trooped out the door and into the biting wind.

"The Lord be with you!" he called, his breath forming gray puffs on the stinging air. "And also with you!"

For a long time afterward, he sat by the fire, feeling the joy of Christmas, and knowing with unsearchable happiness that Christ did, indeed, live in his heart. Not because he was a "preacher." Not because he was, after a fashion, "good." But because, long ago, he had asked Him to.

—*At Home in Mitford*, Chapter Eleven

Puny's Curried Shrimp

4 tablespoons	unsalted butter
½ cup	chopped onions
½ cup	chopped Granny Smith apples
1 clove	garlic, crushed
2 tablespoons	all-purpose flour
1 (14½-ounce) can	petite diced tomatoes in juice
2 teaspoons	curry powder
1 teaspoon	salt
½ teaspoon	freshly ground black pepper
1½ cups	Hellmann's mayonnaise
1 tablespoon	fresh lemon juice
3 pounds	shrimp, cooked, peeled and deveined
1 cup	grated coconut
1 cup	chopped peanuts

Warm the butter in a large sauté pan over medium heat. Add the onions, apples, and garlic and sauté for 8 to 10 minutes, until softened. Stir in the flour and cook 1 minute. Add the tomatoes (with their juices), curry powder, salt, and pepper. Simmer on low heat for 5 minutes. Let the mixture cool slightly, then transfer to the bowl of a food processor and process the mixture until smooth. Pour into a large bowl and stir in the mayonnaise and lemon juice. Refrigerate until completely cool. Add the shrimp to the chilled sauce, cover with plastic, and refrigerate for at least 3 hours to allow the flavors to blend.

To serve, spoon the shrimp onto a serving platter and top with the grated coconut and chopped peanuts.

Puny's Cranberry Salad

3 (3-ounce) packages	orange flavor Jell-O
3 cups	boiling water
2 tablespoons	fresh lemon juice
1 cup	sugar
⅛ teaspoon	salt
2 tablespoons	orange zest (see below)
2½ cups	fresh cranberries, coarsely chopped
2 large	navel oranges, peeled and sectioned
1½ cups	finely chopped celery
1 cup	crushed pineapple in juice
½ cup	chopped walnuts
	Leafy green lettuce

Place the Jell-O in a large bowl and pour in the boiling water. Add the lemon juice, sugar, and salt. Stir for a couple of minutes, until the Jell-O is dissolved. Add the orange zest, cranberries, orange pieces, celery, pineapple, and nuts and mix until well combined. Pour into a 9 x 13-inch Pyrex dish and chill until set. Place a square of the salad over a piece of green leafy lettuce on individual serving plates. This salad is best made 2 days before serving.

HOW TO ZEST AN ORANGE OR LEMON

To zest an orange or lemon (or lime), use a vegetable peeler to remove the outer (colored) peel, leaving the bitter white pith, and use a chef's knife to mince the peel. You may also use a kitchen utensil called an orange zester, which produces finely grated orange peel.

Puny's Brandied Fruit Compote

1½ cups	coarsely chopped dried apricots
1 cup	coarsely chopped dried pears
1 cup	coarsely chopped pitted prunes
1½ cups	dried cranberries
2 cups	coarsely chopped dried apples
1 cup	dried cherries
½ cup	brown sugar
½ cup	brandy
¼ cup	unsalted butter
½ teaspoon	salt
1 tablespoon	fresh lemon juice
1 tablespoon	lemon zest (see page 52)
1 tablespoon	orange zest (see page 52)
3 cups	water

Combine the dried fruit in a large bowl and add enough hot water to cover by 1 inch. Let the fruit soak for 25 minutes, then drain well.

Place the soaked fruit, brown sugar, brandy, butter, salt, lemon juice, lemon zest, orange zest, and water in a large saucepan over high heat. Bring the mixture to a boil, reduce the heat, and simmer for 30 minutes. Pour the compote into a bowl, cool, and refrigerate until ready to serve. Or you may also serve the compote warm.

❖ *The compote is delicious served as a side dish to roasted meats, especially Emma's Pork Roast (page 17) or Lottie Greer's Roasted Lamb (page 59). It is also very good served as a topping for ice cream.*

At six-thirty, he and Barnabas woke Dooley.

"I don't want t' git up!" he wailed. "You done wore me out goin' t' church. I ain't never been t' s' much church in my life. I didn't know they was that much church in th' whole dern world."

"My friend, you will be pleased to know that Santa Claus visited this humble rectory last night and left something in the study for one Dooley Barlowe."

"They ain't no Santy. I don't believe 'at old poop."

"Well, then, lie there and believe what you like. I'm going downstairs and have my famous Christmas morning casserole."

Barnabas leaped on Dooley's bed and began licking his ear.

"'is ol' dog is th' hatefulest thing I ever seen!" Dooley moaned, turning his face to the wall.

"Come, Barnabas. Leave him be."

Barnabas lay resolutely on Dooley's bed and stared at his master.

Barnabas, at least, was determined to execute Puny's good idea.

He set two places at the counter and took the bubbling sausage casserole from the oven. There would be no diet this day. Then, he turned on the record player and heard the familiar, if scratchy, strains of the *Messiah.*

Dooley appeared at the kitchen door, dressed in the burgundy robe. "Sounds like a' army's moved in down here."

"My friend, you have hit the nail on the head. It is an army of the most glorious voices in recent history, singing one of the most majestic musical works ever written!"

—*At Home in Mitford,* Chapter Twelve

Father Tim's Christmas Morning Breakfast Casserole

	Nonstick cooking spray for the baking dish
1 pound	ground pork sausage
¼ cup	chopped shallots or green onions
10 pieces	challah or white bread, torn into small pieces
1 cup	shredded cheddar cheese
1 cup	shredded Monterey Jack cheese
8 large	eggs
2½ cups	milk
1 teaspoon	salt
1¼ teaspoons	dry mustard
¼ teaspoon	Worcestershire sauce

Coat a 9 x 13-inch baking dish with nonstick cooking spray and set aside.

Place the sausage in a large skillet over medium heat and brown the sausage, stirring, until it crumbles. Add the shallots a few minutes before the sausage is done. Drain the sausage and shallots on a paper towel–lined plate.

Place the torn bread pieces in the baking dish and sprinkle the cheese evenly over the bread. Spoon the sausage evenly over the cheese.

In a medium bowl, whisk the eggs, milk, salt, mustard, and Worcestershire sauce together. Pour evenly over the sausage and bread mixture. Cover and chill the casserole for at least 4 hours, or up to 8 hours.

When you are ready to bake the casserole, preheat the oven to 350°F. Remove the dish from the refrigerator and allow it to come to room temperature for at least 30 minutes before baking. Bake for 45 minutes, or until set.

Russell Jacks's Livermush Breakfast Supreme

We never know how Dooley's grandfather, Russell Jacks, eats his livermush; we know only that he craves it. If I were Russell, here's how I'd enjoy this rare and delicious comestible.

Cut three ½-inch thick slices from a loaf of Neese's or Jenkins livermush. Fry in sizzling hot, but not smoking, bacon grease, until golden brown (about 60 seconds each side). Turn the slices over and repeat. Drain your livermush on a paper towel, and spread mayonnaise on two slices of white bread. Whole wheat is too strongly flavored— you want the taste of livermush to predominate.

(I'm rolling on the floor as I imagine your reaction to this piece of wisdom. Let us, however, continue.)

Put two slices of livermush on a slice of bread. Put the third slice of livermush on top of the other two. Add the top slice of bread. With the heel of your hand, mash down the whole caboodle as flat as it will go.

Enjoy this with a cup of strong, black coffee in the morning, or, if your tastes are so inclined, with a cold Dr Pepper.

—Jan Karon

Livermush: The Scoop, the Skinny, and Possibly More Than You Ever Wanted to Know

There are no livermush Web sites, which is one more example of how far we've fallen as a civilization, but if you want to taste livermush for yourself, I'll tell you what I know about how to find it.

Livermush may be found principally in North Carolina, though scrapple may be found more widely throughout the South, including Washington, D.C., which mistakenly thinks of itself as "up north." Scrapple is simply a first-cousin form of livermush, in that it contains less liver, and more cornmeal. (My sister finds scrapple infinitely superior to livermush, while I enjoy both with great happiness and appetite.)

Livermush. Scrapple. If you ask me, both names are quite equal in their ability to amuse, but the point of this piece is to tell you where and how to locate these culinary anomalies.

I find livermush at most western North Carolina grocery stores, but have seen neither hide nor hair of it in central Virginia. In North Carolina, look for Nesse's Liver Pudding (merely another name for livermush), Jenkins Livermush, or Jenkins Country Scrapple. (The fact that there's no such thing as City Scrapple is hardly worth pondering, and it's no use looking for an apostrophe in Jenkins.)

Martha and I tried to find out how you can order any of the above in bulk or by the case, but we failed to locate this information. Aren't you glad?

Want to talk about livermush? Go to www.mitfordbooks.com, and post your livermush opinions, poems, experiences, and recipes. —Jan Karon

Nurse Herman said he had sent his dinner back, barely touched, insisting that he could have cooked it better himself, so she figured he was improving, and could the rector please bring a pound of livermush the next time he came to the hospital, as it wasn't something they ordinarily bought, and Russell said he would give a war pension for some.

"He also insisted," reported Nurse Herman, "that he would go down to the kitchen and personally fry it himself, and Dr. Harper said fine, fry him some too. Can you imagine?"

"LIVERMUSH," Father Tim wrote on his list of things to do.

—*At Home in Mitford*, Chapter Thirteen

I left school when I was twelve," said Absalom Greer over dinner, "to help my daddy in the store, and I got along pretty good teaching myself at night. One evenin', along about the age of fourteen—I was back here in this very room, studyin' a book— the wind got to howling and blowing as bad as you ever heard.

"Lottie was a baby in my mother's arms. I can see them now, my mother sitting by the fire, rocking Lottie, and humming a tune, and I was settin' right there on a little bed.

"My eyes were as wide open as they are now, when suddenly I saw a great band of angels. This room was filled with the brightness of angels!

"They were pure white, with color only in their wings, color like a prism casts when the sun shines through it. I never saw anything so beautiful in my life, before or since. I couldn't speak a word, and my mother went on rocking and humming, with her eyes closed, and there were angels standing over her, and all around us was this shining, heavenly host.

"Then, it seemed as if a golden stair let down there by the door, and the angels turned and swarmed up that staircase, and were gone. I remember I went to sobbing, but my mother didn't hear it. And I reached up to wipe my tears, but there weren't any there.

"I've thought about it many a time over the years, and I think it was my spirit that was weeping with joy."

Lottie Miller had not spoken, but had passed each dish and platter, it seemed to the rector, at just the right time. He had a second helping of potatoes that had been sliced and fried with rock salt and chives, and another helping of roasted lamb, which was as fine as any lamb he'd tasted in a very long time.

"It's a mystery how I could have done it, but I completely forgot that heavenly vision," said the preacher, who was buttering a biscuit.

—*At Home in Mitford*, Chapter Fourteen

Lottie Greer's Roasted Lamb

1 cup	red wine vinegar
1½ cups	vegetable oil
1 tablespoon	honey
3 cloves	garlic, pressed
1 tablespoon	Dijon mustard
2 teaspoons	salt
1 teaspoon	freshly ground black pepper
1 tablespoon	chopped fresh rosemary (or 1 teaspoon dried)
1 (4 to 5 pound)	leg of lamb, boned and butterflied
4 cloves	garlic, thinly sliced
1 tablespoon	Morton Nature's Seasons Seasoning Blend
	Pepper jelly, for serving

Combine the vinegar, oil, honey, pressed garlic, mustard, salt, pepper, and rosemary in a large bowl. Make several small slits in the meat and press the garlic slices into the slits. Place the meat in a shallow dish and pour the marinade over it. Cover with plastic wrap and place the meat in the refrigerator overnight to marinate.

Preheat the oven to 425°F. Remove the lamb from the refrigerator. Truss the lamb with kitchen string. Rub the seasoning blend all over the lamb. Place the lamb on a roasting rack placed in a shallow pan and roast for 30 minutes. Turn the heat down to 350°F and continue to bake for at least 30 more minutes, or until the internal temperature of the thickest part of the lamb reads 130° (medium rare) on an instant-read thermometer. Remove the lamb from the oven; let it rest for 10 minutes before carving. Serve with pepper jelly.

❖ *The meat is trussed (tied up) with kitchen string to make sure it stays together while it's cooking.*

Lottie Greer's Fried Potatoes with Rock Salt and Chives

2½ pounds (about 7 medium)	red potatoes, peeled
2 tablespoons	vegetable oil
1 tablespoon	unsalted butter
1 tablespoon	rock salt
1 teaspoon	freshly ground black pepper
2 tablespoons	chopped fresh chives (or 2 teaspoons dried)

Preheat the oven to 400°F. Cut the potatoes into 1-inch slices. Heat the vegetable oil in a heavy black iron skillet for 3 minutes. Add the potatoes and sauté, stirring every few minutes, until they start to brown, about 10 minutes. Stir in the butter, cover the skillet, and place in the oven for 30 to 45 minutes. Remove from the oven and add the rock salt and pepper. Sprinkle the chives on top and adjust the seasonings with salt and pepper before serving.

❖ You can peel and slice the potatoes ahead of time; place them in a bowl of cold water and refrigerate. When you're ready to use them, drain well and pat dry with paper towels.

❖ Yukon gold potatoes may be substituted for the red potatoes.

IS IT LOTTIE GREER? OR LOTTIE MILLER?

Actually, it's both. Lottie Greer was Absalom Greer's little sister. Lottie adored her brother, Absalom, who grew up to fall in love with Miss Sadie Baxter, and become a wonderful revival preacher at several small churches in the mountains near Mitford. Lottie married a Miller, who was not so fine of character, who left her. She later resumed her maiden name, and lived with and cared for her brother, Absalom, for the rest of his life. So, sometimes your author has called her Lottie Greer and sometimes Lottie Miller, and you will find this little confusion even in the pages of this cookbook. Just think what it's like to keep up with the many and varied personal details of nearly 700 characters (count 'em!) in nine Mitford novels!

Rain again! he thought, as he put the tea kettle on. But every drop that fell contained the promise of another leaf, another blossom, another blade of grass in the spring. Better still, it would help make Russell Jacks's wish come true, for the buds forming on the rhododendron were as large as old-fashioned Christmas tree lights.

Though it was fairly warm, he had laid a fire, thinking that he and Dooley might have supper in the study. But when he looked in the refrigerator, he found little to inspire him.

"Scraps!" he said, as the phone rang.

"Hello, Father!" said his neighbor. "I remembered that Puny isn't there on Thursdays, and I've made a bouillabaisse with fresh shrimp and mussels from The Local. May I bring you a potful?"

Providence! he thought. And one of his favorite dishes, to boot. "Well, now . . ."

"Oh, and crab meat. I used crab meat, and I promise it isn't scorched or burned."

He laughed.

"I could just pop through the hedge," she said.

"Indeed, not. I'll ask Dooley to come for it. And I have two lemon pies here that Puny baked yesterday. I'll send one over."

"I love lemon pies!" she said.

"Of course, we'd be very glad to have you join us here. Dooley will be getting his science project done on the floor of the study, so if you wouldn't mind a bit of a muddle . . ."

"Oh, but you should see the muddle here! I'd be glad to exchange my muddle for yours!"

"All right, then, fish stew and lemon pie it is! Give us an hour, if you will."

"I will! And I look forward to it," she said.

He couldn't help thinking that his neighbor sounded like a very young girl who'd just been invited to a tea party.

—*At Home in Mitford*, Chapter Fourteen

Jan Karon's
Mitford Cookbook
& Kitchen Reader

61

Cynthia's Bouillabaisse

2 tablespoons	extra-virgin olive oil	4½ cups	*Fish Stock* (see recipe, opposite)
2 medium	onions, diced		
6 large cloves	garlic, pressed	2 pounds	firm white-fleshed fish, cut into 1-inch pieces
½ cup	dry white wine		
1 (28-ounce) can	crushed tomatoes in juice	1 pound	shrimp, peeled and deveined
2 large	bay leaves	1 pound	crab meat
½ teaspoon	fennel seeds, crushed	½ pound	mussels in the shell, cleaned
⅛ teaspoon	cayenne pepper	½ pound	littleneck clams in the shell, cleaned
¼ teaspoon	saffron, crumbled		
1 teaspoon	dried basil	3 tablespoons	chopped fresh parsley
1 teaspoon	dried thyme		*Roasted Red Pepper Rouille* (see recipe, page 64)
1 teaspoon	orange zest (see page 52)		
	Salt and freshly ground black pepper		*Cracked Pepper Toast* (see recipe, page 64)
1 pound	new potatoes, peeled		

Heat the oil in a large soup pot over medium heat. Add the onions and garlic and sauté until softened, about 10 minutes. Add the wine and simmer for 5 minutes. Add the tomatoes (with their juices), bay leaves, fennel seeds, cayenne, saffron, basil, thyme, and orange zest. Simmer over low heat for 15 to 20 minutes. Add salt and black pepper to taste.

Place the potatoes in a medium saucepan, cover with water, and bring to a boil over high heat. Reduce the heat to medium, cover, and simmer until the potatoes are soft when pierced with a sharp knife. Drain the potatoes, cut them into thick slices, and set aside.

Add the fish stock to the tomato mixture. Bring to a boil, then reduce the heat to a simmer. Add the fish pieces and simmer for 8 to 10 minutes. Add the shrimp, crab, mussels, and clams. Simmer for 10 minutes, or until the mussel and clam shells have opened. Discard any mussels or clams that do not open. Adjust the seasonings with salt and black pepper.

To serve, place several potato slices in the bottom of individual serving bowls. Spoon the bouillabaisse into the bowls. Serve with *Roasted Red Pepper Rouille* on the side or drizzled over the bouillabaisse. Top with *Cracked Pepper Toast* and garnish with the parsley.

FISH STOCK

2 tablespoons	extra-virgin olive oil
1 medium	onion, quartered
1 medium	carrot, cut into chunks
4 sprigs	fresh parsley
10 whole	black peppercorns
2 pounds	fish bones (from white-fleshed fish)
1 cup	white wine
1 teaspoon	salt
3 quarts	water

Combine all of the ingredients in a stockpot. Bring to a boil, lower the heat, cover, and simmer for 20 to 25 minutes. Remove the stock from the heat, strain, and allow to cool to room temperature. The stock can be stored for up to 3 days in the refrigerator, or frozen for 3 months. Makes about 2½ quarts.

For each new morning with its light,
For rest and shelter of the night.
For health and food, for love and friends,
For everything Thy goodness sends.

—Ralph Waldo Emerson

ROASTED RED PEPPER ROUILLE

3 large cloves	garlic
1 (½-inch) slice	French bread
1	red pepper, roasted, peeled, and seeded
⅛ teaspoon	cayenne pepper
⅛ teaspoon	saffron
1 large	egg yolk
½ cup	extra-virgin olive oil
¼ teaspoon	sea salt

Place the garlic and bread in the bowl of a food processor fitted with the metal blade and process into fine crumbs. Add the red pepper, cayenne, saffron, and egg yolk. Process until pureed. Use a rubber spatula to wipe down the sides of the bowl. With the motor running, add the olive oil in a thin drizzle until the mixture thickens to the consistency of mayonnaise. Add salt and additional cayenne pepper to taste. Makes about 1 cup.

❖ *Rouille is a traditional topping for bouillabaisse.*

CRACKED PEPPER TOAST

1 loaf	French bread, cut horizontally into ¼-inch slices
	Extra-virgin olive oil
	Sea salt
	Freshly ground black pepper

Preheat the oven to 350°F. Place the sliced bread in a single layer on a cookie sheet. Brush each slice with the oil. Sprinkle sea salt and pepper over the bread slices. Bake until crisp, 7 to 10 minutes.

Puny's Lemon Pie

1 (8-ounce) package	cream cheese, softened
1 (14-ounce) can	sweetened condensed milk
1 (6-ounce) can	frozen lemonade, thawed
¼ cup	fresh lemon juice
1	prepared graham cracker crust
1 cup	whipping cream
2 tablespoons	confectioners' sugar

In a large bowl, combine the cream cheese and condensed milk and stir until smooth. Add the lemonade and lemon juice and mix well. Spoon the lemon filling into the prepared crust and chill until set, at least 4 hours. In the bowl of an electric mixer, whip the cream with the confectioners' sugar until stiff peaks form. Serve the pie with whipped cream on top.

After Dooley had gone, he found the ecru lace cloth that a former bishop's wife had given Lord's Chapel. He would use that over the rose-colored damask that Puny had laundered after Christmas.

He would call Jena at Mitford Blossoms first thing in the morning and order . . . what? Roses, of course.

He polished the brass candlesticks that Walter and Katherine had given him for his fortieth birthday. Forty! He could scarcely remember anything about that turning point, except that he thought he was getting old. Now, he knew the truth. Forty was not old, not in the least. It was sixty that was old, and sixty-one was coming straight at him. He decided not to think further on this sore subject.

He would make something simple to serve before dinner. Perhaps the pâté. But he did not, at all costs, want to seem . . . what was it he did not want to seem? Forward, perhaps, as if the evening had been too carefully arranged.

He put the tablecloths on, and set out his grandmother's Haviland china, and the napkins. Then he went to his study to plan the rest of the meal. For dessert, he thought, maybe pears.

—*At Home in Mitford*, Chapter Sixteen

A Pinch of This, a Dash of That

TABLE LINENS

You'll fight me on this, but table linens civilize and enhance our meals, and our kids need to know about such things. Absolutely worth the starching and ironing, and if you can't use them every day, use them on Sunday!

FAVORITE MEALS

New potatoes, boiled in their jackets and enrobed with butter, served with a simple salad. Roast chicken and good bread, nothing more. Small, crisp french fries with a lightly dressed salad. Saltine crackers crumbled in milk. Cold cornbread crumbled in milk. Sliced, homegrown tomatoes with mayonnaise—on a cold, homemade biscuit. Fried chicken. Fried oysters. Homegrown lettuce and spring onions, wilted with a deft shot of smoking-hot oil and a sharp, quick blast of vinegar.

Then, of course, there's fresh lobster and drawn butter, with champagne.

CHOCOLATE

You can rhapsodize all day about chocolate, yes? I cannot. Instead, I dream of toffee, and clearly remember my first taste of it. I found a candy bar, wrapped and pristine, lying on the playground at school. It was a Heath bar. Heaven!

At home, my sister and I were allowed almost no candy, hardly ever were we allowed store-bought ice cream, and never, ever were we permitted to drink Coca-Cola. I was told that Coca-Cola (which I thought was spelled and pronounced Co-Cola) would rot my teeth, corrode the lining of my stomach, and utterly destroy my brain.

I do not, to this day, drink soda pop, except for an occasional Sprite or ginger ale, nor do I crave chocolate. But then, I'm also the one who actually likes to wash dishes—in a sink.

Standing at the sink and washing dishes is a type of meditation for me, an interlude during which I ponder and dream. I can hardly recount what I ponder, for my mind seems to wander off, untethered as a goat, and this is good for someone who uses her mind so intensely in her work.

BACON

I love it. About once every two months, I buy a pound of Oscar Mayer center-cut bacon and eat it all up over a period of several days. I love it fried very crisp, with all the grease patted off with a paper towel. I do not, at this time, have my cholesterol checked.

—Jan Karon

Father Tim's Poached Pears with Chocolate Sauce

2 to 3 cups	water	*For the chocolate sauce*	
2 cups	dry white wine	1 cup	water
1½ cups	granulated sugar	1 cup	granulated sugar
½ cup	fresh lemon juice	½ cup	unsweetened cocoa powder
2 long strips	lemon peel (yellow outer skin only)	½ cup	heavy cream
2 tablespoons	vanilla extract		
4 to 6 firm	Bartlett, Bosc, or Anjou pears		

Place 2 cups of the water, the wine, 1½ cups sugar, lemon juice, lemon peel, and vanilla in a large saucepan.

Peel the pears, leaving the core and the stem intact. Cut a small piece off the bottom of each pear, so they can stand up. Dip the pears in the poaching liquid before you heat it to keep the pears from turning brown.

There should be enough liquid to cover the pears by ½ inch. If not, add more water. Bring the liquid to a boil over medium-high heat in the saucepan, swirling the pan to dissolve the sugar. Turn the heat down to just below a simmer—do not allow the liquid to boil. Add the pears and cook for 15 minutes, or until a thin blade is easily inserted into a pear. Remove the pot from the heat and let the pears cool in the syrup for 30 to 40 minutes.

Make the chocolate sauce: Place 1 cup water and 1 cup sugar in a medium saucepan and bring to a boil, mixing the sugar in until dissolved. Remove from the heat and whisk in the cocoa powder and cream. Heat the chocolate sauce over very low heat, stirring constantly, until thickened.

To serve, spoon warm chocolate sauce on a dessert plate and place a pear on the sauce.

Father! You've brought your famous gloxinia. Louella, if Father ever brings you a gloxinia, you are officially sick."

"Miss Sadie, you ain't officially sick."

"Oh, well, whatever. Sit down right here, Father." She patted the arm of a chair that had been pulled up to the bed. He put the flower pot on her sunny windowsill and happily did as he was told.

"Well, now, tell me," he said, unbuttoning his jacket, "*are* you sick?"

"Not one bit. I'm just tired. Some people get sick confused with tired. But I know tired when I see it, and that's what I am."

"All those years of eatin' froze' pies and white bread will make you tired," said Louella, putting her hands on her hips. "I'm goin' down and get lunch ready, and it's goin' to be greens cooked with a nice piece of side meat. Greens is full of iron, even if they do smell up the place, and they'll be good for what ails you, ain't that right, Father?"

—*At Home in Mitford,* Chapter Nineteen

Jan Karon's
Mitford Cookbook
& Kitchen Reader

69

Louella's Cornbread

½ cup	bacon drippings or vegetable oil
½ cup	self-rising flour
1½ cups	self-rising cornmeal
1 tablespoon	granulated sugar
½ teaspoon	salt
½ teaspoon	baking soda
2 large	eggs, lightly beaten
1½ cups	buttermilk

Preheat the oven to 400°F. Pour the bacon drippings into a 9-inch black iron skillet and heat in the oven for 3 to 5 minutes. In a large bowl, combine the flour, cornmeal, sugar, salt, and baking soda. In a smaller bowl, whisk together the eggs and buttermilk. Add the wet ingredients to the dry and mix well. Pour the hot bacon drippings from the skillet into the batter and mix well. Immediately pour the batter into the hot skillet and return to the oven. Turn the temperature down to 350°F and bake for 40 to 45 minutes, or until browned. Remove from the oven and immediately turn the cornbread out onto a plate to serve.

THE BLACK IRON SKILLET

You simply cannot cook like Father Tim or Louella or Puny without a seasoned, broken-in, black iron skillet, which absorbs heat gradually and spreads it consistently.

You need one that's "as old as dirt," as Moms Mabley used to say. If you don't know who Moms Mabley was, it will not help in any way for me to tell you.

First of all, let me share this quote:

"I raised three children and five grandchildren out of my black iron skillet."

I don't remember who said this, but her statement is full of wisdom.

First of all, you can cook most anything but soup in a black iron skillet, and second of all, what you cook will not only taste better (a known fact!), but will be good for you because of the trace amounts of iron you'll take into your system.

That said, a black iron skillet must first be seasoned, as a new one will stick, burn your cornbread, give your pork chops an odd taste, and generally cause you to be known as a well-meaning but trifling cook.

Here's the scoop:

Purchase a 10-inch skillet at a hardware store. At home, wash it in warm water, dry it thoroughly, and rub a thin coat of vegetable oil over the entire inside surface. Heat it in a 275°F oven for an hour, which will give the skillet a shiny glaze.

Remove the skillet from the oven and let it cool on the stovetop. Then, when you're ready to cook, it will be ready to get the job done, and then some.

One last word: Never put your skillet in the dishwasher. In truth, iron skillets prefer to be wiped clean, not washed clean. To get rid of any rust spots, pour salt on the skillet, rub in and wipe off. Then re-season.

(If you simply can't sit around seasoning a skillet all weekend, you can buy a skillet by Le Creuset, which you can easily find in the pages of a Williams-Sonoma catalog. No seasoning required because of the exterior coating of porcelain enamel.)

—Jan Karon

Louella's Greens

2 pounds	turnip greens or collard greens
2 ounces	salt pork, chopped
2 ounces	smoked bacon, chopped
⅓ cup	chopped onions
¼ teaspoon	Tabasco sauce
	Salt and freshly ground black pepper taste

Remove the stems from the greens. Wash the leaves well by plunging them in a sink full of water. Drain the water, rinse the sand from the sink, and repeat several times, until the water is clear. Bring a large pot of water to a boil. Add the greens and boil for 2 minutes. Drain the greens and discard the water. Bring a fresh pot of water to a rolling boil. Add the salt pork, smoked bacon, chopped onions, and Tabasco. Add the greens, cover, reduce the heat, and simmer for 1 to 2 hours, or until the greens are tender. Add salt and pepper to taste.

❖ *Boiling the greens a second time for 2 minutes in fresh water will remove some of their bitter taste.*

❖ *The juice from the greens is called "pot likker." It is delicious poured over a piece of cornbread.*

He gazed out on Baxter Park, half-hidden from view behind the rhododendron hedge. The light had stolen softly across the wide, open park bordered on all sides by darkly green hedges. What a treasure, that park, and yet he never used it, nor even encouraged Dooley to go there. A perfect place to sit and read. To sit and think. To have a picnic.

A picnic?

He looked in the refrigerator and found four lemons and made a jar of lemonade. He found cold chicken, and then, a fine wedge of Brie and French rolls. There were berries left from breakfast, and Puny's banana bread that hadn't even been cut.

He put it all into a picnic basket with damask napkins and fetched a starched tablecloth out of the bottom drawer of the buffet.

He stopped suddenly and shook his head. Once again, he had put the cart before the horse.

"Cynthia?" he said, when she answered the phone, "would you like to go on a picnic?" He feared the worst. She was probably off to the country club, perhaps to a dinner dance with a full orchestra.

"You would?" He had certainly not meant to sound so joyful.

—*At Home in Mitford,* Chapter Twenty

Fresh Squeezed Lemonade

2 cups	granulated sugar
6 cups	water
⅛ teaspoon	salt
1¼ cups	fresh lemon juice (from 7 or 8 lemons)
	Lemon slices
	Lime slices

Prepare a simple syrup by combining the sugar and 1 cup of the water in a small saucepan. Place over high heat and boil for 5 minutes. Remove from the heat and let the sugar syrup cool.

Pour the simple syrup into a large pitcher and add the salt, lemon juice, and the remaining 5 cups water. Stir until combined. Just before serving, add lemon and lime slices to the pitcher and serve over ice.

Puny's Banana Bread

	Nonstick cooking spray for the pan
⅓ cup	vegetable oil
1¼ cups	granulated sugar
2 large	eggs, beaten
3 large	very ripe bananas, mashed with a fork
1½ cups	White Lily all-purpose flour
1 teaspoon	baking soda
¼ teaspoon	salt
⅓ cup	buttermilk

Preheat the oven to 350°F. Spray a 9 x 5-inch loaf pan with nonstick cooking spray. Cream the oil and sugar together in the bowl of an electric mixer until light and creamy. Beat in the eggs. Add the bananas and mix well. In a separate bowl, sift together the flour, baking soda, and salt. Add 1 cup of the flour mixture to the banana mixture, mix well, then add half of the buttermilk and mix well. Add the remaining flour, and then the buttermilk and mix just until blended. Pour the batter into the pan, smooth the top, and bake for 45 minutes, or until a toothpick comes out clean when inserted into the center of the bread. Cool in the pan for 5 minutes, then invert onto a wire cooling rack.

PUNY'S SAVING GRACE #2

"When your bananas get too ripe, don't throw 'em in th' compost can. Peel 'em an' freeze in a Ziploc 'til its time to bake bread or cake."

Viewed from the site of the burned church, where Hope House would be built, the valley spread below like an emerald carpet, dotted with gardens that stocked the coolers of The Local twice a week.

Already, the Silver Queen corn had started coming up the mountain every Tuesday and Friday, to be unloaded into the wooden bins. And, as always, the villagers could be counted on to clean out the entire truckload in a single day, so that everybody knew what everybody else was having for dinner.

He was happy to stand in line at the sidewalk corn bins holding his paper bag, though, inevitably, someone offered him their place toward the front of the queue. No, he did not want to move through the corn line quickly, he wanted to savor the little hum of excitement that always came, and the fellowship, and the laughter.

He wanted time to get a good look at Avis Packard's face as he peeled back shuck and tassel to display seed-pearl kernels. "Ain't a worm in 'em. You find a worm, you got yourself a free ear."

Miss Rose came, intently looking for worms, while Uncle Billy sat on the bench by the street lamp and told his latest joke to a captive audience. Winnie Ivey closed the bakery and filled a sack for herself and her brother.

While Louella hunted for a dozen perfect ears, Miss Sadie sat in the car, which she had pulled onto the sidewalk in front of the library next door, and Percy Mosely walked across the street in his apron to pick up the bushel Avis had earmarked for the Grill.

A tourist once asked a local, "Is there a festival in town?"

"Nope, it's just that th' corn's come in."

"How quaint! Perhaps I should get some."

"Don't know if I'd do that," the local cautioned, darkly. "They say it sours if it travels in a car." Mitford did not like to sell its early corn to outsiders, who, they said, would only overcook it, and couldn't appreciate it, anyway.

—*At Home in Mitford,* Chapter Twenty-Two

Silver Queen Corn

2 tablespoons	granulated sugar
6 ears	fresh Silver Queen Corn, shucked and silked
½ cup	unsalted butter, melted
	Salt and freshly ground pepper

Bring a large pot of water with the sugar added to a rolling boil. Add the corn and allow the water to come back to a rolling boil. Cook for another 4 minutes after the water returns to a boil. Drain the corn, roll it in melted butter and season with salt and pepper.

"Sex is good, but not as good as fresh sweet corn."

—Garrison Keillor

❖ *Fresh corn is best cooked immediately after it is picked. Since this is not always possible, adding sugar to the water will restore some of its natural sweetness.*

Puny's Saving Grace #3

"When boilin' corn, add a little sugar to th' water instead of salt. Don't never use salt while you're cookin' corn, it makes it tough."

He wrote George Gaynor and gave him a complete update on all church doings, including one death and two new members of the nursery.

"Who're you writing?" asked Emma.

"The man in the attic."

"Do you think I ought to send him some fudge?"

"That's a splendid thought."

"I'm makin' Harold a big batch tonight, he's so skinny I have to shake th' sheets to find him. I'll just make a double batch, and mail it tomorrow. Do you think they'll X-ray it for files or razor blades or whatever?"

"Probably."

"If they're doin' their job, they will," she said with authority. "Do you know what we sang Sunday?"

"What's that?" he muttered, looking in his desk drawer for some glue to repair his bookend.

"'Amazing Grace.'"

"Aha."

"If Episcopalians would sing that more, instead of all that stuff with no tune, you'd be amazed how people would flock in."

"Is that a fact? I suppose you think a Baptist wrote that hymn."

"Well, of course a Baptist wrote it, they sing it all th' time."

"My dear Emma," he said with obvious impatience, "that hymn was written by an Episcopal clergyman."

"He was prob'ly raised Baptist," she said, huffily.

—*At Home in Mitford*, Chapter Twenty-Three

Jan Karon's
Mitford Cookbook
& Kitchen Reader

Emma's Fudge

1 cup	unsalted butter, cut into small pieces, plus more for greasing the pan
4½ cups	granulated sugar
1 (12-ounce) can	evaporated milk
¼ teaspoon	salt
18 ounces (2¼ cups)	semisweet chocolate chips
1 (7-ounce) jar	marshmallow cream
4 cups	chopped pecans
2 teaspoons	vanilla extract

Lightly butter a 9 x 13-inch pan and set aside. Place the sugar and evaporated milk in a large saucepan over medium heat and cook for 11 minutes, stirring constantly. Remove from the heat, add the butter, salt, chocolate chips, and marshmallow cream and stir until well combined. Add the pecans and vanilla and mix well. Pour into the pan and allow to cool completely. Refrigerate overnight and then cut into squares. Store in the refrigerator or freezer.

I vote that the best picnic lunch of my life!" she declared. "The best cold chicken, the best French bread, the best cheese, the best raspberry tart!"

"I agree with all of that!" he said, trying to ignore his increasing appetite for holding her in his arms.

She took a small sketchbook out of her skirt pocket, and a box of pencils. "I don't suppose you'd care to put one corner of the quilt over your head?"

"Not particularly. Why, for heaven's sake?"

"I'm starting on the wise men, and this is my very last chance at you, you know. All you have to do is sit over there and pull the quilt up around your head, like this."

"That's all? How long will it take?"

"Five minutes! I'll hurry. Then, when I get to my drawing board, I'll use the sketch as a model for the watercolor." She peered at him. "Actually, if you get on your knees, it will be easier."

"For who?"

"For me, I think. Here, get on your knees, and I'll fix the quilt like a burnoose, sort of." She took the raffia that he'd used to keep the napkin wrapped around the bread, put the quilt over his head, and tied it.

"There!" she said approvingly. "You look just like you've come from afar!"

He was relieved that the ordeal was nearly over, when he looked up to see an old man and woman coming along the path leading from the woods to the knoll. They were carrying burlap sacks filled with newly dug ferns, an occupation pursued by a number of locals.

As oddly stricken as if he'd been caught thieving chickens, he could not seem to budge from his knees, nor remove his burnoose. "Good afternoon!" he called, weakly. They paused, looked at him quizzically, then turned and hurried back into the woods.

"An' that feller's a preacher!" he heard the man say to his wife.

—*At Home in Mitford*, Chapter Twenty-Four

Cynthia's Raspberry Tart

	Nonstick cooking spray for the pan
6 tablespoons	unsalted butter, at room temperature
1 cup	White Lily all-purpose flour
1¼ cups	chopped pecans
2 tablespoons	brown sugar
½ teaspoon	salt
1 large	egg
½ teaspoon	vanilla extract
1 cup	seedless raspberry preserves
2 (6-ounce) containers	fresh raspberries
1 cup	whipping cream
2 tablespoons	confectioners' sugar

Preheat the oven to 350°F. Coat an 8- to 10-inch tart pan with a removable bottom with nonstick cooking spray. Place the butter, flour, pecans, sugar, salt, egg, and vanilla in the bowl of a food processor fitted with the metal blade and pulse until well blended. Press the nut mixture into the prepared pan. Bake the crust for 20 to 25 minutes, or until it turns a light brown color. Set aside to cool completely before adding the filling.

Spoon the raspberry preserves onto the crust, making sure to spread to the edges. Arrange the fresh raspberries stem side down in circles (if using a round pan) or rows (if using a square pan) and chill. Just before serving whip the cream with the confectioners' sugar until soft peaks form. Serve garnished with a dollop of whipped cream.

The rector grinned. How accustomed he'd grown to the simple familiarity of friends in this small place on the map. Mitford had given him an extended family, with cousins galore, and no two alike.

"The usual," Mule told Percy, "an' squeeze th' grease out."

"I'll squeeze you some grease—on your bald head."

What would he find in Sligo? Considering that half of Mitford had Irish blood, with a liberal dose of Scottish thrift, what he'd find might not be so different, after all. He hoped there would be a warm place like the Grill, in the village near the farmhouse.

"Percy," said J.C., "there's somethin' unusual about these grits."

"Oh, yeah?" Percy said suspiciously.

"They're real good 'n' thick an' got plenty of butter, th' way I like 'em."

Percy beamed. "I never used t' eat grits, but now that I've started eatin' 'em of a mornin', I make 'em th' way they taste good t' me."

Was something different about J.C.? Father Tim wondered. Maybe so, but he couldn't put his finger on it.

"Th' only thing is," said J.C., "this gravy's got lumps the size of banty eggs."

The rector finished his coffee and got up from the booth. "Boys, I've got more to do than I can shake a stick at, and Emma's picking me up at the crack of dawn tomorrow. Hold it in the road 'til I get back."

They all got out of the booth and stood up. It wasn't every day that one of their own went off to a foreign country.

Mule slapped him on the back. "Don't take any wooden nickels, buddyroe."

"Drop us a line," said J.C., "but keep it short and axe th' big words."

Rodney shook his hand. "Take it easy, Father. I'll miss all th' business you've been givin' me lately."

"God bless you," said Percy, choking up. "And put y'r money back in y'r pocket, it's on th' house."

There, he thought, untying Barnabas from the bench leg on the sidewalk. It's official. I'm really going to go through with this thing.

—*At Home in Mitford,* Chapter Twenty-Four

Percy's Grits

4 cups	whole milk
1 cup	quick-cooking grits
4 tablespoons	unsalted butter
1 cup	grated cheddar cheese
	Salt and freshly ground black pepper

Pour the milk into a heavy saucepan over medium-high heat and heat until bubbles appear on the edges of the pan (just before the milk is ready to boil). Stir in the grits using a wire whisk. Reduce the heat to medium-low and cover. Cook for 5 to 7 minutes, stirring occasionally. Add the butter and cheese and stir until melted. Add salt and pepper to taste.

A Light in the Window

He had missed the old rectory, too, with its clamor and quiet, its sunshine and shadow. Never before in his life as a rector had he found a home so welcoming or comfortable—a home that seemed, somehow, like a friend.

He spied the thing on his counter at once. It was Edith Mallory's signature blue casserole dish.

He was afraid of that.

Emma had written to Sligo to say that Pat Mallory had died soon after he left for Ireland. Heart attack. No warning. Pat, she said, had felt a wrenching chest pain, had sat down on the top step outside his bedroom, and after dropping dead sitting up, had toppled to the foot of the stairs, where the Mallorys' maid of thirty years had found him just before dinner.

"Oh, Mr. Mallory," she was reported to have said, "you shouldn't have gone and done that. We're havin' lasagna."

Sitting there on the farmhouse window seat, reading Emma's five-page letter, he had known that Edith Mallory would not waste any time when he returned.

Long before Pat's death, he'd been profoundly unsteadied when she had slipped her hand into his or let her fingers run along his arm. At one point, she began winking at him during sermons, which distracted him to such a degree that he resumed his old habit of preaching over the heads of the congregation, literally.

So far, he had escaped her random snares but had once dreamed he was locked with her in the parish-hall coat closet, pounding desperately on the door and pleading with the sexton to let him out.

Now Pat, good soul, was cold in the grave, and Edith's casserole was hot on his counter.

Casseroles! Their seduction had long been used on men of the cloth, often with rewarding results for the cook.

Casseroles, after all, were a gesture that on the surface could not be mistaken for anything other than righteous goodwill. And, once one had consumed and exclaimed over the initial offering, along would come another on its very heels, until the bachelor curate ended up a married curate or the divorced deacon a fellow so skillfully ensnared that he never knew what hit him.

In the language of food, there were casseroles, and there were casseroles. Most were used to comfort the sick or inspire the downhearted. But certain others, in his long experience, were so filled with allure and innuendo that they ceased to be Broccoli Cheese Delight intended for the stomach and became arrows aimed straight for the heart.

In any case, there was always the problem of what to do with the dish. Decent people returned it full of something else. Which meant that the person to whom you returned it would be required, at some point, to give you another food item, all of which produced a cycle that was unimaginably tedious.

Clergy, of course, were never required to fill the dish before returning it, but either way, it had to be returned. And there, clearly, was the rub.

He approached the unwelcome surprise as if a snake might have been coiled inside. His note of thanks, which he would send over tomorrow by Puny, would be short and to the point:

Dear Edith: Suffice it to say that you remain one of the finest cooks in the county. That was no lie; it was undeniably true.

Your way with (blank, blank) is exceeded only by your graciousness. A thousand thanks. In His peace, Fr. Tim.

There.

He lifted the lid. Instantly, his mouth began to water, and his heart gave a small leap of joy.

Crab cobbler! One of his favorites. He stared with wonder at the dozen flaky homemade biscuits poised on the bed of fresh crab meat and fragrant sauce.

Perhaps, he thought with sudden abandon, he should give Edith Mallory a ring this very moment and express his thanks.

As he reached for the phone, he realized what he was doing—he was placing his foot squarely in a bear trap.

He hastily clamped the lid on the steaming dish. "You see?" he muttered darkly. "That's the way it happens."

Where casseroles were concerned, one must constantly be on guard.

—*A Light in the Window*, Chapter One

Jan Karon's
Mitford Cookbook
& Kitchen Reader

Edith's Crab Casserole

½ cup plus 1 tablespoon	unsalted butter, more for greasing the casserole
½ cup	sliced green onions
¼ cup	finely chopped onions
2 pounds	lump crab meat, drained
1 (14-ounce) can	artichoke hearts, drained and finely chopped
½ cup	all-purpose flour
3 cups	half-and-half
¾ cup	white wine
2 tablespoons	chopped fresh parsley (or 2 teaspoons dried)
2 tablespoons	fresh lemon juice
2 teaspoons	salt
½ teaspoon	freshly ground white pepper
¼ teaspoon	cayenne pepper

For the biscuit topping

2 cups	White Lily self-rising flour
¼ cup	shortening, chilled
1¼ cups	buttermilk, chilled
1 cup	grated white cheddar cheese

Lightly butter a 13 x 9-inch casserole and set aside. Warm 1 tablespoon of the butter in a large skillet over medium heat, add the green onions and onions and sauté until soft, about 10 minutes. Using paper towels, pat the crab meat and artichoke hearts to remove excess moisture. Melt the remaining ½ cup of the butter in a medium saucepan over low heat, then add the flour, stirring until smooth. Gradually add the half-and-half, and continue cooking over medium heat, stirring constantly, until the mixture is thick and bubbly. Stir in the wine, parsley, lemon juice, salt, white pepper, and cayenne.

Layer half of the crab meat, followed by the artichoke hearts, and then the onions in the casserole and top with half of the sauce. Repeat with the remaining crab meat, artichokes, and onions and top with the rest of the sauce.

Make the biscuit topping:
Preheat the oven to 375°F. Place the 2 cups flour in a large bowl, and using a pastry blender or two knives, cut the shortening into the flour until the mixture looks like small peas. Add the buttermilk and grated cheese and stir until just mixed. Turn out onto a lightly floured surface. Pat the dough into a ½-inch thick round. Cut out biscuits with a 2-inch round cookie cutter and place on top of the casserole. Make sure the biscuit edges are touching each other.

Place in the oven and bake for 35 to 40 minutes, or until the casserole is bubbly and the biscuits are just brown on top.

❖ *Be sure to use self-rising flour for this recipe—it comes with salt and leavening already mixed in.*

Going to a town council meeting was decidedly not what he wanted to do with his evening. After two months away, he hardly knew what was going on. And he was still feeling oddly jet-lagged, shaking his head vigorously on occasion with some hope of clearing it. But he would go; it might put him back in the swing of things, and frankly, he was curious why the mayor, Esther Cunningham, had called an unofficial meeting and why it might concern him.

"Don't eat," Esther told him on the phone. "Ray's bringin' baked beans, cole slaw, and ribs from home. Been cookin' all day."

"Hallelujah," he said with feeling.

There was a quickening in the air of the mayor's office. Ray was setting out his home-cooked supper on the vast desktop, overlooked by pictures of their twenty-one grandchildren at the far end.

"Mayor," said Leonard Bostick, "it's a cryin' shame you cain't cook as good as Ray."

"I've got better things to do," she snapped. "I did the cookin' for forty years. Now it's his turn."

Ray grinned. "You tell 'em, honey."

"Whooee!" said Paul Hartley. "Baby backs! Get over here, Father, and give us a blessin'."

"Come on!" shouted the mayor to the group lingering in the hall, "it's blessin' time!"

Esther Cunningham held out her hands, and the group eagerly formed a circle. "Our Lord," said the rector, "we're grateful for the gift of friends and neighbors and those willing to lend their hand to the welfare of this place. We thank you for the peace of this village and for your grace to do the work that lies ahead. We thank you, too, for this food and ask a special blessing on the one who prepared it. In Jesus' name."

"Amen!" said the assembly.

"Edith Mallory's lookin' to give you th' big whang-do," said Emma.

Until this inappropriate remark, there had been a resonant peace in the small office. The windows were open to morning air embroidered with birdsong. His sermon notes were going at a pace. And the familiar comfort of his old swivel chair was sheer bliss.

"And what, exactly, is that supposed to mean?"

His part-time church secretary glanced up from her ledger. "It means she's going to cook your goose."

—EMMA GARRETT AND FATHER TIM

The mayor was the first in line. "You're goin' t' get a blessing, all right," she told her husband. "Just look at this sauce! You've done it again, sweet face."

Ray winked at the rector. There, thought the rector, is a happy man if I ever saw one.

"How's your diabetes, Father?"

"It won't tolerate the torque you've put under the hood of that pot, I regret to say."

"Take doubles on m' slaw, then," said Ray, heaping the rector's plate.

—*A LIGHT IN THE WINDOW*, CHAPTER ONE

Ray's Barbecue Ribs

4 pounds	pork spareribs
2 cups	apple cider vinegar
1 cup	water
2 cups	chopped onions
2 cloves	garlic, minced
2 teaspoons	salt
2 teaspoons	freshly ground black pepper
1 tablespoon	red pepper flakes
2 teaspoons	granulated sugar
2	bay leaves
2 teaspoons	dried thyme
½ cup	vegetable oil
2 tablespoons	dry mustard

Place the spareribs in a large pot and cover with cold water. Bring to a boil over high heat and boil for 5 minutes. (Boiling the ribs before baking removes some of the unwanted fat.) Remove the ribs from the boiling water, drain, and place in large baking pan.

In a large saucepan over high heat, combine the vinegar, water, onions, garlic, salt, pepper, red pepper flakes, sugar, bay leaves, thyme, oil, and dry mustard. Bring to a boil, lower the heat, and simmer for 10 minutes.

Preheat the oven to 300°F. Pour 2 cups of the barbecue sauce over the ribs. Cover with aluminum foil and bake until the ribs are tender and brown, 2½ to 3 hours. Add water to the pan while cooking if the ribs become dry.

Serve the ribs topped with the extra sauce.

Ray's Cole Slaw

8 to 10 cups	grated cabbage, or 2 (1-pound) bags pre-cut slaw mix
4 teaspoons	salt
1 bunch	green onions, sliced
½ cup	sour cream
½ cup	Hellmann's mayonnaise
3 tablespoons	apple cider vinegar
1 tablespoon	fresh lemon juice
¼ cup	granulated sugar
⅛ teaspoon	freshly ground black pepper

Toss the cabbage with the salt in a colander set over a medium bowl. Cover with plastic wrap and place a heavy plate on top. Place in the refrigerator for at least 1 hour, allowing the excess water to drain from the cabbage. Pat the cabbage dry with paper towels. Mix together the cabbage and green onions in a large bowl.

In a small bowl, combine the sour cream, mayonnaise, vinegar, lemon juice, sugar, and pepper. Add the dressing to the cabbage and green onions and mix well. Refrigerate until chilled. Adjust the seasonings with salt and pepper before serving.

W hang-do," said Emma sourly, handing him the phone.

"I've invited the building committee to meet here on Wednesday evening." Edith Mallory sounded pleased with herself. "Of course, they loved the idea. Magdolen will do her famous spoonbread but I'll do the tenderloin."

Tenderloin!

"I know how you enjoy a tenderloin. I've had it sent from New York."

"That's very generous of you. Of course, there's really no need to impose for a dinner meeting . . ."

"But life is so short," she said, sniffing. "Why have a dull meeting when you can have a dinner party?"

He didn't know why. Why, indeed?

"You can see the trump lloyd I had painted in the study. It looks just like old books on a shelf."

"Aha."

"I'll have Ed pick you up at a quarter 'til," she said. He could hear the little sucking noise that came from dragging on that blasted cigarette.

"No!" he nearly shouted. His car was still sitting in the garage with a dead battery. "Ah, no thanks. I'll come with Ron. We have a lot to discuss . . ."

"Of course, but Ron is coming with Tad Sherrill, he said, because his pickup . . . what did he say . . . blew a gasket, I think."

"Well, then, I'll just squeeze in with them. And thank you, Edith. It's more than good of you." He hung up at once, not surprised to find his forehead slightly damp.

—*A Light in the Window*, Chapter One

Emma peered at him over her glasses. "Just remember," she muttered. "Remember what?" "Forearmed is forewarned." "No, Emma. Forewarned is forearmed."

—Emma Garrett and Father Tim

Edith's Beef Tenderloin

2 cups	white wine
2 cups	white vinegar
1 (10-ounce) bottle	Heinz 57 Steak Sauce
1 (3½ to 5 pound)	beef tenderloin
1 large	white onion, sliced
½ cup	unsalted butter, at room temperature
	Lowry's Seasoned Pepper
	McCormick Season-All

Pour the wine, vinegar, and Heinz 57 sauce into a large bowl and mix well. Place the tenderloin in a large zip-top bag. Pour the wine mixture into the bag, add the onions, and seal the bag. Place in the refrigerator for 48 hours to marinate.

Remove the tenderloin from the marinade, pat dry, and place in a roasting pan. Rub the tenderloin with the butter, and coat with Seasoned Pepper and Season-All. Cover, place in the refrigerator, and let sit for 4 hours.

Preheat the oven to 450°F. Roast the meat, uncovered, for 30 to 40 minutes. Using a meat thermometer to determine desired doneness, cook the meat to: 120° to 130° for rare, 130° to 140° for medium rare, 140° to 155° for medium, 155° to 160° for well done.

Let stand at room temperature for 45 minutes before slicing and serving.

Magdolen's Spoon Bread

2 tablespoons	unsalted butter, more for greasing the soufflé dish
1 cup	plain cornmeal
1 teaspoon	salt
1 tablespoon	granulated sugar
1¼ cups	boiling water
3 large	eggs, separated
1 cup	buttermilk
1 teaspoon	baking soda
½ teaspoon	baking powder

Preheat the oven to 350°F. Lightly butter a soufflé dish and set aside. Place the cornmeal, salt, and sugar in a large bowl and mix well. Slowly add the boiling water, stirring constantly. Add the butter and stir until the butter is melted. In a separate small bowl, lightly beat the egg yolks. Add a small amount of the hot meal mixture to the egg yolks, then add the egg yolks to the remaining hot meal mixture and mix well.

Add the buttermilk, baking soda, and baking powder to the batter and mix well. In the bowl of an electric mixer, beat the egg whites until stiff. Gently fold in the beaten egg whites. Pour into the soufflé dish and bake for 25 to 30 minutes.

But who would have sent me a microwave?" he wanted to know.

Puny threw up her hands. "Don't ask me."

"And who am I to ask, for heaven's sake? Weren't you here when it was delivered?"

She shrugged.

"Come on, Puny. Who did this low thing?"

"They was goin' to give you a VCR," she said, "so I told 'em t' send a microwave."

"I won't have it in my kitchen. I knew this would happen someday. It's insidious the way these things take over people's lives."

"How can it take over your dern life if you don't even use it? Who does most of th' cookin' around here, anyway? If I want to heat up some soup for your lunch, I can do it while you're comin' through th' door. If Dooley wants a hamburger, whap, in it goes, out it comes, instead of me slavin' over a hot stove to feed that bottomless pit.

"You don't have to touch it. You don't have to lay a finger on it. I'll cover it with a sheet when I leave of an evenin' if that'll suit you any better."

"Who?" he asked darkly.

"Those vestry people."

"Them again," he said.

"They were jis' tryin' to be helpful."

Helpful! Since when did a vestry have the right to violate a man's kitchen? Was nothing sacred?

"I hope you don't mind my sayin' this . . ."

He knew he would mind.

"You prob'ly ought to take you a laxative."

—*A Light in the Window*, Chapter Two

Jan Karon's
Mitford Cookbook
& Kitchen Reader

99

Indian summer was a glad fifth season that didn't come every year. It stepped in without warning, as an inexpressibly welcome bonus, a gift that made limbs lighter, minds clearer, steps quicker.

Absalom Greer bounded from behind the counter of his country store as if all the bonuses of the season resided in him.

"To my mind, preachin' is like soup. They want a little chunk of meat in it, an' they like it seasoned good. Don't hold back on th' pepper, don't be scant with th' salt, and make sure it ain't watery. They'll turn it down if it's watery, even on an empty stomach."

—Homeless Hobbes

They shook hands warmly and embraced. "Preacher Greer has sent his son to greet me," said the rector.

The old man laughed. "You're a fine one to talk, seein' as Ireland knocked a decade or two off your own years."

"What's that wondrous smell? Wait! Don't tell me. Fried chicken!"

"Sure as you're born. Crisp and brown, with a mess of green beans and a bowl of mashed potatoes and gravy. We won't even talk about the biscuits stacked up on our best china platter, already buttered."

"Hallelujah and four amens," said the rector, who refused to consider the lethal consequences of that particular menu on his diabetes.

"Lottie has cooked all morning, and don't be sayin' you wish she hadn't gone to any trouble. It's my sister's joy to go to trouble when the town priest is comin'. Did you bring your dog?"

"I did. In the car."

"Our cat's off on a toot, so bring him in. We'll give him a home-cooked dinner."

Absalom put the handwritten *Closed* sign on the knob of the front door, and all three of them walked the length of the creaking floor to the back rooms. Though the rector had been here but once before, he felt instantly at home.

After the meal the Greers called dinner and the rector called lunch, Lottie went to the garden to clean out the vegetable beds, and Barnabas lay with his head on Absalom's foot.

—*A Light in the Window*, Chapter Three

Lottie Greer's Fried Chicken

1 whole	chicken, cut into 8 pieces
¼ cup	salt
	Ice water, to cover the chicken
¼ cup	granulated sugar
1 quart	buttermilk
2 tablespoons	seasoned salt
2 cups	all-purpose flour
3 tablespoons	bacon drippings
	Vegetable shortening, for frying

Place the chicken pieces in a large bowl; add the salt and enough ice water to cover the chicken. Cover with plastic wrap and place in the refrigerator for at least 8 hours, or overnight. Drain the chicken and pat dry. Wipe out the bowl, add the sugar, buttermilk, and 1 tablespoon of the seasoned salt, and mix well. Add the chicken and place in the refrigerator to soak for 2 to 4 hours.

Combine the flour and the remaining 1 tablespoon of the seasoned salt in a brown paper bag. Remove the chicken pieces from the buttermilk. Place the chicken in batches in the paper bag and shake to coat the chicken.

Place the bacon drippings and enough shortening to reach 1 inch of melted fat in a large black iron skillet. Heat the fat to 360°F over medium-high heat.

Add the chicken pieces to the skillet, a few pieces at a time (do not crowd the skillet), and cook for 15 to 20 minutes on each side, or until golden brown. Drain the chicken on paper towels before serving.

Lottie Greer's Mashed Potatoes

5 to 6 medium	russet potatoes, peeled and quartered
2 teaspoons	salt
¼ cup	unsalted butter
½ cup	sour cream
¼ to ½ cup	milk
	Freshly ground black pepper to taste

Place the potatoes in a large saucepan. Cover with water, add the salt, and bring to a boil over high heat. Lower the heat and simmer until the potatoes are completely tender when pierced with a knife. Drain the potatoes in a colander and return them to the saucepan. Add the butter and sour cream and mash with a potato masher. Add milk as needed until the potatoes are soft and creamy. Add salt and pepper to taste before serving.

PUNY'S SAVING GRACE #4

"Let's say you're makin' gravy and you've got it way too salty. Stir in a little instant mashed p'tatoes, and add a little more liquid to offset th' thickenin'. My granmaw taught me this, 'cept she didn't use instant, she used real.

"An' speakin' of p'tatoes, if you soak p'tatoes in salt water for twenty minutes before bakin', they'll bake a lot faster. Plus, if you're goin' to make french fries—Joe Joe an' th' twins love it when I make french fries—let th' cut p'tatoes stand in cold water for a half-hour. Then get 'em good an' dry before fryin' an' they'll be a whole lot crispier."

Lottie Greer's Country Biscuits

8 tablespoons	shortening, chilled, more for greasing the baking sheets
3¼ cups	White Lily self-rising flour, more for rolling out the dough
½ teaspoon	salt
2 tablespoons	granulated sugar
½ teaspoon	baking soda
2 cups	buttermilk, chilled

Preheat the oven to 475°F. Grease a couple of baking sheets and set aside. Combine the flour, salt, sugar, and baking soda in a large bowl. Cut in the shortening with a pastry blender until the shortening is the size of small peas. Add the buttermilk and stir until just mixed. The dough should be very wet.

Place some flour in a shallow bowl. Spoon a heaping tablespoon of wet dough into the flour. Flour your fingers and sprinkle flour on the top of the wet dough. Roll the dough gently in flour just to coat the outside. Try not to mix too much extra flour into the dough. Shape into biscuits, using floured hands, working the dough as little as possible. Arrange the biscuits, touching each other, on the baking sheets. Bake for 15 to 20 minutes, or until just brown on top.

Clearly, Ireland had given him a sense of wholeness he'd longed for, and the mass gathering at Erin's of near and distant cousins had been a high point. The Irish were known to grumble about the hordes of Americans who stumbled through parish graveyards, rubbing stones, trampling flowers, looking for their roots. But once connected, it was a different story—one was taken in and cosseted like the biblical prodigal.

Yet, if the cousins had been a high point, one event had been higher still—the day he'd taken the rented car with Katherine and Walter and the picnic basket with the rhubarb tart. The landlady had wrapped the tart, hot from the oven, and for miles they salivated as the aroma crept out of the basket and filled the car.

With a sudden screech of tires, Katherine had pulled off the narrow road and looked them dead in the eye. "I can't wait another minute," she said. Excited as children, they peeled the tea towel from around the still-warm delicacy and devoured every crumb.

"There!" Katherine had said, recklessly wiping her mouth on the hem of her dress. "That's how I want to live for the rest of my life!"

—*A Light in the Window*, Chapter Three

The Irish Lady's Rhubarb Tart

	Unsalted butter for greasing the pan	*For the topping*	
½ recipe	*Pastry for a Double Crust Pie* (page 4) (Halve the recipe, or make the whole recipe and freeze half)	¼ cup	all-purpose flour
		2 tablespoons	light brown sugar
		2 tablespoons	rolled oats
		2 tablespoons	sliced almonds
		½ teaspoon	ground cinnamon
1 large	egg, lightly beaten	⅛ teaspoon	ground cloves
2½ cups	halved hulled strawberries	⅛ teaspoon	salt
4 cups	chopped rhubarb	3 tablespoons	unsalted butter
1¼ cups	granulated sugar	1 cup	whipping cream
3 tablespoons	cornstarch	3 tablespoons	confectioners' sugar

Preheat the oven to 400°F. Butter a 9-inch tart pan with a removable bottom. Roll out the pastry dough and fit it into the tart pan. Cover the dough with aluminum foil and fill with pie weights or dried beans. Bake for 15 minutes. Remove crust from the oven and remove the pie weights and foil. Brush the crust with the beaten egg and return to the oven for 5 minutes. Remove from the oven and turn the temperature down to 350°F.

Combine the strawberries, rhubarb, granulated sugar, and cornstarch in a medium bowl. Pour the fruit mixture into the prepared pie shell.

Make the topping: Place the flour, brown sugar, rolled oats, almonds, cinnamon, cloves, and salt in a separate large bowl, and mix well. Cut the butter into the mixture with a pastry blender or two knives until it resembles coarse meal. Sprinkle the topping over the fruit. Bake for 40 to 45 minutes, until the crumb topping is browned. Remove the tart from the oven to a cooling rack, and cool completely before serving.

Whip the cream with the confectioners' sugar in the bowl of an electric mixer until soft peaks form. Serve tart slices topped with whipped cream.

❖ *If you are in a hurry and don't have time to prepare the homemade pie crust, use a Pillsbury prepared pie crust.*

You remember Father Tim's Irish cousin in *A Light in the Window* who, as it turned out, wasn't Irish in the least, much less his cousin. What a pain in the neck. As was her recipe for lunch:

Remove tab from can of Coke, leave tab on drain board, in sink, or on floor. Open pack of cheese Nabs and eat one while standing at sink, dropping part of wrapper on floor. Open bread drawer and take out bar of Kit Kat candy, stick in robe pocket and head upstairs where you climb into bed with a derelict typewriter and eat and drink all of the above while working on a trashy novel.

Let crumbs fall where they may.

—JAN KARON

On the sidewalk at the Grill, they met Buck Leeper. "Mr. Leeper, my cousin, Meg Patrick."

"Pleased," she said, thrusting her hands into the pockets of her trench coat.

The Hope House superintendent nodded and flipped his cigarette over the curb. "Miss Patrick."

"Things are looking good on the hill," said the rector.

"Not good enough."

Leeper sauntered through the door ahead of them and went to his table at the window.

The rector greeted the Collar Button and Irish Woolen crowd who were sitting at the counter. He felt every head in the place turn as they walked to the rear booth.

After Velma poured their coffee, Percy came around, wide-eyed with curiosity.

"Percy, meet my cousin, Meg Patrick. From Ireland."

"Ireland, is it?" Percy peered into the booth as if into a cage containing a rare panda. "Mule Skinner claims t' be Irish."

"We're distantly related to Skinners," she said, adjusting her bifocals. "Very distantly."

"This one ain't so distant. Here he comes now. How d'you like your eggs?"

"Fried," she said, "and a broiled tomato."

"A what?"

"A broiled tomato."

Saying "tomahto" did not cut it with Percy Mosely.

"Grits or hash browns is all we got." Percy appeared to pronounce this through his teeth.

"Are your hash browns freshly peeled and cut, or are they . . . packaged?"

Father Tim stirred his coffee, though there was nothing in it to stir.

"Packaged, like every other hash brown from here t' California."

"Is your cooking oil saturated?"

"You better believe it."

"Just eggs, thank you, and whole-wheat toast. Unbuttered."

"Better have you some of Percy's good sausage t' go with that," said Mule, slipping into the booth.

Please don't say it, thought the rector. But, of course, she did.

"I eat flesh foods only on Sunday."

Percy Mosely would not let him forget this anytime soon.

—*A Light in the Window*, Chapter Twelve

W ill you have dinner with me on Friday evening?"

   She looked into his eyes and smiled. "I would love to have dinner with you on Friday evening."

   "How do you like your peanut butter-and-banana sandwiches?"

   "With the bananas cut in thick slices and smashed into the peanut butter."

   "Smooth or crunchy?"

   "Crunchy."

   "White or dark?"

   "White."

   "With or without crusts?"

   "With!"

   With such knowledge now his forever, he felt invincible.

—*A Light in the Window*, Chapter Four

Jan Karon's
Mitford Cookbook
& Kitchen Reader

Jan Karon's Banana and Peanut Butter Sandwiches

1 large	banana
¼ teaspoon	fresh lemon juice
4 tablespoons	peanut butter
6 slices	sandwich bread
	Miniature chocolate chips, optional
	Miniature marshmallows, optional

In a small bowl mash the banana with the lemon juice. Add the peanut butter and mix until smooth. Divide the mixture up between 3 sandwiches, adding miniature chocolate chips or marshmallows if desired. Cut each sandwich in half or into 4 triangles.

❖ *Author's note: On the preceding page, Cynthia gives Father Tim her "recipe." It sounds good to me, but here's one I like even better. (No crusts for me, please. This is a party sandwich!)*

The Sunday of the Village Advent Walk was bright with sun, yet bitterly cold. He was glad to put on the camel topcoat Puny had brushed and hung on the closet door. He had let it hang there for more than two weeks, eagerly waiting for the weather to turn cold. Winters had become so mild, he had scarcely had it on his back in recent years. Let the hard winter come! he thought, whistling the morning anthem.

At four o'clock, the villagers poured into Lord's Chapel, teeth chattering, to stand expectantly in the pews as the choir processed along the aisle. "O Zion, that bringest good tidings, get thee up to the heights and sing!" Rays of afternoon light poured through the stained glass windows, drenching the sanctuary with splashes of color. It was enough, he thought, if no word were spoken or hymn sung.

After the service, he and Dooley followed the singing procession to the Methodist chapel, where the children's choir met them on the steps. "Hark, the Herald Angels Sing," they warbled, sending puffs of warm breath into the freezing air. People filled the nave and were standing in the churchyard as the ancient story of Christmas was read from Luke, and candles were lighted in every window.

Afterward, they trooped down the alleyway and across Main Street, singing to the tops of their voices in wildly random keys. They were led, at this point, by J.C. Hogan, who was walking backwards at a heedless trot while snapping pictures of the oncoming throng.

The Presbyterians joined them on the corner of Main Street and Lilac Road with ten pieces of brass, and led the frozen, exhilarated regiment across the street to First Baptist, where the lower grades sang "O Little Town of Bethlehem," accompanied by their preacher on the guitar. They also saw a re-enactment of the manger scene, for which the preacher's wife had made all the costumes.

Then, everyone clattered to the fellowship hall, where the brass band was rattling the cupboards with "Joy to the World!" The women of the church had set out an awesome array of sandwiches, cookies, cake, homemade candy, hot chocolate, and steaming apple cider.

"I think we're about to get our second wind," said the rector to his Presbyterian colleague.

"One more denomination in this town and some of us couldn't make it around. We've just clocked a mile and a quarter."

—*A Light in the Window*, Chapter Four

Advent Walk Hot Apple Cider

2 teaspoons	whole cloves
2 teaspoons	whole allspice
6	cinnamon sticks
1 gallon	apple cider
1 cup	brown sugar
½ teaspoon	salt
¼ teaspoon	ground nutmeg
2	oranges, sliced thin

Tie the cloves, allspice, and cinnamon sticks in cheesecloth. Pour the cider into a large pan. Add the brown sugar, salt, nutmeg, and spice bag. Stir to combine and heat to a rolling boil over high heat. Immediately reduce the heat and simmer for 30 minutes. Remove the spice bag and add the orange slices before serving.

tuart Cullen would arrive on Thursday for an overnight at the rectory on his way to a meeting down the mountain.

"Th' pope's comin'," he heard Puny announce to her sister on the phone.

"Stuart's not a pope," he told her, "he's a bishop. It's the Catholics that have a pope."

"My grandpa said he never met a Catholic that knew pea turkey about th' Bible . . ."

"Well, then," he said, heading off a diatribe, "let's do something with the guest room. It's been awhile since we had a guest."

"Never had one, period, since I been here. Needs airin' out, turnin' th' mattress, needs flowers—where'll they come from in th' dead of winter? Holly! We could use holly and save you th' florist bill."

"You're a good one! Let's do it. And let's put a copy of the *Muse* by the bed. Stuart likes a good laugh."

Puny would spend Thursday baking bread and a cake, and he would roast a tenderloin and do the potatoes. When he went by the Local, Avis gave him a bottle of Bordeaux, on the house.

"Seein' as it's th' pope," he said.

—*A Light in the Window*, Chapter Five

Father Tim's Beef Tenderloin

2 tablespoons	salt	1 tablespoon	Italian seasoning
1 tablespoon	paprika	1 teaspoon	Creole seasoning
1 tablespoon	garlic powder	1 (4 to 5 pounds)	beef tenderloin
2 teaspoons	ground black pepper	½ cup	extra-virgin olive oil
2 teaspoons	cayenne pepper		*Mustard Horseradish Sauce*

Combine the salt, paprika, garlic powder, black pepper, cayenne, Italian seasoning, and Creole seasoning in a small bowl. Rub the beef with the oil. Coat both sides of the beef with the spice mixture. Wrap tightly in aluminum foil and refrigerate for at least 8 hours or overnight.

Preheat the oven to 500°F. Remove the beef from the refrigerator, remove the foil, and place on a rack on a roasting pan. Roast for 15 minutes, then reduce the temperature to 375°F and continue to bake until desired doneness is reached. Use an instant-read thermometer to test the internal temperature of the meat. A temperature reading of 125°F indicates the meat is rare, 130–135°F for medium-rare, 135–140°F for medium, 140–150°F for medium-well.

Remove from the oven and let the meat rest for 10 to 15 minutes before slicing and serving.

Serve with *Mustard Horseradish Sauce*.

MUSTARD HORSERADISH SAUCE

⅔ cup	sour cream	2 tablespoons	prepared horseradish
¼ cup	Dijon mustard	½ teaspoon	salt
1 cup	Hellmann's mayonnaise	¼ teaspoon	freshly ground black pepper

In a small bowl mix all of the ingredients to blend. Adjust the seasonings before serving. Makes about 2 cups.

Father Tim's Scalloped Potatoes

4 cups	half-and-half
2 large	cloves garlic, pressed
1	bay leaf
1 teaspoon	salt
½ teaspoon	freshly ground white pepper
2½ to 3 pounds	red potatoes, peeled and sliced ⅛ inch thick
	Vegetable oil for the baking dish
3 tablespoons	freshly grated Parmesan cheese

In a large saucepan over medium heat, combine the half-and-half, garlic, bay leaf, salt, and pepper. Add the potatoes. Bring to a simmer and simmer for 30 minutes, or until the potatoes are tender. Make sure the liquid is just simmering and not scorching on the bottom of the pan.

Preheat the oven to 425°F. Coat a large baking dish with vegetable oil. Adjust the seasoning with salt and pepper and transfer the potatoes and sauce to the baking dish. Sprinkle the Parmesan on top and bake for 20 to 25 minutes, or until the cream is bubbling and the top is lightly browned.

❖ *The potatoes can be prepared up to several hours in advance. Cover cooked potatoes and refrigerate until ready to bake.*

"I ain't doin' this n' more," said Dooley, whose face was red as a lobster. He stomped along, carrying a doll and a wagon in a sack on his back. The rector's sack contained a dress, socks, and nurse's set, plus the doll carriage Margaret Ann had forgotten to mention.

"You fall and bust your butt," said Dooley, "and you cain't preach. I bust mine, I cain't play football."

"Good thinking." He had to stomp hard on the crust of ice with each step in order to keep from falling. He would pay for this by morning in every aching muscle. "We've only got three more blocks to go. Just keep in mind those steaks sizzling in the skillet . . . those oven-roasted potatoes with all the sour cream you can eat . . . and that triple-chocolate cake, sent by some well-meaning parishioner, which is currently hidden in the freezer. You can devour the whole thing!"

—*A Light in the Window*, Chapter Six

*"Do all the good you can
In all the ways you can
As long as ever you can
By all the means you can,
In all the places you can."*

—John Wesley

Jan Karon's
Mitford Cookbook
& Kitchen Reader

Steaks in the Skillet

<table>
<tr><td>2</td><td>New York strip or rib-eye steaks</td></tr>
<tr><td>1 tablespoon</td><td>vegetable oil</td></tr>
<tr><td></td><td>Salt</td></tr>
<tr><td></td><td>Freshly ground black pepper</td></tr>
<tr><td></td><td>*Horseradish Sauce*</td></tr>
</table>

Heat a black iron skillet over medium heat for 10 minutes. Brush the steaks on both sides with the oil. Season each side generously with salt and pepper.

Place the steaks in the skillet and cook on one side for 5 minutes. Turn the steaks over and cook 4 minutes for rare, 5 minutes for medium, and 7 to 8 minutes for medium-well. Serve with *Horseradish Sauce*.

HORSERADISH SAUCE

<table>
<tr><td>¼ cup</td><td>sour cream</td></tr>
<tr><td>¼ cup</td><td>prepared horseradish</td></tr>
<tr><td></td><td>Salt and freshly ground black pepper</td></tr>
</table>

Combine the sour cream and horseradish in a small bowl. Add salt and pepper to taste. Serve with the skillet steaks. Makes ½ cup.

Father Tim's
Twice Baked Potatoes

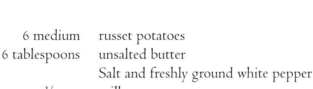

6 medium	russet potatoes
6 tablespoons	unsalted butter
	Salt and freshly ground white pepper
½ cup	milk
1½ cups	grated sharp cheddar cheese
	Sour cream, for serving
	Chopped scallions, for serving

Preheat the oven to 400°F. Pierce the potatoes with a fork and place them on a baking sheet. Place the potatoes in the oven and bake for 1 hour, or until the potatoes are soft when pierced with a fork. When the potatoes are just cool enough to handle, halve them lengthwise and carefully scoop the flesh into a large bowl, leaving ¼-inch-thick potato shells.

In a small saucepan melt 2 tablespoons of the butter. Brush on the potato shells and season with salt and pepper. Bake the potato shells for 15 minutes.

While the potato shells are baking, add the remaining 4 tablespoons of the butter, the milk, and cheese to the potatoes. Mix just until well blended (do not beat). Season with salt and pepper to taste. Spoon the potato mixture into the potato shells and bake for 10 to 15 minutes, or until browned.

Serve each potato topped with a dollop of sour cream and some scallions.

Andrew Gregory stopped in for a glass of Italian wine before meeting friends for dinner at the club.

Roberto had put on the rector's favorite apron, tucked his tie into his shirt pocket, and was busy creating the most seductive aromas in the rectory's history.

"Osso buco!" Roberto announced, removing the pot lid with one hand and waving a wooden spoon with the other.

"Ummmm!" cried Cynthia, coming through the back door with an armful of flowers. "Ravishing!"

"Man!" exclaimed Dooley, lured downstairs.

"Oh, my gracious!" gasped Miss Sadie, who arrived with her usual hostess gift of Swanson's Chicken Pie and a Sara Lee pound cake for his freezer.

Louella sniffed the air, appreciatively. "That ain't no collards and pigs' feet!"

The toasts flew as thick as snowflakes during last year's blizzard.

To Leonardo, who lay crippled with rheumatism in Florence!

To Roberto's happiness in Mitford!

To Miss Sadie's good health!

To Louella's quick recovery from an impending knee operation!

To Dooley's prospects for a new school!

To the hospitality of the host!

To the charm and beauty of the hostess!

To Olivia and Hoppy at Brown's Hotel in London!

Avis Packard called to find out if everything was going all right, thrilled with having cut veal for a real Italian who knew what was what.

Roberto showed photos of his wife and three beautiful children, of his grandfather's work in the homes and churches of Florence, and of Leonardo himself, wearing the same boyish smile Miss Sadie remembered from his long-ago visit to Fernbank.

The rector had never seen so much toasting and cooking and pouring of olive oil and peeling of garlic, nor heard so much laughing and joking.

It was as if Roberto were one of their very own and had come home to them all,
at last.

—*A Light in the Window*, Chapter Twenty-One

Jan Karon's
Mitford Cookbook
& Kitchen Reader

Roberto's Osso Buco

3 pounds	veal shanks
1 teaspoon	salt, plus more for seasoning the veal
½ teaspoon	black pepper, plus more for seasoning the veal
	All-purpose flour, for dredging
2 tablespoons	extra-virgin olive oil
2 tablespoons	unsalted butter
1 large	onion, chopped
4 cloves	garlic, minced
2 large	carrots, coarsely chopped
2 ribs	celery, coarsely chopped
1 cup	dry white wine
1 (14½-ounce) can	chopped tomatoes in juice
1 cup	*Chicken Stock* (see page 137)
1 teaspoon	dried thyme
1	bay leaf
1 teaspoon	dried basil
2 teaspoons	lemon zest (see page 52)
	Gremolata, for serving

Preheat the oven to 325°F.

Rinse the shanks, pat dry, and season with salt and pepper. Place some flour in large zip-top bag. Add the shanks to the bag, one at a time, and shake to coat with flour. Shake off excess flour as you remove the shanks from the bag. Heat the oil and 1 tablespoon of the butter in a large Dutch oven over medium-high heat. Brown the shanks on both sides, then transfer to a plate.

Lower the heat to medium and add the remaining 1 tablespoon of the butter to the Dutch oven, along with the onions, garlic, carrots, and celery. Sauté the vegetables for about 5 minutes, or until soft.

Add the wine, tomatoes (with their juices), chicken stock, thyme, bay leaf, basil, lemon zest, salt, and pepper to the Dutch oven. Arrange the shanks in the Dutch oven in one layer. Cover the Dutch oven and place in the oven. Braise the shanks for 2½ hours, or until very tender.

Serve on individual plates with a sprinkling of *Gremolata* (recipe opposite).

GREMOLATA

Gremolata is a traditional topping for Osso Buco.

1 bunch	fresh flat-leaf parsley
4 cloves	garlic
2 tablespoons	lemon zest (see page 52)

Pull the parsley leaves from the stems. Finely chop the parsley leaves and the garlic together. Combine the parsley, garlic, and lemon zest in a small bowl.

A Common Life

Miss Sadie and Louella were sitting on the porch, fanning and rocking.

Each time he came to Fernbank's front porch, the years automatically rolled away. With these two old friends, he felt twelve, or possibly ten. Fernbank was his fountain of youth.

His heart pounding, he sat on the top step and panted. Barnabas lay beside him, doing the same.

"Father," said Miss Sadie, "aren't you too old for this running business?"

"Not by a long shot. I do it to keep young, as a matter of fact."

"Pshaw! Too much is made of running up hill and down dale. I've never done such a thing in my life, and I'm coming up on ninety and healthy as a horse."

Louella rocked. "That's right."

"Is that lemonade?" asked Father Tim, eyeing the pitcher on the wicker table.

"Louella, what's happened to our manners?" asked Miss Sadie.

"I don't know, Miss Sadie. I 'spec' we don' get enough comp'ny t' hardly need manners."

Louella put ice in a glass and handed it to Fernbank's mistress, who, ever conserving, poured the glass half full.

He got up and fetched the lemonade from her, wondering what on earth they would think about his announcement. He'd envisioned them as happy about it, but now he wasn't so sure. He drank the lemonade in two gulps and stood on one foot, then the other.

"You itchy," said Louella.

They could read him like a book.

"Miss Sadie, Louella, are you sitting down?"

The two women looked at each other, puzzled.

Of course they were sitting down, how stupid of him to ask such a thing, it had flown out of his mouth.

"Joke!" he said feebly.

"Father, why don't *you* sit down? Get in this chair next to me and start rocking!"

He did as he was told. "Yes, ma'am." Eight years old.

"Louella and I like to rock in harmony, you pay a penny if you get off track."

"Who's leading?"

Miss Sadie looked at him as if he were dumb as a gourd.

"Honey, Miss Sadie always lead."

"Here we go," said Miss Sadie, looking bright and expectant. Since her feet barely touched the floor, this would be no small accomplishment.

After a ragged start, they nailed their synchronization, then worked on building momentum. Miss Sadie was flying in that rocker. . . .

Lord knows he couldn't sit around on porches all day like some jackleg priest, he had things to do, people to see, and besides, he was getting married. . . .

"Miss Sadie, Louella, I have great news."

The two women looked at him eagerly, never missing a beat.

"I'm getting married!" he shouted over the roar of six wooden rockers whipping along on aged white pine.

Miss Sadie's feet hit the floor, Louella's feet hit the floor. Their rockers came to a dead stop. His was still going.

"To Miss Cynthia?" asked Louella, who was generally suspicious of good news.

"The very one!" he said, feeling a stab of happiness and pride.

Louella whooped and clapped her hands. "Thank you, Jesus! Thank you, *thank* you, Jesus!"

Miss Sadie dug a handkerchief from the sleeve of her dress and pressed it to her eyes. "This is a happy day, Father. I can't tell you how happy we are for you. Cynthia is the loveliest imaginable lady, so bright and positive, just what you need. I hope you've been on your knees thanking the Lord!"

He had, actually.

Louella was beaming. "Miss Sadie, I'm goin' t' cut us all some pie." As she opened the screen door to go inside, she turned and said, "An' remember you owe me five dollars!"

They heard Miss Sadie's longtime companion shuffling down the hall in her slippers.

"Why, may I ask, do you owe Louella five dollars?"

She looked at him, barely able to conceal her mirth. "Because, Father, I bet five dollars you didn't have it in you to marry that lovely woman!"

Knowing how dear five dollars was to Sadie Baxter, he smiled at his favorite parishioner and said, "I suppose I could say I'm sorry you lost."

She patted his arm fondly. "Actually, Father, your good news declares that we've all won."

—*A Common Life*, Chapter Two

Louella's Buttermilk Chess Pie

½ cup	unsalted butter, melted and cooled, more for greasing the pan
½ recipe	*Pastry for a Double Crust Pie* (page 4) (Halve the recipe, or make the whole recipe and freeze half)
1¼ cups	granulated sugar
3 tablespoons	all-purpose flour
4 large	eggs, lightly beaten
1 cup	buttermilk
1 tablespoon	fresh lemon juice
1 teaspoon	vanilla extract
Dash	ground nutmeg
Dash	salt

Preheat the oven to 400°F. Lightly butter a 9-inch pie pan. Roll out the pastry dough and fit it into the pie pan. Mix the sugar and flour together in a large bowl. Add the beaten eggs and mix well. Add the butter and buttermilk and mix well. Stir in the lemon juice, vanilla, nutmeg, and salt. Pour into the unbaked pie shell. Bake for 15 minutes at 400°F, then turn the oven temperature down to 350°F and continue baking for 35 to 40 minutes, or until browned on top. Remove the pie from the oven to a cooling rack, and cool completely before serving.

I t *will* be September, you know."
Hessie Mayhew—*Mitford Muse* reporter, Presbyterian mover and shaker, and gifted flower arranger—had come to consult with Cynthia in the rectory living room. As Father Tim served them lemonade and shortbread, he couldn't help but listen. After all, wasn't he a gardener? Wasn't he interested in flowers?

He crept to a corner of the room with a glass of lemonade and appeared to be wholly absorbed in scratching his dog behind the ears.

"And in September," said Hessie, "there's precious little that's worth picking." Hessie had staked her reputation on what she foraged from meadow and pasture, roadside and bank. Her loose, informal bouquets were quite the hit at every spring and summer function, and her knowledge of where the laciest wild carrot bloomed and the showiest hydrangeas grew was both extensive and highly secret. However, as autumn drew on and blooms began to vanish, she hedged her bets—by dashing cold water on her clients' heady expectations, she was usually able to come up with something agreeably breathtaking.

"What does this mean?" asked Cynthia, looking worried.

"It means that what we mostly have to deal with is pods."

"*Pods?*" His fiancée was aghast.

Hessie shrugged. "Pods, seeds, berries," she said, expanding the list of possibilities. "Unless you'd like *mums.*" Hessie said this word with undisguised derision.

Mums. He noted that the very word made his neighbor blanch.

Cynthia looked his way, imploring, but he did not make eye contact. No, indeed, he would not get in the middle of a discussion about pods and berries, much less mums.

"Pods and berries *can* be wonderful," Hessie stated, as if she were the full authority, which she was. "Mixed with what's blooming and tied in enormous bunches, they can look very rich hanging on the pew ends. Of course, we'll use wide ribbons, I'd suggest French-wired velvet, possibly in sage and even something the color of the shu-

make berry." As a bow to tradition, Hessie enjoyed using the mountain pronunciation for sumac.

He stole a glance at Cynthia from the corner of his eye. How had that gone down? She seemed uncertain.

"Why can't we just order dozens of roses and armloads of lilacs and be done with it?"

Hessie sucked in her breath. "Well," she said, "if you want to spend *that* kind of money . . ."

And let the word get out that his bride was a spendthrift? That was Hessie's deeper meaning; he knew Hessie Mayhew like a book. He knew, too, that Hessie considered the ordering of lilacs in September to be something akin to criminal—not only would they cost a royal fortune, they were *out of season in the mountains!*

"Not to mention," said Hessie, pursing her lips, "they're out of season in the mountains."

"Excuse me for living," said his fiancée. "Anyway, we *don't* want to spend that kind of money." In truth, his bride-to-be had the capability to spend whatever she wished, being a successful children's book author and illustrator. Besides, thought the rector, wasn't it her wedding? Wasn't it their money to spend however they liked? He hunkered down in the chair, anonymous, invisible, less than a speck on the wall.

Cynthia heaved a sigh. "So, Hessie, whatever you think. Sage and burgundy . . . or let's call it claret, shall we? Burgundy sounds so . . . *heavy.* Do you think we should intermix the ribbon colors along the aisle or put sage on one side and claret on the other?"

The color deepened in Hessie's ample cheeks. "Sage for the bride's side and claret for the groom's side, is my opinion!"

"Of course, I don't have any family for the bride's side. Only a nephew who isn't really a nephew, and the last I heard, he was in the Congo."

His heart was touched by the small sadness he heard in her voice, and so, apparently, was Hessie's.

> He helped her from the footstool and she sat beside him on the love seat and breathed the peace that settled over them like a shawl.
>
> "There will be many times when fear breaks in," he said, holding her close. "We can never be taken prisoner if we greet it with prayer."
>
> "Yes!" she whispered, feeling a weight rolled away like the stone from the sepulcher.
>
> "I smelled the chicken as I came through the hedge."
>
> "Dinner in twenty minutes," she murmured.
>
> "I thought you'd never ask," he said.
>
> —FATHER TIM AND CYNTHIA

"Oh, but you *do* have family!" Hessie threw her head back, eyes flashing. "The entire parish is your family!"

Cynthia pondered this extravagant remark. "Do you really think so?"

"*Think* so?" boomed Hessie. "I *know* so! Everyone says you're the brightest thing to happen to Lord's Chapel in an *eon,* and you must *not* forget it, my dear!" Mitford's foremost, all-around go-getter patted Cynthia's arm with considerable feeling.

Click! Something wonderful had just taken place. Hessie Mayhew, sensitive to the bone underneath her take-charge manner, had for some reason decided to be his fiancée's shield and buckler from this moment on; and nobody messed with Hessie.

"We'll fill every pew on the bride's side," Hessie predicted. "We'll be falling over ourselves to sit there! It's certainly where *I'm* sitting—no offense, Father."

Cynthia took Hessie's rough hand. "Thank you, Hessie!"

Thank you, Lord, he thought, forsaking his invisibility by bolting from the chair to refill their glasses all around.

"And what," inquired Hessie, "are you planning to do, Father, other than show up?"

Hessie Mayhew was smiling, but he knew she was dead serious. Hessie believed that every man, woman, and child, including the halt and lame, should participate in all parish-wide events to the fullest.

"I'm doing the usual," he said, casting a grin in the direction of his neighbor. "I'm baking a ham!"

—*A Common Life,* Chapter Three

Father Tim's Baked Ham

	Vegetable oil for greasing the pan
1 cup	brown sugar
½ cup	molasses
½ cup	bourbon
1 cup	orange juice
2 tablespoons	Dijon mustard
1 tablespoon	whole cloves
1 (6 to 8 pound)	smoked ham

Preheat the oven to 350°F. Lightly grease a large baking dish and set aside. Combine the brown sugar and molasses in small saucepan and melt over low heat. Remove from the heat, add the bourbon, orange juice, mustard, and cloves and mix well.

Remove the skin and fat from the ham and place in the baking dish. Make ¼-inch cuts in the ham in a diamond pattern. Pour the glaze over the ham.

Bake for 2 to 2½ hours, or until an instant-read thermometer inserted into the thickest portion of the ham registers 140°F, basting every 15 minutes with the glaze.

Remove the ham from the oven and cool in the pan. Remove from the pan and refrigerate. Pour the pan drippings into a bowl and refrigerate. When ready to serve the ham, remove the fat from the top of the drippings, remove the whole cloves, warm it up, and serve it with the ham.

They sat on the bench and listened for a moment to the birds and a light wind that stirred the leaves in Baxter Park. He kissed her, lingering. She kissed him back, lingering still more. She drew away and fanned herself with the notebook, laughing.

"On to more serious matters!" he exclaimed. "First order of business—pew bulletin or invitations, what do you think?"

"Pew bulletin! That way everyone knows, and those few who aren't in the parish, we'll call. I'll try to reach David, though I can't imagine he'd trek all the way from the Congo to Mitford!"

"Where shall we put Walter and Katherine? Your place or mine?"

"First things first," she said. "We need to know where we're spending our wedding night."

"The rectory?"

"But darling, your bed is so small."

"Yes, but your bed is so *big.*" In his view, they could hold a fox hunt on the vast territory she called a bed.

"Draw straws!" she said, leaning from the bench to pluck two tall spears of grass. She fiddled with them a moment, asked him to close his eyes, then presented them in her fist.

"Gambling again," he said.

"Long one, my house, short one, your house."

He drew the short one.

"Rats in a poke!" fumed his neighbor.

"Watch your language, Kavanagh."

"Isn't it a tad early to call me Kavanagh?"

"I'm practicing."

"Anyway, there's your answer. Walter and Katherine spend the night at my house."

"Done!" He checked the topic off his list. "Have you thought any more about flower girls?"

"Amy Larkin and Rebecca Owen!"

"Perfect. Music?"

"Richard and I are just beginning to work on it—let's definitely ask Dooley to sing."

"Splendid. Should have thought of it myself."

"A cappella."

"He doesn't go for a cappella."

"He'll get over it, darling, I promise, and it will be wonderful, a true highlight for everyone. 'O Perfect Love,' what do you think?"

"There won't be a dry eye in the house. By the way, we're scheduled for the bishop on Wednesday at eleven o'clock."

"What are you wearing?" she asked.

"Oh, something casual. A pink curler in my hair, perhaps."

She swatted his arm over this old joke.

"I love you madly," she said.

"I love you madlier."

"Do not!"

"Do, too!"

"Prove it!"

"I shall. I'm serving you dinner tonight, Puny made chicken and dumplings."

"Chicken and dumplings!" she crowed.

"With fresh lima beans."

"I'm your slave!"

"I'll remember that," he said.

—*A Common Life*, Chapter Four

Puny's Chicken and Dumplings

2 cups	White Lily self-rising flour, more for rolling out the dough
½ teaspoon	salt
¼ teaspoon	freshly ground black pepper
½ teaspoon	granulated sugar
⅓ cup	vegetable shortening
¾ cup	buttermilk
4½ cups	*Puny's Chicken Stock*
3 tablespoons	unsalted butter
4 cups	cooked chicken meat (from the chicken stock)
1 cup	milk

In a large bowl, combine the flour, salt, pepper, and sugar. Cut the shortening in with a pastry blender until the mixture resembles coarse meal. Add the buttermilk and stir with a fork just until the dough forms a ball. On a lightly floured surface, roll out the pastry until it is ⅛ inch thick and cut into 1-inch squares.

In a large pot bring 4 cups of the chicken stock to a rolling boil, add the butter, and continue to keep the stock at a rolling boil. Gradually drop the dumplings in, one at a time, stirring to prevent sticking. Place the chicken meat on top of the dumplings and pour the milk over all. Cover, reduce the heat to medium-low, and simmer for 20 minutes, or until dumplings are cooked through. Do not remove the cover while the dumplings are cooking. After 20 minutes, remove the top and add more milk if the mixture is too dry. Adjust the seasonings with salt and pepper and serve immediately.

PUNY'S CHICKEN STOCK

1 (3 to 4 pound)	chicken, rinsed and giblets removed
2 large	onions, quartered
2 large	carrots, sliced thick
3 ribs	celery, sliced thick
10	black peppercorns
2 teaspoons	salt
3 sprigs	fresh parsley
4 quarts	cold water

In a tall, narrow stockpot, combine the chicken, onions, carrots, celery, peppercorns, salt, and parsley. Add the water and bring to a rolling boil. Cover the pot, reduce the heat to very low and simmer for 2 to 3 hours.

Remove the chicken, strain the liquid, and pour into small containers (no deeper than 4 inches). Let the stock cool to room temperature. Cover and refrigerate overnight. When the chicken has cooled, remove and discard the skin, then remove the meat and refrigerate. Before using the stock, skim any hardened fat from the surface and bring back to a rolling boil.

Thank you for the world so sweet,
Thank you for the food we eat.
Thank you for the birds that sing,
Thank you, God, for everything.
Amen

—AUTHOR UNKNOWN

❖ *The stock may be kept in the refrigerator for 3 to 4 days, or frozen up to 3 months.*

Louella held the catalog closer to the window and squinted at the picture. She wished Moses Marshall could see her all dressed up for the father's wedding. He would look at her and be so proud. Oh, how she'd loved that man from the day she laid eyes on him!

She closed her eyes to rest them and held the picture against her heart, and saw her husband-to-be walking into the kitchen of the Atlanta boardinghouse.

She was fifteen years old, with her hair in cornrows and the sense that something wonderful was about to happen.

Moses Marshall flashed a smile that nearly knocked her winding. She had never seen anybody who looked like this when she was growing up in Mitford. The only people of color in Mitford were old and stooped over.

"Who's th' one baked them good biscuits for supper?" he asked.

She'd been scarcely able to speak. "What you want to know for?"

"'Cause th' one baked them good biscuits, that's th' one I'm goin' to marry."

She had looked at old Miss Sally Lou, who had to stand on tiptoe to peer into a pot on the stove. She was so little and dried up, some said she was a hundred, but Louella knew she was only eighty-two, and still the boss cook of three meals a day at the boardinghouse.

She had pointed to Miss Sally Lou, afraid to say the plain truth—that she, Louella Baxter, had baked the biscuits herself, three pans full and not one left begging.

Moses Marshall looked his bright, happy look at Miss Sally Lou and walked over and picked her up and swung her around twice before he set her down like a doll. "Fine biscuits, ma'am. Will you jump th' broom wit' me?"

"Git out of my way 'fore I knock you in th' head!" said Miss Sally Lou. "Marry that 'un yonder, she th' one do biscuits, I does yeast rolls."

She was sixteen when they were married at her grandmother's house in Atlanta, where she'd gone to live after leaving Mitford. Her grandmother had cooked the wedding feast, which was topped off with fresh peach cobbler. "Why eat cake when you can eat cobbler?" was what her grandmother always said.

Her years with Moses had been the happiest years of her life, next to those with Miss Sadie. But the Lord had taken Moses home when he was just thirty-nine, and then He'd taken her precious boy in a terrible wreck, leaving her a grandson living in Los Angeles. . . .

She looked out to the green orchard and nodded her head and smiled. "Moses Marshall," she said, "I invite you to sit wit' me at th' weddin', an' don' be pinchin' and kissin' on me in front of th' good Lord an' ever'body. . . ."

—*A Common Life*, Chapter Five

A Soupçon of This, a Dollop of That

PIE

I've baked a few pies in my time. But only a few.

The trouble with pie is this: if you bake one, you will eat it.

Therefore, you must bake it and, while it's still hot, immediately get it out of the house. This can make you popular with your neighbors.

CAKE

I baked a cake in third grade. My grandmother, who, by the way, is the chief character in my children's book *Miss Fannie's Hat,* let me think I'd created the recipe myself. She even assured me that this cake, which I remember being egg-y, very sweet, and heavily textured, was marvelous indeed.

To prove her great excitement for, and her belief in, this cake, Mama invited my first grade teacher, Nan Downs, to our home to sample it.

I remember being perfectly intoxicated with the thought, much less the experience, of having a teacher *visit our house!* We hardly ever had company from another gene pool, and so this was an event. The thrill of having my teacher actually come into our home and sit down at the back porch table with us was similar to what some people say of their wedding— *afterward, I couldn't remember a thing!* I only recall that we ate cake on the big farm table that was always covered with oil cloth.

What a triumph that day was. And what a lovely grandmother to let me believe I'd done it on my own, when I couldn't have done any of it without her.

ICE CREAM

I have ice cream about twice a year, more's the pity. That's because nothing today tastes so good as—can you believe it?—ice cream made in an ice tray. Here's my grandmother's recipe, and believe me, I don't give this to just everybody.

When you serve it, most people will say "What is *this*?" Because most people have never tasted, much less heard of, Ice Cream in a Tray. It's fabulous.

But let's say you don't have any condensed milk or strong coffee, or even any ice trays, and you're craving a really super ice cream. Get in the car and drive to Blowing Rock in the high, green hills of North Carolina.

(From Los Angeles, that's about two and a half days. From New York, roughly eleven hours. From Topeka, maybe a day and three quarters.)

When you reach Blowing Rock, look for Kilwin's on Main Street. Now, everybody pile out of the car and get waffle cones loaded with Kilwin's wildly popular, family-made ice cream. Spend the night in one of Blowing Rock's charming inns, log cabins, or wonderfully old-fashioned motels, and next morning, have breakfast at Sonny's Grill where the only thing to order, as far I'm concerned, is a livermush sandwich. Sonny's holds about eighteen people sitting and three or four standing, so get there early.

—Jan Karon

Mama's Ice Cream in a Tray

1⅓ cups	sweetened condensed milk
1 cup	water
1 tablespoon	vanilla extract
2 cups	heavy cream

In a large bowl, combine all the ingredients and freeze in ice trays. Stir several times as it freezes. For coffee flavor, substitute 1 cup strong coffee for the water and use evaporated milk instead of the cream. Reduce the vanilla to 2 teaspoons.

"I doubt the world holds for anyone a more soul-stirring surprise than their first adventure with ice cream."

—Heywood Broun

A FINAL WORD ON ICE CREAM

How on earth did vanilla fall into such latter day disgrace? Let me tell you, I have had it with the Rocky Roads, Mango Passions, and Killer Chocolates of this world! Give me a bowl of Ben and Jerry's vanilla ice cream spritzed with fresh lemon juice. That, and nothing more. (Speaking of this delectable, did you know that Thomas Jefferson is the good fellow who, following one of his many European sojourns, introduced America to ice cream?)

—Jan Karon

Louella's Grandmother's Peach Cobbler

1 recipe	*Pastry for a Double Crust Pie* (page 4)	½ teaspoon	ground nutmeg
10 cups (12 to 14)	peeled and sliced fresh peaches	¼ teaspoon	salt
2½ cups	granulated sugar, more for sprinkling on top	½ cup	unsalted butter, melted
1 tablespoon	fresh lemon juice	1 teaspoon	vanilla extract
3 tablespoons	all-purpose flour		Nonstick cooking spray for the baking dish
¾ teaspoon	ground cinnamon		Vanilla ice cream, for serving (optional)

Prepare the pastry and refrigerate the dough for 30 minutes before rolling it out.

In a large bowl, combine the peaches, ½ cup of the granulated sugar, and lemon juice. Let the fruit sit for 20 minutes. In a small bowl, combine the flour, the remaining 2 cups of the sugar, the cinnamon, nutmeg, salt, butter, and vanilla. Add to the peaches and mix well.

Preheat the oven to 400°F. Spray a 12 x 8-inch baking dish with nonstick cooking spray. Roll half of the pastry into a ⅛-inch thick large rectangle. Spoon half of the fruit mixture into the prepared dish. Cut the pastry into 2-inch squares and place on top of peaches. Bake the first layer for 10 minutes, then turn on the broiler and broil for 5 more minutes, or until golden brown on top. Remove from the oven, lower the temperature back down to 400°F, and spoon the remaining fruit on top. Roll the remaining pastry into another ⅛-inch thick large rectangle and cut into 1-inch strips. Arrange the strips in a lattice design over the peaches. Sprinkle with sugar and bake another 30 to 35 minutes, or until golden brown on top.

Serve warm, topped with vanilla ice cream.

❖ *If you are in a hurry and don't have time to prepare the pastry, use a Pillsbury prepared pie crust.*

It had been years since Elliott walked out—the divorce papers arrived by certified mail the following day—and in those years, not one soul had made her mouth go dry as cotton and her knees turn to water. Oh, how she despised the torment of loving like a girl instead of like . . . like a sophisticated woman, whatever that might be.

That early, awkward time had also been irresistibly sweet. But now this—confusion and distress and alarm, and yes, the oddly scary thoughts of the women of Lord's Chapel who for years had stood around him like a hedge of thorns, protecting him as their very own; keeping him, they liked to believe, from foolish stumbles; feeding him meringues and layer cake at every turn; mothering and sistering him as if this were their life's calling. She saw, now, something she'd only glimpsed before, and that was the way an unmarried priest is thought to belong to the matrons of the church, lock, stock, and barrel.

Give them wisdom and devotion in the ordering of their common life, that each may be to the other a strength in need, a counselor in perplexity, a comfort in sorrow, and a companion in joy. Amen.

—THE BOOK OF COMMON PRAYER

More than once she'd waited at his side, feeling gauche and adolescent, as they clucked over him—inquiring after his blood sugar, flicking an imaginary hair from his lapel, ordering him to take a week off, and coyly insisting he never stray beyond the town limits. They were perfectly harmless, every one, and she despised herself for such cheap and petty thoughts, but they were real thoughts, and now that the word was out, she felt his flock sizing her up in a fresh, even severe way.

Yet, for all their maternal indulgence of their priest, she knew they underestimated him most awfully. She had heard a member of the Altar Guild wondering how anyone "so youthful and sure of herself" could be attracted to their "dear old priest who is going bald as a hen egg and diabetic to boot."

Jan Karon's
Mitford Cookbook
& Kitchen Reader

143

Indeed, he wasn't merely the mild and agreeable man they perceived him to be; he was instead a man of the richest reserves of strength and poise, of the deepest tenderness and most enormous wit and gallantry.

From the beginning, she found him to possess an ardor for his calling that spoke to her heart and mind and soul in such a deep and familiar way, she felt as if he were long-lost kin, returned at last from a distant shore. He had felt this, too, this connection of some vital force in himself with her own vitality, and he had been knocked back, literally, as if by the thunder-striking power of a summer storm.

She had known she would never again be given such a connection, and she had moved bravely toward it, toward its heat, toward its center, while he had drawn back, shaken.

"'Love bade me welcome,'" he had once quoted from George Herbert, "'but my soul drew back.'" She found a delicate irony in the fact that George Herbert had been a clergyman.

She looked at the handwritten sheet pinned above her drawing board, something she had copied at the Mitford library from an old book by Elizabeth Goudge:

> She had long accepted the fact that happiness is like a swallow in spring. It may come and nest under your eaves or it may not. You cannot command it. When you expect to be happy you are not, when you don't expect to be happy there is suddenly Easter in your soul, though it be midwinter. Something, you do not know what, has broken the seal upon that door in the depth of your being that opens upon eternity.

Eternity!

She moved from the window and walked quickly to the kitchen. She would do something that, if only for the briefest hour, had the power to solve everything, to offer certain and absolute consolation.

She would cook.

—*A Common Life*, Chapter Seven

Cynthia's Roasted Chicken

2 tablespoons	extra-virgin olive oil
5 cloves	garlic, crushed
1 large	roasting chicken, soaked in brine
1	lemon
1 bunch	fresh rosemary
	Sea salt and freshly ground black pepper

Preheat the oven to 450°F. Rub the olive oil and 3 of the crushed garlic cloves over the chicken. Cut the lemon in half and place in the cavity of the chicken, along with the remaining 2 garlic cloves and a sprig of rosemary. Sprinkle salt and pepper over the chicken and stick one of the rosemary stalks under the skin. Place the chicken on a rack in a black iron skillet or heavy roasting pan. Roast for 30 minutes, then turn the oven temperature down to 350°F and bake for an additional hour, or until an instant-read thermometer inserted in the breast portion registers 150 to 154°.

HOW TO BRINE A CHICKEN

Remove the chicken giblets and rinse the chicken inside and out. Place 1 cup salt and 5 quarts water in a large container and stir to dissolve the salt. Submerge the chicken in the brine, making sure it is completely covered with brine. Cover and refrigerate for at least 3 or up to 8 hours.

Remove the chicken from the brine, rinse well, and pat dry.

❖ *Brining chicken ensures meat that's juicy and not dry.*

In her home a half mile from town, Puny Guthrie crumbled two dozen strips of crisp, center-cut bacon into the potato salad and gave it one last, heaving stir. Everybody would be plenty hungry by six or six-thirty, and she'd made enough to feed a corn shuckin', as her granpaw used to say. She had decided to leave out the onions, since it was a wedding reception and very dressy. She'd never thought dressing up and eating onions were compatible; onions were for picnics and eating at home in the privacy of your own family.

Because Cynthia and the father didn't want people to turn out for the reception and go home hungry, finger foods were banned. They wanted to give everybody a decent supper, even if they would have to eat it sitting on folding chairs from Sunday School. What with the father's ham, Miss Louella's yeast rolls, Miss Olivia's raw vegetables and dip, her potato salad, and Esther Bolick's three-layer orange marmalade, she didn't think they'd have any complaints. Plus, there would be ten gallons of tea, not to mention decaf, and sherry if anybody wanted any, but she couldn't imagine why anybody would. She'd once taken a sip from the father's decanter, and thought it tasted exactly like aluminum foil, though she'd never personally tasted aluminum foil except when it got stuck to a baked potato.

—*A Common Life*, Chapter Eight

Puny's Potato Salad

7 medium	russet potatoes
1 tablespoon plus 1¼ teaspoons	salt
2 tablespoons	bacon drippings
4 medium	hard-cooked eggs (see page 158), mashed
2 tablespoons	red onions, chopped
½ cup	thinly sliced celery
1¾ cups	Hellmann's mayonnaise
2 teaspoons	yellow mustard
2 tablespoons	sour cream
2½ teaspoons	apple cider vinegar
½ teaspoon	freshly ground black pepper
6 slices	cooked bacon, crumbled
	Parsley flakes, for garnish
	Paprika, for garnish

Peel and cube the potatoes. Place the potatoes in a large saucepan, and add water to cover along with 1 tablespoon salt. Bring to a boil over high heat, reduce the heat, cover, and simmer until the potatoes are just tender. Drain the potatoes in a colander. Add the bacon drippings and shake the colander to coat. Cover loosely and let the potatoes cool completely.

In a large bowl, combine the potatoes, mashed eggs, red onions, and celery. In a separate bowl, combine the mayonnaise, mustard, sour cream, and vinegar and stir it into the potatoes. Add 1¼ teaspoons salt and ½ teaspoon pepper. Just before serving, adjust the seasonings with salt and pepper. Garnish the salad with the crumbled bacon, parsley flakes, and paprika.

Louella's Yeast Rolls

2½ cups	milk
½ cup	granulated sugar
2 packages	dry yeast
½ cup	vegetable shortening
5 cups	bread flour, more for rolling out the dough
2 large	eggs
¼ cup	unsalted butter, at room temperature, more for greasing the bowl and baking sheet
½ teaspoon	baking soda
1 teaspoon	baking powder
2 teaspoons	salt
	Melted butter for dipping the dough

In a medium saucepan over low heat, heat the milk until bubbles just start to form around the edges. Pour ½ cup of the heated milk into a 2-cup measuring cup, stir in 1 teaspoon sugar, and let the mixture cool to 115°F. Stir in the yeast. Allow the yeast to proof (bubble). Add the remaining sugar and the shortening to the saucepan of milk and stir until the shortening is melted. Let this mixture cool to 115°F as well.

In a large mixing bowl, combine 2 cups of the flour, the yeast mixture, and the milk mixture. Mix well until thoroughly combined. Cover with a kitchen towel and let the dough rise for 1 hour, until doubled in bulk. Punch down the dough and add the eggs, butter, and 1 cup of the flour, and mix well. Add the baking soda, baking powder, salt, and the remaining 2 cups of the flour, and mix well. Coat the inside of a large bowl with butter and transfer the dough to the greased bowl. Cover and place in a warm spot free of drafts and let rise for another hour. Punch the dough down, cover with plastic wrap, and refrigerate overnight.

Bring the dough to room temperature before working with it. Grease a cookie sheet. Roll the dough out on a lightly floured surface until it is about ⅛ inch thick. Cut the dough out with a 2-inch cookie cutter and dip the pieces in melted butter. Place the rolls on the cookie sheet, fold over, and pinch the edges of the dough to form a pocketbook roll. Cover with a kitchen towel and let rise for 1½ hours, until doubled in bulk, before baking.

Preheat the oven to 450°F. Just before placing the rolls in the oven, turn the temperature down to 375°F. Bake for 15 to 20 minutes, until the rolls are lightly browned or they sound hollow when tapped on the bottom. Set on a rack to cool or serve right out of the oven.

Louella's Cinnamon Rolls

1 cup	brown sugar
½ cup	granulated sugar
½ cup	unsalted butter, softened
1 tablespoon	ground cinnamon
½ teaspoon	salt
1 recipe	dough for *Louella's Yeast Rolls* (opposite)

Prepare the filling by combining the brown sugar, granulated sugar, butter, cinnamon, and salt in a large bowl. Bring the dough to room temperature and roll it out on a lightly floured surface into a 24 x 12-inch rectangle that is about ⅛ inch thick. Spread filling on the the lower half of one of the 24-inch sides of the dough. Fold the other half over the filling and pinch the edges to seal. Cut cross-wise into 1-inch strips and twist each strip into a circle, tucking under the ends to shape a pinwheel. Cover with a kitchen towel and let the rolls rise until doubled in bulk, about 1 hour.

Preheat the oven to 375°F. Bake the rolls for 15 to 20 minutes, or until lightly browned.

These High, Green Hills

M iss Sadie," he said when she answered the phone at Fernbank, "I've had a note from Dooley. He says he doesn't like it in that fancy school."

"He can like it or lump it," she said pleasantly.

"When you're dishing out twenty thousand a year, you sure can be tough, Miss Sadie."

"If I couldn't be tough, Father, I wouldn't have twenty thousand to dish out."

"You'll be glad to know the headmaster says he's doing all right. A little slow on the uptake, but holding his own with those rich kids. In fact, they're not all rich. Several are there on scholarship, with no more assets than our Dooley."

"Good! You mark my words, he'll be better for it. And don't you go soft on me, Father, and let him talk you into bailing him out in the middle of the night."

"You can count on it," he said.

"Louella and I have nearly recovered from all the doings in June. . . ."

"June was a whopper, all right."

"We're no spring chickens, you know."

"You could have fooled me."

"I'll be ninety my next birthday, but Louella doesn't tell her age. Anyway, we're going to have you and Cynthia up for supper. What did we say we'd have, Louella?"

FACING PAGE: *My mother's hand-painted pitcher holds the flowers; my sister gave me the Early American compote; and the silver service was made by a Philadelphia company with the same name as my father: Robert Wilson.*

He heard Louella's mezzo voice boom from a corner of the big kitchen, "Fried chicken, mashed potatoes, gravy, an' cole slaw!"

"Man!" he exclaimed, quoting Dooley.

The announcement rolled on. "Hot biscuits, cooked apples, deviled eggs, bread and butter pickles . . ."

Good Lord! The flare-up from his diabetes would have him in the emergency room before the rest of them pushed back from the table.

"And what did we say for dessert?" Miss Sadie warbled into the distance.

"Homemade coconut cake!"

Ah, well, that was a full coma right there. Hardly any of his parishioners could remember he had this blasted disease. The information seemed to go in one ear and out the other.

"Ask Louella if she'll marry me," he said.

"Louella, the Father wants to know if you'll marry him."

"Tell 'im he got a short mem'ry, he done married Miss Cynthia."

He laughed, contented with the sweetness of this old friendship. "Just name the time," he said. "We'll be there."

—*These High, Green Hills*, Chapter One

MEMORIES ARE MADE OF THIS

Some of my sweetest childhood memories are of fried chicken on Sunday afternoons.

How on earth my grandmother ever scrubbed two little girls and brushed their hair (and stuck ribbons in it), and made breakfast and got my grandfather's shirts and socks and underwear laid out, and arranged herself to look beautiful and went to Sunday School and church and came home and prepared a full and blessed Sunday dinner with the whole works including mashed potates and gravy with yeast rolls or biscuits, is a mystery to me.

When I think of fried chicken (and believe me, I often do), I think of Sunday and Mama. "What keeps me motivated," said Michael Chiarello, "is not the food itself, but all the memories the food represents."

I used to believe I'd like nothing better than a full-time hairdresser. Then, I thought I'd like nothing better than a full-time gardener. Now, years later, I'm done with such foolishness! What I would really like is a full-time cook—one who, need it be said, fries chicken every Sunday.

—Jan Karon

Louella's Fried Chicken

1 (2½ to 3 pound)	broiler chicken, cut up and soaked in brine (see page 145)
1 quart	buttermilk
2 cups	White Lily self-rising flour
1½ teaspoons	salt
1 teaspoon	freshly ground black pepper
½ cup	bacon drippings
¾ to 1 cup	lard

Place the chicken pieces in a large bowl, pour in the buttermilk and place in the refrigerator to soak for 2 to 4 hours.

Combine the flour, 1½ teaspoons salt, and pepper in a shallow dish such as a pie plate. Drain the chicken and dredge in the flour mixture. Shake off excess flour.

Heat the bacon drippings and lard in a black iron skillet over medium-high heat until a small bit of flour pops when dropped in the fat. Add the chicken, a few pieces at a time, skin side down. Cover and cook the chicken for 15 to 20 minutes. Remove the cover and turn the chicken over. Cook for another 15 to 20 minutes. The chicken is done when it is a light golden brown color.

Drain the chicken on paper towels before serving.

Louella's Cole Slaw

4 to 5 cups (about 1 pound)	shredded cabbage
2 teaspoons	salt
½ cup	granulated sugar
¼ cup	white vinegar
1 cup	Hellmann's mayonnaise
¼ teaspoon	freshly ground black pepper

Combine the shredded cabbage and salt in a colander set over a large bowl. Cover with plastic wrap, place a heavy plate on top, and refrigerate for at least 1 hour, or up to 4 hours, allowing the excess water to drain. Pat the cabbage dry with paper towels and place in a large bowl.

In a small bowl combine the sugar, vinegar, mayonnaise, and pepper and stir into the cabbage. Refrigerate for at least 2 hours. Before serving, adjust the seasonings with salt and pepper.

❖ *Salting and draining the cabbage removes excess water and produces pickle-crisp cabbage.*

Louella's Mashed Potatoes

4 to 5 medium	russet potatoes, peeled and cut into
	⅓-inch-thick slices
4 teaspoons	salt
¼ cup	unsalted butter
1 (12-ounce) can	evaporated milk
1 teaspoon	freshly ground black pepper

Place the potatoes in a large saucepan and add enough water to cover. Bring the water to a boil over high heat, then immediately turn down the heat until the water is just simmering. Add 2 teaspoons salt and simmer for about 20 minutes, or until fork-tender. Drain the potatoes and return them to the saucepan. In a separate small saucepan, gently heat the butter, evaporated milk, the remaining 2 teaspoons salt, and the pepper. Add to the potatoes and mash with a potato masher. Adjust the seasonings, adding more salt and pepper if needed before serving.

Louella's Cooked Apples

5 medium	Granny Smith apples, peeled and sliced
1 tablespoon	fresh lemon juice
¾ cup	brown sugar
¾ teaspoon	ground cinnamon
¼ teaspoon	salt
⅛ teaspoon	ground nutmeg
¼ cup	unsalted butter

In a large skillet over medium heat toss the apples with the lemon juice. Add the brown sugar, cinnamon, salt, nutmeg, and butter, stirring to combine. Cover and cook for 30 minutes, or until the apples have softened.

THE JOHNNY APPLESEED PRAYER

Sometimes it's fun, especially at a family gathering with lots of children, to sing the table prayer. Here's one I enjoy. Since I can't sing it for you, I hope you have a friend who knows it who can share it with you.

"Oh the Lord is good to me,
and so I thank the Lord,
for giving me the things I need,
the sun and the rain and the appleseed,
the Lord is good to me.
Amen, amen, amen, amen, amen."

Louella's Deviled Eggs

6 large	hard-cooked eggs, peeled
2 tablespoons	Hellmann's mayonnaise
2 tablespoons	sour cream
1 teaspoon	apple cider vinegar
1 teaspoon	prepared mustard
⅛ teaspoon	salt
⅛ teaspoon	freshly ground black pepper
	Paprika, for garnish

Slice the eggs in half lengthwise and carefully remove the yolks. In a small bowl, use a fork to mash the egg yolks with the mayonnaise, sour cream, vinegar, mustard, salt, and pepper.

Spoon the filling back into the egg white halves. You can also spoon the filling into a sandwich size zip-top bag, cut a small opening in one corner of the bag, and pipe the filling into the egg white halves.

Refrigerate until ready to serve, garnish with a sprinkle of paprika, and serve on a deviled egg plate.

PERFECT HARD-COOKED EGGS

Place eggs in a single layer in a large saucepan. Add enough cold water to cover the eggs. Bring the water to a rolling boil. Remove the saucepan from the heat, cover, and allow the eggs and water to stand for 17 minutes. Drain the water immediately after 17 minutes and add cold water and ice cubes. After the eggs have cooled, peel under cold running water.

Louella's Bread and Butter Pickles

4 quarts	thinly sliced cucumbers
8 small	onions, thinly sliced
2 large	bell peppers, cored, seeded, and thinly sliced
½ cup	salt
1 quart	water
	Ice cubes
5 cups	white vinegar
4 cups	granulated sugar
1½ teaspoons	turmeric
½ teaspoon	ground cloves
2 tablespoons	mustard seeds
1 teaspoon	celery seeds

Combine the cucumbers, onions, and peppers in a large bowl. Sprinkle the salt over the mixture and add the water and ice cubes to cover. Let stand for 3 hours, stirring several times.

In a large saucepan over high heat, combine the vinegar, sugar, turmeric, cloves, mustard seeds, and celery seeds. Bring to a boil, reduce the heat, and simmer for 5 minutes. Drain the vegetable mixture well and pack the vegetables into sterilized jars. Pour the liquid over the vegetables, seal, and sterilize the jars for 15 minutes according to the instructions included with the box of canning jars.

Louella's Coconut Cake

For the cake		For the filling	
	Nonstick cooking spray for the pans	½ cup	unsalted butter, at room temperature
2 cups	White Lily all-purpose flour, more for dusting the pans	4 ounces	cream cheese
		1½ cups	confectioners' sugar
1 teaspoon	baking soda	1 tablespoon	lemon zest (see page 52)
½ teaspoon	salt	2 tablespoons	fresh lemon juice
5 large	eggs, at room temperature, separated	2 tablespoons	milk
2 cups	granulated sugar	*For the icing*	
½ cup	unsalted butter, at room temperature	1½ cups	confectioners' sugar
½ cup	vegetable oil	1 (16-ounce) container	sour cream
1 cup	buttermilk	2 cups	freshly grated coconut (see page 161)
2 cups	freshly grated coconut (opposite)	1 teaspoon	vanilla extract

The cake Preheat the oven to 350°F. Coat three 9-inch round cake pans with nonstick cooking spray, then dust with flour. Set aside. In a large bowl, sift together the flour, baking soda, and salt. In the bowl of an electric mixer, beat the egg whites on medium speed until stiff peaks form. Using another bowl with the electric mixer on medium speed, cream the 2 cups granulated sugar and ½ cup butter until light in color, about 4 minutes. With the mixer running, add the oil and combine thoroughly, scraping down the sides of the bowl so all of the batter is mixed properly. Add the egg yolks, one at a time, beating well (about 30 seconds) after each addition. Continue beating for 2 minutes after adding the last egg yolk.

Remove the bowl from the mixer. Fold in half of the flour mixture with a large rubber spatula. Scrape down the sides of the bowl and add half of the buttermilk. Fold in the remaining flour mixture, scrape down the sides, and add the remaining buttermilk. Fold in the 2 cups of grated coconut. Scrape down the sides and fold in the beaten egg whites. Pour the batter into the pans and bake for 25 to 30 minutes, or until a toothpick inserted in the center of the cakes comes out clean.

Let the cakes cool in the pans for 15 minutes, then run a small knife around the sides of the pans and invert the cakes onto cooling racks and cool completely before icing.

The filling In the bowl of an electric mixer, cream the ½ cup butter and the cream cheese together until fluffy. Add the confectioners' sugar, lemon zest, lemon juice, and milk and mix well.

The icing In a large bowl combine the 1½ cups confectioners' sugar, the sour cream, the 2 cups coconut, and the vanilla. Refrigerate for at least 30 minutes before using.

To assemble the cake Spread half of the filling on top of one cake layer. Place a second layer on top and spread the other half of the filling on top. Place the third layer on top, then finish with the icing. Refrigerate overnight before serving.

HOW TO CRACK AND GRATE
A FRESH COCONUT

Pierce two of the three "eyes" on the fresh coconut with an ice pick or screwdriver. Drain the liquid. Place the coconut on a hard surface and gently tap all over with a hammer to crack the shell. Break the shell apart and remove the coconut meat. Peel the brown skin from the white meat using a vegetable peeler. Grate the coconut meat with a hand grater or the shredding blade of a food processor. One medium coconut yields 3 to 4 cups grated coconut.

❖ *This cake is better if made one to two days before serving.*
❖ *Packaged grated coconut may be substituted for the fresh coconut.*

POLITICAL CHICKEN

I've noticed that once it hits the table, fried chicken becomes highly political.

Honored guests are always offered the breast, as this is the part our society deems superior.

It's all downhill after the breast is carved away and distributed to the bigwigs and high muckety-mucks. If you are a child, you will end up with the drumstick (a playful and childlike name, in fact). Or, if you are a mother who is sacrificial, you will end up with the drumstick. Politics will have been served.

I have never preferred the breast; in fact, I consider it fairly tasteless and mundane. My sworn favorites are the thigh and drumstick, the dark meat in which all the succulent flavors reside.

I recall Daniel D'Arezzo's visit to my home when I was starting as *Victoria* magazine's writer-in-residence. I had made a salad, roast potatoes, and a roast chicken for Daniel, who was then deputy editor of *Victoria*. "Daniel," I called from the kitchen, "would you like white or dark meat?"

"Dark!" he exclaimed at once. I had found a rare soulmate—someone who actually preferred the socially outcast parts, and was man enough to admit it!

My grandmother, reared in a farm family of eleven, professed a love for the chicken back. Several things were happening here, I think. In a family of eleven, this piece may be all that's left on the platter. In a family of eleven, it is one way, however odd, to gain some precise identity ("Fannie always likes the back," her mother must have said more than once). It is also, in its humble way, quite a misunderstood piece of chicken, for, after all, it does have those delicious morsels, one on either side, that make the most perfect and savory bites. There are other morsels to be found on the back of a chicken, but they are small and pathetic. It is these two pearls of perfection that one wishes for and may be quite fully satisfied to get.

And now, to the wing, which is very far down on the political rung, and often falls to young children (being careful of the bones, of course) or self-effacing elderly people ("Oh, no, dear, not the breast, just a wing for me," which means, *I certainly don't want to be any trouble or cause anyone to go hungry*).

With the wing, all is not as it may appear. It is a scrawny thing, given that chickens hardly ever fly (only over an occasional puddle or just for the heck of it), so this part of their anatomy is seldom exercised.

However, if you roast a chicken on its back with the wings sticking up (as wings are prone to do), you will then have two of the most crispy, golden, and delicious delicacies in the kingdom of fowl cookery. My advice is, if no company is at the table, just remove the wings in the kitchen and hide them for the one who washes up, which will, of course, be yourself.

Years ago, I heard a great-aunt confess, to everyone's consternation, that she liked "the part that goes over the fence last."

(Squeamish readers may wish to turn the page.)

And why not? On either side of this piece, which is as low as you can go in the game of Political

Chicken, is a juicy morsel, always a treat to my cats and dog. I have never seen them walk away in a huff when offered these lovely portions.

Suffice it to say that I have pondered chicken all my life, on the table and in the farmyard. And, while chickens are said to be dumb, in my personal opinion they are not. In truth, I find chickens to be soulful and gay (in the lovely, old-fashioned sense, of course). Few things please me more than to sit and watch the behavior of chickens, especially the fluffy, yellow, innocent biddies. And I love the mothering wings that sweep them all together and hold them close to a beating heart, covered ever so nicely by feathers.

Another way to enjoy chicken, albeit roasted, is in a sandwich, thus:

Cold and sliced, the bread slathered with orange marmalade (a variation of the more traditional mayonnaise). The garlicky, lemony flavor of roast chicken goes happily with the tangy taste of orange marmalade, especially if the marmalade is rough cut with those chewy morsels of rind. Roast chicken is also splendid with a nice slab of tangy goat cheese and some fresh mesclun, sprinkled with a lively squeeze of lemon juice.

And that, gentle reader, is all I know about chicken.

—Jan Karon

Cynthia gave him a hug as he came in the back door. "We've been invited to Miss Rose's and Uncle Billy's for banana pudding this evening."

"Oh, no! Please, no!"

"Dearest, don't be stuffy."

"Stuffy? Miss Rose has been hospitalized with ptomaine poisoning twice—and nearly sent a Presbyterian parishioner to her reward. You're the only person in town who'd put your feet under her table."

"So, pray for protection and let's go," she said, looking eager.

It didn't take much to delight Cynthia Kavanagh. No, indeed, it hardly took anything at all. What's more, she loved flying in the face of mortal danger.

—*THESE HIGH, GREEN HILLS*, CHAPTER TWO

Miss Rose's Banana Pudding

⅓ cup	all-purpose flour
⅛ teaspoon	salt
4 cups	milk
1 (14-ounce) can	sweetened condensed milk
4 large	egg yolks
1 tablespoon	vanilla extract
6 medium	ripe bananas, sliced
60 to 70	vanilla wafers
8 large	egg whites, at room temperature
½ cup	granulated sugar

Combine the flour and salt in a large saucepan. Turn the heat on to medium and add the milk, condensed milk, and egg yolks, stirring constantly until thickened. Remove from the heat and add the vanilla. Let the custard cool briefly. To prevent a thick skin from forming on top of the custard, place a piece of plastic wrap directly on top of the custard until completely cooled.

Arrange half of the banana slices on the bottom of a baking dish, top with half of the wafers, and spoon half of the custard mixture on top. Repeat with remaining bananas, wafers, and custard.

Preheat the oven to 325°F. In the bowl of an electric mixer, beat the egg whites on medium speed until foamy. Slowly add the sugar while the mixer is still running. Continue to beat until soft peaks are formed. Spread the meringue over the pudding, making sure to seal in the edges. Bake until the meringue is brown on top, 5 to 8 minutes. Cool for at least 30 minutes, then chill before serving.

❖ *This is how Miss Rose's Banana Pudding is supposed to taste, when prepared properly and refrigerated (rather than left out on the countertop for several days).*

I'll be et for a tater if it ain't th' preacher! Rose, come and look, he's got 'is missus with 'im."

They stood at the back door of the museum that led to the apartment the town had remodeled for Miss Rose and Uncle Billy Watson.

The old man's schizophrenic wife of nearly fifty years peered around the door. The rector thought she looked fiercer than ever.

"What do they want?" she demanded, staring directly at the shivering couple on the steps.

Uncle Billy appeared bewildered.

"You invited us for banana pudding!" said Cynthia. "Yesterday, when I saw you on the street."

"I did?" Miss Rose put her hands on her hips and gave them a withering look. "Well, I don't have any banana pudding!"

"Oh, law," said Uncle Billy, "did you go an' forget you invited th' preacher and 'is missus?"

"I certainly did not forget. It's too close to Thanksgiving to make banana pudding. I would never have had such an idea."

—*These High, Green Hills,* Chapter Two

SAYING GRACE

Think about it. If it weren't for the goodness of God, would we have that heaping plate in front of us?

Grace can be short, sweet, and simple, and does not have to cover petitions for all the nations of the world, the circumstances of the entire family, and the misguided path of the modern church. This kind of prayer is best done at one's bedside.

People seem to enjoy holding hands around a table and bowing their heads in a moment of recognition that God faithfully provides our needs.

I think it's wonderful when such a prayer pours straight from the heart, but if you'd feel more comfortable using one of Father Tim's, there are several to be found in the series.

This, for example, was his blessing when he went to visit Miss Sadie and Louella in *These High, Green Hills.*

"Lord, we thank You for the richness of this life and our friendship, and for this golden-crusted cornbread. Please bless the hands that prepared it, and make us ever mindful of the needs of others, through Christ our Lord, amen."

You can, of course, substitute anything you like for "golden-crusted cornbread," but be careful. Soon after this blessing, you may recall, Louella voiced her grave disappointment that Father Tim "didn't say nothin' to th' Lord 'bout my beans!"

There are wonderful prayers for every occasion in the back of the *Book of Common Prayer*, or help yourself to this simple and lovely grace of Martin Luther's, often used by the Reverend Roald Carlson, the father of my literary editor, Carolyn Carlson.

Great is the Lord, and greatly to be praised,
The eyes of all look to thee,
And thou givest them their food in due season.
Thou openest thy hand,
Thou satisfieth the desire of every living thing.
My mouth shall speak the praise of the Lord
And let all flesh bless his holy name forever and ever. Amen.

Roald Carlson taught this prayer to his four young daughters, using hand gestures to help them memorize the words and meaning. Certainly you may change thee and thy to you and your, though I love the King Jamesian language.

This is the one my little sister, Brenda, and I were taught to say:

God is great, God is good,
Let us thank Him for our food.
By His hands we all are fed,
Give us, Lord, our daily bread.
In Jesus' name, amen.

I'm trying to remember how it felt to pray when I was a child. First, I think it made me feel happy that, when called upon, I had something special to say. Better still, it gave me an introduction, however small, to God—I learned that He was great, that He was good, and I knew, in some way I couldn't really understand, that He had provided for us.

Come to think of it, that's a lot for a little prayer to accomplish.

—JAN KARON

The annual All-Church Feast, convening this Thanksgiving Day at Lord's Chapel, was drawing its largest crowd in years. Villagers trooped across the churchyard hooting and laughing, as if to a long-awaited family reunion.

It was one of his favorite times of the year, hands down.

People he saw only at the post office or The Local were, on this day, eager to give him the details of their gallbladder operation, inquire how he liked married life, boast of their grandchildren, and debate the virtues of pan dressing over stuffing.

This year, the Presbyterians were kicking in the turkeys, which were, by one account, "three whoppers."

Esther Bolick had made two towering orange marmalade cakes, to the vast relief of all who had heard she'd given up baking and was crocheting afghans.

"Afghans?" said Esther with disgust. "I don't know who started such a tale as that. I crocheted some pot holders for Christmas, but that's a far cry from *afghans.*"

Miss Rose Watson marched into the parish hall and marked her place at a table by plunking her pocketbook in a chair. She then placed a half dozen large Ziploc plastic containers on the table, which announced her intent to do doggie bags again this year.

Ray Cunningham came in with a ham that he had personally smoked with hickory chips, and the mayor, who had renounced cooking years ago, contributed a sack of Winesaps.

Every table in the Lord's Chapel storage closets had been set up, and the Presbyterians had trucked in four dozen extra chairs. The only way to walk through the room, everyone discovered, was sideways.

Cynthia Kavanagh appeared with two pumpkin chiffon pies in a carrier, Dooley Barlowe followed with a tray of yeast rolls still hot from the oven, and the rector brought up the rear with a pan of sausage dressing and a bowl of cranberry relish.

Sophia and Liza arrived with a dish of cinnamon stickies that Liza had baked on her own. Handing them off to her mother, she ran to catch Rebecca Jane Owen, who had grown three new teeth and was toddling headlong toward the back door, which was propped open with a broom handle.

Evie Adams helped her mother, Miss Pattie, up the parish hall steps, while lugging a gallon jar of green beans in the other arm.

Mule and Fancy Skinner, part of the Baptist contingent, came in with a sheet cake from the Sweet Stuff Bakery.

And Dora Pugh, of Pugh's Hardware, brought a pot of stewed apples, picked in August from her own tree. "Get a blast of that," she said, lifting the lid. The aroma of cinnamon and allspice permeated the air like so much incense from a thurible.

In the commotion, George Hollifield's grandchildren raced from table to table, plunking nuts and apples in the center of each, as Wanda Hollifield came behind with orange candles in glass holders.

In his long memory of Mitford's All-Church Feasts, the rector thought he'd never seen such bounty. He thought he'd never seen so many beaming faces, either—or was that merely the flush from the village ovens that had been cranked on 350 since daybreak?

—*These High, Green Hills*, Chapter Three

Jan Karon's
Mitford Cookbook
& Kitchen Reader

Cynthia's Pumpkin Pie

3 tablespoons	unsalted butter, melted and cooled, more for greasing the pan
½ recipe	*Pastry for a Double Crust Pie* (page 4) (Halve the recipe, or make the whole recipe and freeze half)
3 large	eggs
⅓ cup	granulated sugar
1 (14-ounce) can	sweetened condensed milk
1½ cups	pumpkin puree
1 tablespoon	all-purpose flour
¼ teaspoon	ground ginger
½ teaspoon	ground cinnamon
¼ teaspoon	ground mace
¼ teaspoon	ground cloves
⅛ teaspoon	salt
	Sweetened whipped cream, for serving

Preheat the oven to 325°F. Lightly butter a 9-inch pie pan. Roll out the dough and fit it into the pie pan, and set aside.

In the bowl of an electric mixer mix the eggs, sugar, condensed milk, and pumpkin puree on medium speed until well combined. Add the butter and mix until well combined.

In a separate bowl combine the flour, ginger, cinnamon, mace, cloves, and salt. Add to the pumpkin mixture and stir until combined.

Pour the filling into the unbaked pie crust and bake for 45 to 50 minutes, or until the pie is set in the middle. Cool completely before slicing and serve with a dollop of whipped cream.

"Line up and collect your baskets," hollered Esther Cunningham, "and hot foot it out of here! This is not a cold-cut dinner you're deliverin'."

The delivery squad obediently queued up at the kitchen door.

"If you could knock th' Baptists out of this deal," said Charlie Tucker, "we'd have somethin' left to go *in* these baskets. Baptists eat like they're bein' raptured before dark."

"It wasn't the *Baptists* who gobbled up the turkey," said Esther Bolick, appearing to know.

"In Mitford, we take care of our own."

—Mayor Esther Cunningham

"Well, it sure wasn't the Methodists," retorted Jena Ivey, taking it personally. "We like fried chicken!"

"It was the dadgum Lutherans!" announced Mule, picking up the basket for Coot Hendrick's mother. "Outlanders from Wesley!"

Everyone howled with laughter, including the Lutherans, who had personally observed the Episcopalians eating enough turkey to sink an oil freighter.

—*These High, Green Hills,* Chapter Three

The rectory dining room and kitchen were upside down and backward, and the plunder from the two rooms had been scattered throughout the parlor and along the hallway, not to mention dumped on either side of the steps all the way to the landing.

On Easter Monday, his dining chairs and china dresser had been hauled to the foyer, along with a stack of pots, pans, dishes, and nine boxes of oatmeal. As he hadn't cooked oatmeal in two or three years, he had no idea where it came from, and was afraid to ask.

He saw his wife on occasion, but hardly recognized her, smeared as she was with pumpkin-colored paint, and her hair tied back with a rag.

"Cynthia?" he said, peering into the dining room. He might have stuck his head inside a cantaloupe, for all the brazen new color on his walls.

She looked down from the top rung of a ladder. "H'lo, dearest. What do you think?"

"Lord!" she said. "What I wouldn't give for a chocolate Little Debbie, to celebrate!" Emma had given up Little Debbies for Lent three years ago, a sacrifice he deeply appreciated. Being in the same room with a Little Debbie of any variety was more temptation than he could handle.

—Emma Garrett and Father Tim

He honestly didn't know what he thought.

What he wondered was how much longer they'd be dodging around paint buckets and ladders, not to mention that he'd stepped in a skillet last night as he went up to bed. His study was the only place on the ground floor that hadn't been invaded by the haste to transform the rectory into an old Italian villa before May fifteenth.

The kitchen, which certainly hadn't been painted in his fourteen-year tenure, was becoming the color of "clotted Devon cream," according to Cynthia. She was also doing something with a hammer and sponge that made the walls look positively ancient.

If anything, shouldn't they be trying to make the place look more up-to-date?

As worthless as guilt was known to be, he couldn't help feeling it, seeing his wife work herself to exhaustion for a parish tea that would last only two hours.

"Yes," said their friend Marge Owen, "but they'll talk about it for two years!"

He tried once to help her, but he'd never held a paintbrush in his life.

"You bake," she finally said, exasperated, "and I'll paint. For starters, I need ten dozen lemon squares—they freeze beautifully. When you're through with those, I need ten dozen raspberry tarts and fourteen dozen cookies, assorted . . ."

She rattled off a baking list that sounded like the quarterly output of Pepperidge Farm.

Why couldn't they just do vegetable sandwiches and strawberries dipped in chocolate?

"We're also doing those, but not until the last minute," she said, peering down at him from a ladder. She was always on a ladder. Except, of course, for the times she popped through the hedge to work on her book, which had an ominous deadline.

"I can't even *think* about the deadline," she wailed. "I can't even think about it!"

At night, she rolled over and expired, while he stared at dancing shadows on the ceiling and listened to Barnabas snore in the hall.

~

"We're thrilled," said Esther Bolick. "I can't remember when something this big has happened and I didn't have to bake a cake for it!"

"You're not hurt that we didn't ask you to bake?"

"Hurt? I should say not!"

He could tell, however, that Esther wouldn't have minded doing a two-layer orange marmalade.

He was relieved to see that Emma was softening toward the coming event. But she made it clear to him that Cynthia should at least get involved in Sunday School and chair the parish brunches.

The ECW called to offer help in serving and pouring, and promised to line up four or five husbands to keep the tea traffic untangled on the street in front of the rectory.

Hessie Mayhew stopped by, wanting an interview, just as Father Tim trekked home to pick up his sermon notebook.

"Talk to my wife," he said, "it's all her doing." He hoped that Hessie would not read any Coleridge before she wrote the story.

Clutching her note pad, Hessie grilled Cynthia, who was painting dentil molding from the top rung of a ladder. "What are you serving? How many people? What time of day? Any special colors? Do you have a theme?"

He ran from the room.

Going out the back door five minutes later, he heard Cynthia announce that the event would be called the "First Annual Primrose Tea."

Hessie gave a squeal of delight, which was definitely a good sign.

—*These High, Green Hills*, Chapter Seven

Cynthia's Lemon Squares

	Nonstick cooking spray for the pan
2 cups	White Lily all-purpose flour
½ cup plus 2 to 4 tablespoons	confectioners' sugar
1 cup plus 2 tablespoons	unsalted butter
1 teaspoon	vanilla extract
¼ teaspoon plus ⅛ teaspoon	salt
2 cups	granulated sugar
2 tablespoons	cornstarch
5 large	eggs, at room temperature
1 tablespoon	grated lemon zest (see page 52)
½ cup	fresh lemon juice

Preheat the oven to 350°F. Coat a 9 x 13-inch baking pan with nonstick cooking spray. Place the flour, ½ cup of the confectioners' sugar, 1 cup of the butter, the vanilla, and ¼ teaspoon salt in the bowl of an electric mixer and mix on medium speed until combined. Pat the batter into the pan and bake for 18 minutes, or until a light gold color. Melt the remaining 2 tablespoons butter in a small saucepan over low heat. Set aside to cool slightly.

Meanwhile, in the bowl of an electric mixer, combine the granulated sugar and cornstarch. Add the eggs, one at a time, beating well after each addition. Add the lemon zest, lemon juice, ⅛ teaspoon salt, and the melted butter and beat well. Pour the lemon mixture over the crust and bake for another 20 to 25 minutes, or until set. Let cool completely, then sift 2 to 4 tablespoons of confectioners' sugar over the lemon squares. Chill and cut into squares.

Primrose Tea Raspberry Tarts

3 ounces	cream cheese, softened
½ cup	unsalted butter, softened
1 cup	White Lily all-purpose flour
½ teaspoon	salt
	Nonstick cooking spray for the pan

For the filling

½ cup	granulated sugar
1 large	egg
2 tablespoons	unsalted butter, softened
2 tablespoons	heavy cream
2 tablespoons	fresh orange juice
1 teaspoon	grated orange zest (see page 52)
½ teaspoon	vanilla extract
24	fresh raspberries

Preheat the oven to 325°F. In the bowl of an electric mixer combine the cream cheese and ½ cup butter. Add the flour and ¼ teaspoon of the salt and mix until just combined. Place the dough in the refrigerator to chill for 15 minutes. Remove the dough from the refrigerator and divide it into 24 balls. Chill the dough balls briefly. Coat the cups of a mini muffin pan with nonstick cooking spray. Place a ball of dough in each cup and press the dough on the bottom and up the sides of the cup and use a tart tamper to shape the mini tarts in the pan. Refrigerate while you prepare the filling.

The filling In the bowl of an electric mixer, beat the sugar, egg, 2 tablespoons butter, the cream, orange juice, orange zest, the remaining ¼ teaspoon salt, and vanilla until creamy. Spoon into the prepared mini crusts and bake for 25 to 30 minutes, or until the filling is set. Cool completely before removing from the muffin pans. Place a raspberry in the center of each tart and refrigerate until ready to serve.

Cucumber Tea Sandwiches

1	seedless cucumber, sliced thin
¼ cup	white wine vinegar
1 tablespoon	salt
4 ounces	cream cheese, softened
½ cup	unsalted butter, softened
1 clove	garlic, minced
6	green onions, roughly chopped
1 tablespoon	fresh lemon juice
1 teaspoon	lemon zest (see page 52)
½ teaspoon	freshly ground black pepper
1 teaspoon	fresh dill (or ¼ teaspoon dried), plus dill sprigs for garnish
1 loaf	thinly sliced white bread

Place the cucumber slices in a colander set in the sink. Pour the vinegar and 2 teaspoons of the salt over them. Drain for at least 20 minutes, then remove the cucumber slices from the colander and pat dry.

In the bowl of a food processor fitted with the metal blade, combine the cream cheese, butter, garlic, green onions, lemon juice, lemon zest, the remaining 1 teaspoon salt, the pepper, and dill. Process until the mixture is smooth.

Cut into the bread slices with a 2-inch round cookie cutter. Place the rounds in an airtight zip-top bag until you're ready to assemble the sandwiches.

Spread the cream cheese mixture on the bread slices. Top with cucumber slices and garnish with a sprig of fresh dill. Serve immediately.

Tomato Basil Tea Sandwiches

1 pint carton	cherry tomatoes
8 ounces	cream cheese, softened
1 bunch	green onions, roughly chopped
½ teaspoon	salt
8 to 10	fresh basil leaves, more for garnish
1 loaf	thinly sliced white bread
¼ teaspoon	freshly ground black pepper
1 pound	bacon strips, cooked and crumbled

Cut the cherry tomatoes in very thin slices. Place the slices, cut side down, in a single layer on paper towels to drain.

In the bowl of a food processor fitted with the metal blade, combine the cream cheese, green onions, salt, and basil. Pulse until the mixture is combined.

Spread a small amount of the cream cheese mixture on a slice of bread. Cut each slice of bread into 3 fingers, removing the crusts. Top each slice of bread with a layer of cherry tomatoes. Season with salt and pepper, top with bacon, and garnish with a fresh basil leaf.

❖ *These sandwiches are best if served immediately after assembling. The cream cheese mixture can be made ahead of time and the bacon can be cooked and crumbled ahead of time.*

Chocolate-Dipped Strawberries

48 large	strawberries
12 ounces	semisweet chocolate chips
1 tablespoon	vegetable shortening

Line a large baking sheet with wax paper. Rinse the strawberries and pat dry. Leave the stems on. Make sure the strawberries are completely dry before dipping them in the chocolate.

Place the chocolate chips and the shortening in a microwave-safe bowl and microwave at medium power for 2 minutes. Stir, then return to the microwave and melt for another 1½ minutes. Stir well.

Dip the strawberries into the chocolate: hold each strawberry by its green top and dip three-quarters of the way down into the chocolate mixture. Let the excess chocolate drip into the bowl. Place the strawberries on the wax paper–lined baking sheet. Repeat the dipping process with the remaining strawberries. Refrigerate until the chocolate coating is firm, about 1 hour. The strawberries can be prepared up to 4 to 6 hours before serving.

PUNY'S SAVING GRACE #5

"You can keep strawberries fresh for ten days if you do this: wash 'em, put 'em between layers of paper towels, then stick in a Ziploc bag and store in th' refrigerator. Rinse when you take 'em out."

T hat was some shindig at your place."

He had wondered when Emma would at last bring up the social event that was still the talk of the town. "So I hear."

"Cynthia did a good job."

"Thank you. I hear that, too."

"A little too much sugar in the lemon squares."

"I see it failed to sweeten your disposition."

"Ha ha. What do you think about your kitchen walls being banged up with a hammer?"

"The best thing to happen to the rectory since Father Hanes installed a fireplace in the study."

"I didn't think you'd go much for that deal."

"I hope you know the ruined look is the very thing to give mundane surfaces a mellow, weathered appeal. Take your old villas in Italy, for example, where the plaster is put on thickly, without superficial concern for perfection, where the surfaces ripple and change like . . . like life itself . . ."

She peered at him over her glasses.

". . . where buildings shift and settle with the passage of years, where a century is but a fleeting moment in time . . ."

"I *get* it!" she said, wanting him to stop at once.

". . . where decades of smoking olive oil and burning wood wash the walls with a palette of color as subtle as the nuances of old stone or ancient marble—where, indeed, the very movement of light and shadow are captured in the golden glow of the walls, grown as redolent with history as trade routes worn by ancient Romans. . . ." He had no idea what he was saying, but he was enjoying it immensely.

She stared at him with her mouth slightly agape.

That ought to fix her.

—*These High, Green Hills*, Chapter Nine

When he arrived home at five-thirty, he thought he had never smelled such a seductive aroma in his life, though something in his stomach was definitely off.

"Leg of lamb!" exclaimed Cynthia.

"Man!" Sometimes there was nothing else to do but quote Dooley Barlowe.

"And glazed carrots, and roasted potatoes with rosemary."

"The very gates of heaven."

"Dearest," she said, putting her arms around his neck, "there's something different about you. . . ."

"What? Exhaustion, maybe, from only four hours of sleep."

She kissed his chin. "No. Something deeper. I don't know what it is."

"Something good, I fondly hope."

"Yes. Very good. I can't put my finger on it, exactly. Oh, I forgot—and a salad with oranges and scallions, and your favorite dressing."

"But why all this?"

"Because you were so brave when we were lost in that horrible cave."

The payoff was definitely improving. He brushed her hair back and kissed her forehead. "It wasn't so horrible."

"Timothy . . ."

"OK," he said. "I was scared out of my wits."

She laughed. "I knew that!"

"You did not."

"Did so."

"Did not."

Jan Karon's
Mitford Cookbook
& Kitchen Reader

—*These High, Green Hills, Chapter Eleven*

Cynthia's Leg of Lamb

1 (4½ to 5 pound)	butterflied leg of lamb		2 tablespoons	balsamic vinegar
⅔ cup	extra-virgin olive oil		4 tablespoons	Dijon mustard
⅓ cup	fresh lemon juice		3 tablespoons	minced fresh rosemary
2 teaspoons	grated lemon zest			(or 1 teaspoon dried)
	(see page 52)		3 tablespoons	minced fresh parsley
5 cloves	garlic, minced			(or 1 teaspoon dried)
2 teaspoons	chili powder			*Apple Jelly with Fresh Mint*

Trim the excess fat and silver skin off the lamb.

Combine the rest of the ingredients in a large bowl. Place the lamb in a large zip-top bag and pour the marinade over the meat. Seal the bag and place the lamb in the refrigerator for 24 hours to marinate.

Remove the lamb from the refrigerator 30 minutes before you are ready to cook it.

Heat a gas or charcoal grill to medium-hot. Cook the lamb 15 to 20 minutes per side until nicely browned, basting often with the remaining marinade. Cook the lamb until the internal temperature at the thickest part reaches 130 to 135° for medium-rare or 140 to 145° for medium.

Let the lamb rest on a cutting board for 10 minutes. Carve into thin slices and serve with *Apple Jelly with Fresh Mint*.

APPLE JELLY WITH FRESH MINT

2 cups	apple jelly
½ cup	chopped fresh mint
2 teaspoons	freshly ground black pepper

In a medium bowl, mix together the jelly, mint, and pepper. Cover and refrigerate until ready to use. Makes 2 cups.

Cynthia's Glazed Carrots

6 cups	sliced carrots (sliced ¼ inch thick on the diagonal)
1½ teaspoons	salt
¼ cup plus 2 tablespoons	brown sugar
½ cup	*Chicken Stock* (see recipe, page 137)
¼ cup plus 1 tablespoon	unsalted butter
2 teaspoons	fresh lemon juice
1 teaspoon	grated lemon zest (see page 52)
	Freshly ground black pepper
½ cup	walnuts

Combine the carrots, salt, ¼ cup of the brown sugar, and the chicken stock in a nonstick skillet and bring to a boil over high heat. Cover, reduce the heat, and simmer for about 5 minutes. Uncover the skillet and simmer for about 2 minutes more. Stir in ¼ cup of the butter and the remaining 2 tablespoons of the brown sugar to the skillet. Cook the carrots on low heat, stirring to coat them with the glaze, about 3 minutes. Remove the skillet from the heat and add the lemon juice, lemon zest, and additional salt and pepper to taste.

Place the walnuts and the remaining 1 tablespoon of the butter in a separate skillet over low heat. Sauté the walnuts until toasted, 8 to 10 minutes.

Spoon the carrots into a serving dish and top with the toasted walnuts.

Cynthia's Roasted Potatoes with Rosemary

¼ cup	extra-virgin olive oil, more for the baking dish
8 large	cloves garlic, minced
2 tablespoons	chopped fresh rosemary (or 2½ teaspoons dried)
10	new potatoes, halved
3 medium	sweet potatoes, cut into chunks
	Salt and freshly ground pepper

Preheat the oven to 400°F. Grease a large baking dish. Combine the oil, garlic, and rosemary in a small bowl. Place the potatoes in the baking dish. Pour the olive oil mixture over the potatoes and mix well.

Bake, uncovered, stirring occasionally, for 40 to 45 minutes. Add salt and pepper to taste before serving.

PUNY'S SAVING GRACE #6

"I don't wash lettuce when I bring it home. I put it in th' fridge, then wash it a minute or two before I use it. This'll make it last longer and taste fresher.

"Before th' Father married Cynthia, he'd sometimes let 'is lettuce go 'til it got wilted an' all. I always perked it up by soakin' in cold water with a little lemon juice."

Cynthia's Salad with Oranges and Scallions

1 tablespoon	unsalted butter	*For the dressing*	
½ cup	slivered almonds	2 cloves	garlic, pressed
½ teaspoon	salt	¼ cup	fresh lemon juice
¼ teaspoon	seasoned salt	3 tablespoons	fresh orange juice
1 head	romaine lettuce, torn	1 teaspoon	Dijon mustard
	into small pieces, or	⅛ teaspoon	cayenne pepper
	1 bag prewashed	½ cup	extra-virgin olive oil
	romaine lettuce	½ cup	vegetable oil
	pieces	1 tablespoon	grated orange zest
1 (15-ounce) can	mandarin oranges,		(see page 52)
	drained		Salt and freshly ground black
1 bunch	scallions, sliced		pepper

Warm the butter in a small skillet over medium heat. Add the almonds and sauté until they start to brown, 8 to 10 minutes. (Watch carefully so the almonds don't burn.) Remove from the heat and stir in the salt and the seasoned salt. Drain the nuts on paper towels.

Make the dressing In a bowl of a food processor fitted with the metal blade, combine the garlic, lemon juice, orange juice, mustard, and cayenne. With the machine running, add the olive and vegetable oils slowly in a thin stream until thoroughly incorporated. Pour the dressing into a medium bowl and stir in the orange zest. Add salt and pepper to taste.

In a large serving bowl, combine the lettuce, mandarin oranges, scallions, and almonds. Just before serving, toss with the dressing. Adjust the seasonings with salt and pepper before serving.

"Sissy and Sassy?" he inquired.

"It's really Kaitlin and Kirsten," said Puny, smiling hugely. "But we decided to call 'em Sissy and Sassy." She was holding one infant on either side. The whole lot had mops of red hair like he'd never seen before in his life.

"Which is, ah, Sissy and which is . . . ?"

"This," said Puny, shrugging her right shoulder, "is Sissy. And this," she said, shrugging her left shoulder, "is Sassy. You'll get to know 'em apart when they come to work with me."

"Take your time on that," he said, meaning it. "No hurry. Why not take a month? Or take two—we can manage!"

Puny looked at him, wide-eyed. "We'd never pay our bills if I laid out for a month or two! You know that bathroom we added on, our *own* self? It cost four thousand dollars, and that's without a toilet! Lord only knows when we can git a toilet!"

"Aha."

"They say you fainted when Sassy popped out!"

"Went black," he said, grinning. If Nurse Herman hadn't snatched him up, he might have cracked his skull on the tile floor.

"Don't y'all worry about a thing," Puny assured him. "I'll be back in two weeks, good as new."

He gazed at the new mother and her little brood, feeling a glad delight for the young woman who had taken over his home and his heart, all to his very great relief.

"You're the best, Puny Guthrie."

"I'll bake you a cake of cornbread first thing," she said, smiling happily.

—*These High, Green Hills*, Chapter Eleven

Dooley would be home from school in a matter of days. He'd ride down with a boy and his family on their way to Holding, and be delivered to the rectory. A blessed relief, given the demands of Cynthia's new book and his own commitments, which included plans for a surprise celebration of Miss Sadie's ninetieth birthday, to be held in the parish hall Sunday after next.

There was no question in his mind that a blowout was in order.

Hadn't Sadie Baxter given five million dollars to Lord's Chapel, to build one of the finest nursing homes in the state? And hadn't her father, and then Miss Sadie herself, kept a roof on the church building throughout its long history?

He called the bishop, to ask whether he could attend, but Stuart Cullen had no fewer than four events on the Sunday in question, all of them miles from Mitford.

"Emma," he said, "call the entire parish and tell them they're invited."

Emma's lip curled. "Call th' whole bloomin' mailin' list?"

"The whole blooming list," he said, his excitement mounting.

"That's a hundred and twenty households, you know."

"Oh, I know." He was pleased with the number, especially as it had risen by seven percent in two years, even with the recent loss to the Presbyterian camp.

"I suppose you realize that nobody's ever home anymore, to *answer* the phone."

"I'm excited, Father, I just wanted you to know it." It was Sadie Baxter, and the old zing was back in her voice.

"That's what I like to hear. We're excited, too. It's mighty hard to dig up a brass band these days, but we're trying."

"Don't you go to any trouble, now!"

"Trouble? Why, Miss Sadie, trouble is what it's all about! If nobody went to any trouble in this world, the church would never have a roof. Cornbread would never get baked. Boys would never go to school."

—Miss Sadie and Father Tim

He couldn't argue that point. "So have cards done at QuikCopy. But you'll have to get them in the mail no later than tomorrow. Oh. And remember to say it's a surprise."

"It's certainly a surprise to me."

"When we get our computer," he said jauntily, "it'll knock the labels out in no time. Until then . . ."

She glared at him darkly. "I'll have to address every blasted one by hand."

—*These High, Green Hills*, Chapter Twelve

ooley was arriving at the rectory at two-thirty, and they'd promised to give his friend's parents a quick refreshment before they continued down the mountain to Holding.

Cheese and crackers . . .

He was supposed to pick up cheese and crackers right after the meeting at the hospital—and don't forget livermush. Russell Jacks was primed for livermush, and no two ways about it. The rector determined to buy six pounds and freeze four, and let Dooley make a delivery to his grandfather tomorrow morning. A fine boy in clean clothes, talking like a scholar and bearing two pounds of livermush? It was enough to make a man's heart fairly burst with pride—his own as well as Russell's.

—*These High, Green Hills*, Chapter Thirteen

"You know, Timothy, it's not having someone to love us that's so important—but having someone to love, don't you think?"

—Marge Owen

Jan Karon's
Mitford Cookbook
& Kitchen Reader

Sunday was all the perfection of June rolled into one fragile span of time, a golden day that no one would have end.

They feasted on Marge's chicken pie and raved over the flaky crust, and drank an entire pitcher of iced tea. Dooley rode Goosedown Owen around the barnyard, holding tightly to Rebecca Jane, who shared the saddle. Barnabas caroused with several of the Meadowgate dogs, and returned with a coat full of burrs, twigs, dead leaves, and other cast-offs of nature.

The rector headed for the woods with his wife and her sketchbook, where they found a cushion of moss along the sunlit path.

"Dearest," she said, opening her box of colored pencils, "maybe we should buy a farm when you retire."

"That's a thought."

"I'd love to pick wildflowers and put them in Mason jars on a windowsill!" She peered at a grove of Indian pipes that had pushed through a layer of leaf mold, and sketched quickly. "And I'd love making deep-dish blackberry pies. Would you do the picking?"

"No way," he said.

"Why not?"

"The last time I picked blackberries, I was so covered with chigger bites, I was nearly unrecognizable."

"When was that?"

"Oh, when I was ten or eleven."

"And it put you off blackberry picking for life?"

"Absolutely."

"Maybe we'd better not buy a farm."

"Maybe not," he said, laughing.

—*These High, Green Hills*, Chapter Sixteen

Marge's Chicken Pot Pie

For the chicken

6 large	chicken breasts, bone-in and skin on
2 stalks	celery
3 sprigs	fresh parsley
1 large	onion, quartered
1	bay leaf

For the pot pie

¾ cup plus 3 tablespoons	unsalted butter
¾ cup	all-purpose flour
5 cups	reserved chicken stock, heated

1½ teaspoons	poultry seasoning
4 teaspoons	salt
1 teaspoon	freshly ground black pepper
1 cup	coarsely chopped carrots
2 cups	chopped onions
½ cup	chopped celery
1 cup	frozen English peas, thawed
	Nonstick cooking spray for the pan
2 recipes	*Pastry for a Double Crust Pie* (see page 4)
¼ cup	unsalted butter, melted

The chicken Place the chicken, celery, parsley, onion, and bay leaf in a large pot and cover with cold water. Bring the water to a rolling boil over high heat for 1 minute. Cover and remove from the heat. Let the chicken sit, covered, until completely cooled, at least 2 hours. When cooled, remove the chicken, strain the broth, and refrigerate to use later. Before using the stock, remove the congealed fat from the top. Remove the skin from the chicken, cut the meat off the bones, coarsely chop it, cover, and refrigerate.

The pot pie In a large saucepan over medium heat, stir together the ¾ cup butter and the flour for 5 minutes, making a light roux. Slowly whisk in the warm stock, continuing to stir until the sauce is smooth and thickens. Add the poultry seasoning, 2 teaspoons salt, and pepper.

In a separate large skillet, warm the remaining 3 tablespoons butter, add the carrots, onions, and celery and sauté 8 to 10 minutes, or until softened. Add the sautéed vegetables and peas to the sauce and place in a large bowl. Place plastic wrap directly on top of the sauce and refrigerate to cool completely.

Preheat the oven to 400°F. Coat a 9 x 13-inch baking dish with nonstick cooking spray. Roll out the pastry dough and line the bottom and sides of the baking dish with three-quarters of one whole pie crust recipe. Line the pastry with aluminum foil and fill with pie weights or dried beans and bake for 15 minutes. Remove the crust from the oven and remove the pie weights and aluminum foil.

Add the reserved chicken to the vegetable mixture and pour into the prepared crust. Cover with one pie crust recipe. Pinch together the edges of the top and bottom crust. Cut out leaf shapes with the remaining one-quarter pastry and place on the edges of pie. Cut a slit in the middle of the pie.

Combine the melted ¼ cup butter and the remaining 2 teaspoons salt. Brush on top of the pastry and place in the oven. Bake at 400°F for 15 minutes, then reduce the oven temperature to 350°F and continue baking for 30 to 45 minutes, or until the crust is lightly browned.

Cynthia's Deep-Dish Blackberry Pie

	Nonstick cooking spray for the pan
1 recipe	*Pastry for a Double Crust Pie* (see page 4)
6 cups	fresh blackberries
2 cups	granulated sugar, more for sprinkling on top
2 tablespoons	White Lily all-purpose flour
½ teaspoon	ground cinnamon
	Vanilla ice cream, for serving

Preheat the oven to 425°F. Coat a 9 x 13-inch baking dish with cooking spray. Roll out half of the pastry dough and fit into the baking dish. Line the pastry with aluminum foil and fill with pie weights or dried beans. Bake for 15 minutes. Remove the crust from the oven and remove the pie weights and aluminum foil. In a large bowl combine the blackberries, sugar, flour, and cinnamon. Pour the filling into the pie shell. Roll out the remaining dough until it is about ¼ inch thick and cut out ½-inch strips. Arrange the strips in a lattice design on top of the filling. Sprinkle a small amount of sugar on top of the pie and bake for 30 to 35 minutes, or until the crust is browned on top. Remove the pie from the oven to a cooling rack. Let the pie cool for 5 to 8 minutes before serving. The pie is very juicy and best served in a bowl topped with vanilla ice cream.

etreat time!" she announced as he came in the back door, ready to do another few hours' work at home.

"Didn't we just have one?" he asked, scratching his head.

"Timothy, that was July! This is October."

"Oh," he said.

"I'm just packing up this hamper and we'll be off. The sunset should be glorious tonight; there was a red sky this morning!"

"Doesn't red sky in morning mean sailor take warning?"

"Whatever," she said happily, stuffing in a wedge of cheese.

Barnabas trudged with them up the hill, where, panting furiously, they all arrived at the stone wall.

"Don't really look at the view just yet, dearest. Let's save it until we finish setting up our picnic, shall we?"

He spread the old fringed cloth, which had belonged to a bishop's wife in the late forties, over the wall, and Cynthia began unpacking what she'd just packed.

Why was he up here on the hill, lolling about like some gigolo, when he had a nursing home to officially open one week hence, and a thousand details to be ironed out, only two of which had kept him up until one o'clock in the morning? But no, let his wife finish a book and she went instantly into the lolling mode. Perhaps it was this

"Lord help! Look at this! Are you practicin' to be John the Baptist in a church play? Remember what happened to him, honey, his hair was so bad-lookin', they cut his head off, how's your wife, I saw her the other day at the food bank givin' a ton of stuff, all I took was cream of mushroom soup, do you think that's OK? Do you know what all you can *do* with cream of mushroom soup? You can pour it over chicken and bake it covered, and Lord, it is the best thing you ever put in your mouth, Mule loves it, you can also pour it over a roast, but you have to wrap that thing like a mummy for it to work, at least two sheets of foil, and let it go on three fifty for two hours."

—Fancy Skinner

very lolling mode of the last two months that had given her countenance the beatific look he'd lately noticed.

"The domestic retreat," she said, setting out a plate of crackers, "is an idea which could literally save the institution of marriage. Do you know that studies say husbands and wives speak to each other a total of only seventeen minutes a week?"

"We're so far over that quota, we've landed in another study."

"I'll say. Roasted garlic. Ripe pears. Toasted pecans. Saga bleu."

She pulled out napkins and two glasses and poured a round of raspberry tea.

"There!" she said. "Now we can look!"

The Land of Counterpane stretched beneath their feet, a wide panorama of rich Flemish colors under a perfectly blue and cloudless sky.

Church steeples poked up from groves of trees.

Plowed farmland appeared like velveteen scraps on a quilt, feather-stitched with hedgerows.

There, puffs of chimney smoke billowed heavenward, and over there, light gleamed on a pond that regularly supplied fresh trout to Avis Packard's Local.

"Look, dearest! Look at our high, green hills."

He gazed across the little valley and up, up to the green hills, where groves of blazing hardwoods topped the ridges, and fences laced the broad, uneven meadows.

"Aren't they beautiful in this light?"

"They are!" he said, meaning it.

"Where's the train?"

He peered at his watch. "Ten minutes!" The little train would come winding through the valley, over the trestle that spanned the gorge, and just as it broke through the trees by the red barn and the silo, they would see it. If providence were with them, they would also hear the long, mournful blast of its horn.

—*These High, Green Hills,* Chapter Twenty-One

Cynthia's Raspberry Tea

3 Lipton family-size teabags, tags removed
1 cup granulated sugar
1 (12-ounce) can frozen raspberry lemonade, thawed
Maraschino cherries

Place the teabags in a pottery or glass pitcher, and pour 2 cups cold water over them. Bring a kettle with 4 cups of water to a rolling boil. Pour over the teabags and cover the pitcher with a small plate. Steep for 10 to 15 minutes, then remove the teabags, add the sugar, and stir until dissolved. Add 3 cups of cold water to the tea and stir in the lemonade until dissolved. Add the cherries before serving. Serve over ice.

Cynthia's Toasted Pecans

4 tablespoons	unsalted butter
2 tablespoons	Worcestershire sauce
½ teaspoon	ground cumin
1 teaspoon	celery salt
1 teaspoon	garlic powder
¼ teaspoon	cayenne pepper
1 teaspoon	seasoned salt
1 pound	whole pecans
2 tablespoons	coarse sea salt

Preheat the oven to 325°F. In a medium saucepan over medium heat combine the butter, Worcestershire sauce, cumin, celery salt, garlic powder, cayenne, and seasoned salt. Simmer for a few minutes for the flavors to combine.

Add the pecans and stir until evenly coated. Spread the pecans on a cookie sheet and bake for 15 to 20 minutes, or until the pecans are browned and crisp.

Transfer the pecans to a large bowl and toss them with the coarse salt. Cool, and store the pecans in an airtight container for up to 1 week.

"There are two cardinal rules from which I will not depart—I will not cook with Cheez Whiz and I will not do drumettes."

—CYNTHIA KAVANAGH

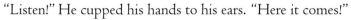

"Listen!" He cupped his hands to his ears. "Here it comes!"

A freight train broke into view at the red barn, blowing its horn as it rushed past a field, disappeared into the trees, and appeared again along a row of tiny houses.

She applauded, and turned to him, laughing. No, indeed, it didn't take much for his wife. . . .

They tried the roasted garlic and spread the Saga bleu on crackers and munched the pecans and emptied the tea container and watched the sky blush with pink, then fuchsia.

—*These High, Green Hills*, Chapter Twenty-One

The following story was published in *Victoria* magazine when Jan Karon served as their writer-in-residence. This is the first time it has appeared in a Mitford book.

The Right Ingredients

Uncle Billy Watson could hardly read the *Mitford Muse* these days. It seemed that awhile back, maybe after the war, the print in the *Muse* had been bigger, much bigger. But now, with things costing so much, maybe they couldn't afford big print.

He held the newspaper close to his face with one hand, and gripped a looking glass in the other, wishing his hand wouldn't shake and cause the words to jump up and down.

Around Town

by Vanita Bentley

Uncle Billy silently formed each word with his mouth.

Is Mitford getting to be the crossroads of the world?

Not too long since Winnie Ivey, now Winnie Kendall, won a cruise with Golden Band Flour Company, here Golden Band turns up in Mitford with a baking contest, can you believe it???!!!

Next Thursday, Golden Band will arrive in Mitford to watch our good cooks strut their stuff. Golden Band is going around to the small towns of America to prove that somebody out there still actually cooks and bakes. I don't, thank goodness, but I hope you do, because . . . first prize in each category is $500.00!!!!!!

The categories are Cakes, Pies, and Bread. Bread is the only category with two divisions—Loaf Bread or Biscuits—so you get two chances to win $500.00!!!!!!

Pick up your entry forms at The Local, today! And start your ovens!

Uncle Billy laid the newspaper in his lap and closed his eyes.

The story had suddenly put him in mind of his mother's kitchen, and the baking and cooking she'd done from sunup to sundown.

Until he was old enough to hunt rabbits in the piney woods, he had hung around the door of the cabin smelling the good smells, eating sweet scraps from his mother's floured hands, stealing sips of her coffee from a cracked blue cup.

As much as he'd like five hundred dollars to jingle in his pocket, he would pay every cent of that amount, if he had it, just to taste one of her pies again.

He patted his foot, and looked out the window without seeing.

Something was throbbing in his right temple, which he knew at once was his blood pressure.

He was going to do it. He was going to enter that contest.

The first thing he wished is that he could get his wife, Rose, out of the house so he could do what he had to do in peace and quiet.

The second thing he wished is that he'd be able to find the twenty dollar bill he hid in the stack of newspapers in the dining room, so he could buy what he needed to make . . . to make what?

Sweet potato pie.

The thought came to him as naturally as breathing.

Esther Bolick refolded the *Muse* and thumped it onto the kitchen table. She rued the day she ever parted with her orange marmalade cake recipe.

It was something she had vowed she'd never do. In fact, she refused to write the recipe down, thinking that would be extra protection against it landing in the wrong hands.

Then, a couple of years ago, just days before the annual Bane and Blessing sale, she'd fallen off that blooming ladder at Lord's Chapel and ended up in the hospital with two broken arms and her jaws wired shut.

The Bane was the biggest fund-raiser in the church's entire history. And everybody and his brother had counted on her to produce the dozen two-layer orange marmalades she'd baked every year for fourteen years.

She shuddered to recall the way the Bane volunteers had descended on her hospital bed like a swarm of vultures, gouging the recipe out of her, teaspoon by teaspoon, you might say, while the pain in her jaws was so searing, the pounding in her head so

blinding, that she wished to the good Lord she'd never heard of orange marmalade cake, much less gotten famous for it.

Naturally, the volunteers had scrambled home and baked off the dozen two-layers in the nick of time, which raised a total of three hundred dollars for digging wells in east Africa. This news had been wonderful medicine for Esther who, lying in the hospital bed, pictured eager children dancing around the well, drinking from dippers and feeling happy.

There was only one problem.

Since that day, half of Mitford had gotten their hands on her recipe.

Esther rose from the kitchen table and yanked open the freezer door.

If she was a betting woman, she'd bet Evie Adams would enter an orange marmalade in the Golden Band flour bake-off. Time and again, she'd been told that Evie not only liked using the orange marmalade recipe, but liked doctoring it up with Cointreau.

Cointreau? thought Esther, jabbing a knife between two cookies that had frozen together. If you couldn't bake a decent cake without resorting to liquor, you had the brains of a chicken.

And hadn't Hessie Mayhew said the hospital supervisor baked Esther's recipe all the time, and just loved adding nuts to the batter?

Nuts? She shivered.

She'd be surprised if her recipe didn't show up forty times in that bloomin' contest, since everybody in creation was walking around with it in their pockets, grinning like apes. Heaven knows, her rector's wife was the only one of the lot who'd ever called and asked permission.

Esther put the bag of cookies back in the freezer and slammed the door.

She wouldn't touch that contest with a ten-foot pole, as she'd never entered a contest less important than the State Fair and didn't expect to start now.

Jan Karon's
Mitford Cookbook
& Kitchen Reader

201

Hope Winchester sat on a stool behind the bookstore cash register, and watched a summer rain lash Main Street.

Through the block lettering, *Happy Endings,* which was painted on the front windows, she could see people dashing along the sidewalk, some with umbrellas, some with today's *Mitford Muse* held over their heads.

She read Vanita Bentley's story for the third time and hoped nobody came in for awhile, because she wanted to think.

What if she entered one of Golden Band's three contest categories? She figured if she got up the nerve to do it at all, she would enter Bread.

She'd never baked a loaf of bread in all her thirty-one years, nor anything else, for that matter, but she desperately needed five hundred dollars.

With a little practice, she could actually *see* the bread in her mind's eye, and the nice, brown crust on top. This was called "imaging." If you can image it, you can do it, she read in a self-help book, which was not a publishing genre she especially cared for.

When she was little, her father had said, "You read too many books. If I catch you reading another book, I'll throw it in the fire. Reading will rot your brain, go help your mother."

She had read in bed for years, under the covers with a flashlight, which was how she'd read every word of her second favorite book, *Jane Eyre.* She had nearly put her eyes out and ended up wearing glasses, which to this day she blamed on small print in paperbacks.

But the point was, hadn't Sir Walter Scott written about "the will to do, the soul to dare"? Just because you'd never done a thing didn't mean you shouldn't dare to do it, maybe she would just *start,* and something in her soul would show her how—she'd heard about people who had never in their lives played the piano, but one day they sat down on the piano bench and touched the keys, and the most beautiful music in the world poured forth.

She had the will to do it, but did she have the soul to dare and enter a contest to be judged at the town hall, with everybody she knew looking on, especially her customers from Happy Endings?

Then she remembered why she needed the five hundred dollars.

During lunch break at the bookstore, she went to The Local and bought everything the James Beard recipe called for.

~

As Lew Boyd read the story in the *Muse,* he got the shivers, thinking how he'd won that pickle-canning contest in 4-H. When he took the blue ribbon to school, Earlene Dickson had kissed him on the mouth and run . . .

And Granmaw Minnie . . . he could see her plain as day, lying on her deathbed and transferring ownership of her recipes to the grandchildren.

"I want Wilma to have the recipe for my chicken pie," his granmaw said, speaking through a tube in her throat.

"Little Sue, I want you to have my chocolate cake recipe . . ."

Overcome with gratitude, Little Sue burst into tears.

"Pearl, where is Pearl?"

"Over here, Big Mama."

"You get th' fried chicken recipe, and if you ever tell a soul th' secret ingredient . . ."

Pearl's eyes were the size of saucers in a doll's tea set. "Oh, no, Big Mama!"

". . . and I want Lew to have th' pickle recipe."

Everyone nodded their agreement. After all, he'd worked with her each summer as a boy, slicing cucumbers into a huge crock that, even when empty, smelled of pickles.

At this point, Lew remembered his granmaw half-sitting up in bed, and looking fierce as anything. The fact that she'd removed her dentures didn't help matters.

"Now listen to me," said Minnie. "These recipes have been in th' family since I was a young 'un. Don't *ever* give 'em out of th' family, or I'll come back and haint ever' one of you!"

"Yes, *ma'am!*" Lew gulped.

Minnie lay back on the pillow. "Now bring me a little touch of whisky and sugar," she said . . .

Lew walked around the gas pumps at his Exxon station, located just beyond the Mitford town monument. He slapped his leg with the rolled-up copy of the *Muse*, thinking hard.

He was barely able to wait till five when the rates went down.

"Little Sue?"

There was a pause at the other end of the line. "Is that you, Lew?"

"It's me, alright."

"You haven't called me in ten years," said Little Sue.

"Well," said Lew, not knowing what else to say. Then he remembered why he hadn't called. "I've been real busy with my gas station."

"Bull. What d'you want?"

"Well . . . I was just thinkin' about Granmaw Minnie."

"Like I said, Lew, what d'you want?"

He hadn't meant to blurt it out. "I want her chocolate cake recipe!"

"What in th' dickens d'you want it for?"

"I want to enter a contest, they don't take pickles!"

"Your brain is pickled, askin' me for that recipe."

"Little Sue, dadgummit, I'm *family*!!"

It was four o'clock at the nursing home on the hill above Mitford.

In Room Number One, Louella Baxter Marshall was tired of watching *All My Children*. She wanted to sing hymns or bake a pan of biscuits or cook a pot of greens, something constructive.

She didn't want to read the *Mitford Muse* that a nurse just delivered to her room.

She didn't want to put in her order for Pokey, either. That little speckled dog would jump in her lap and sleep so long, her bladder would get full and she couldn't get up without dumping him on the floor.

She missed Miss Sadie, who had gone to heaven over two years ago. Except for the short, sweet time she'd been married to Moses Marshall, she had been Miss Sadie's lifelong companion. And never once had Miss Sadie acted like she was boss and Louella was help. Fact is, Miss Sadie had given the money for this very building and everything in it, and had written in her will that the best room in the building was to be reserved for her "sister in the Lord, Louella B. Marshall."

Louella closed her eyes and rocked in her chair, humming.

Just being *around* Miss Sadie had been fun. They used to sing to beat the band, all the hymns they'd been raised with at Lord's Chapel, and then they might have a little game of dominoes or Chinese checkers or read to each other from the Bible. Louella had read to someone from the Bible only last night, someone so old and feeble, it hurt her terribly just to look at the frail figure in the wing chair.

She had taken Violet Larkin's hand in hers, and noted how much it felt like Miss Sadie's, so small and delicate, like a child's hand.

"The Lord is my shepherd," Louella read aloud, "I shall not want. He maketh me to lie down in green pastures, he leadeth me beside still waters, he *restoreth* my soul . . ."

Don't give her any of that modern stuff that leaves out the leadeth and restoreth and the thee and thou, no sir, the language of the old King James was beautiful to her ears, like music.

Speaking of music, that's how she'd read the rest of that psalm—she'd sung it. Something just came over her and she'd started singing the words.

"Surely goodness and mercy
Will *follow* me
All the *days* of my *life*
And I will dwell in the
House of the *Lord*
For*ev*———er-r-r-r!"

She'd really held on to that last note, and the word that contained all of eternity in it.

Miss Larkin had closed her eyes and repeated the last line in a warbly voice, her face beaming like an angel's. Then she looked at the chocolate-colored woman who lived down the hall and was so good to her.

Without meaning to, Violet Larkin told Louella Baxter Marshall her heart's desire—she wanted more than anything on earth to see her grandson again, but he lived so far away, somewhere in Canada, and it would cost nearly five hundred dollars to get him here.

Sitting alone in Room Number One at Hope House, Louella said aloud, "Miss Sadie, I got t' do this thing, an' you an' Jesus got t' help me."

On the high hill above Mitford, Louella Baxter Marshall rang for a nurse to come to Room Number One.

"I want t' go t' th' kitchen," said Louella, easing her heavy frame into the wheel-chair.

"The *kitchen*, Miss Louella?"

"That's right, honey."

"How's your knee today, Miss Louella? Is it hurtin' you bad?"

"Not too bad 'less I stand on it," said Louella. When they arrived at the double doors behind the Hope House dining room, the nurse helped Louella out of the chair. "You go on, now," she told the bewildered young woman, "and come back at ten o'clock."

The Hope House cook didn't know who was blowing through his kitchen door on a walking cane; he never saw the residents, he only got wind of their complaints. It was true he sometimes heard praise, as well—usually when he gave them lasagna, but only if it wasn't too spicy.

"I'm lookin' for th' boss," Louella said, in a mezzo voice that bounced off the sauce pans and made the large kitchen seem smaller.

"That's me," said the cook, who actually preferred to be called a chef. He had an odd compulsion to bow, though he had no idea why.

"I need to bake a pan of biscuits," said Louella, looking him in the eye.

"You need to . . . what?"

"Bake a pan of biscuits," she said as if speaking to the deaf. "I need flour, shortenin', buttermilk, an' the whole caboodle. You can set me up right over there, honey." She waved her cane at a surface he'd just floured down to work croissants for lunch.

"She's Room Number One," whispered his sous chef. "Miz Louella Baxter Marshall."

Room Number One! When he came to work here, he was told that Room Number One could have anything she wanted—at anytime, from anybody—and he wasn't to forget it.

"Yes *ma'am*," he said, stepping out of her way before she mowed him down.

Esther Bolick was not accustomed to having teenagers call her on the phone.

Her grandson used to call at Christmas and Easter, but stopped when he turned twelve and now communicated solely by letters written on his computer in a font called Spiderman.

"Miz Bolick? This is Dooley Barlowe."

Dooley Barlowe was the red-headed mountain boy Father Kavanagh had taken to raise a few years ago; he worked summers at The Local, bagging groceries, and had come a mighty long way, in Esther's opinion.

"Excuse me for calling, but I know . . ." She heard him gulp and swallow. ". . . I know you're the best cake baker in town."

Esther's face flushed.

"Cynthia says so, and my dad does, too."

"Mercy! Really?" She was touched.

"Plus a lot of people who're enterin' the contest talk about your cake when I'm baggin' their groceries."

Thieves, thought Esther.

"That's why I'm callin', because I'm workin' to save money for a car, and my dad says he'll match everything I make."

"My, my," she said, having forgotten entirely what it felt like to be a teenager.

"I also mow yards and clean out attics and basements, and . . ."

She heard him gulp again.

". . . and I've been thinking—would you, I mean, could you tell me how to bake that cake you're famous for? If I could enter that contest and win, that would really help a lot, I mean, if you could maybe give me a few tips on how to do it, I'd really appreciate it."

She heard him breathing as if he'd run a race. She liked Dooley and thought he was made of the right stuff. But more than that, she cared about Father Kavanagh—hadn't he pastored them for years, loving them like his own and never demanding anything back?

As for herself, she had no intention of entering that jackleg contest where half the town was using her recipe without permission.

"Let me think about it," she said, not wanting to think about it at all. On the other hand, here was an innocent boy trying to make a dollar and willing to work for it, unlike some people she knew.

She went in the den and told Gene about the odd request.

"I don't want to enter that bloomin' contest," she said.

"You wouldn't be enterin' it, Dooley would."

She patted her foot, frowning. Why couldn't people let her alone about that cake?

Gene grinned. "I think you should do it."

"You really think so, cross your heart?"

He crossed his heart. "Y'all could blow th' competition out of th' water."

She went back to the kitchen and walked around the cooking island three times before she dialed the number at The Local, which she had memorized years ago.

When Dooley came to the phone, she said, "If you ever breathe to a *soul* that I helped you . . ."

"No *ma'am! I won't.*"

"I wish you'd asked me a couple of days ago, that cake's better if it sets awhile before you eat it."

"Oh," Dooley said, sounding stricken.

"But no use to cry over spilled milk. What d'you want to do, two layers or three?"

"Umm," said Dooley, who didn't have a clue.

"I'd do three-layer for a contest. Showier."

"Great! Thank you, Miz Bolick. I appreciate it a whole lot. I'll do somethin' for you anytime you say, like clean out your basement or your attic, or I could do your yard . . ."

Esther walked around with the cordless, opening cabinets and looking in the refrigerator. "I'm a little low on ingredients. How soon can you get up here with six oranges, a pound of butter and a dozen eggs?"

Since his wife passed four years ago, Lew Boyd had used nothing in his kitchen but a toaster oven and a stove-top percolator. He did not believe in microwaves, in case anybody came to see him who had a pacemaker.

For this reason, he didn't have a clue what might be stored in his kitchen cabinets, and spent four hours on the eve of the contest trying to make sense of the clutter.

He called his sister, Little Sue, three times, and nearly had a stroke when he realized he forgot to grease the cake pans. He poured the batter back into the bowl and washed the pans and started over, speaking aloud to his departed Granma Minnie.

Why in the world he'd ever gotten into this mess was more than he could fathom. Little Sue had nearly laughed her head off about the whole thing and told him to get a life. He thought she said Get a wife, and replied that it was very hard to find one that didn't drink and run around.

He freely admitted he was lonesome, how much time could a man spend at his gas station, anyway? He had to eventually come home to an empty house.

He had developed a ritual for evenings. He walked in the back door, passed through the kitchen where he heated his supper, watched TV in the den, and ended up in the bedroom, all on the back side of the house. In truth, he hadn't seen his living room for months, it seemed as remote as Mesopotamia. And he had no idea what to do, if anything, about the dining room, which had become a year-round storage bin for Christmas ornaments, odd boxes, and a nonflammable tree.

Setting the oven to preheat at 325, he thought again about Earlene Dickson kissing him when he won the pickle contest years and years ago. That had been on his mind a lot lately.

He surveyed what he had done and felt pleased. He might be a pickle man, but he knew a creamy, velvety batter when he saw one.

He could hardly wait to get the brimming cake pans in the oven, so he could go sit in his recliner with the mixing spoon and batter bowl.

Louella felt the sharp, shooting pain in her knee as she rolled out the dough, but she had better things to think about than hurting.

She was thinking about healing, about sending the prize money to Canada so Miss Violet Larkin's grandson could buy a plane ticket and come to Hope House where he would kneel down and kiss his granmaw's hand. Louella didn't know where she got such an image, but she thought it was a good one, Miss Violet being the only granmaw the boy had.

Louella's head and heart seemed suddenly full of images, as if rolling out biscuit dough was returning something to her that was lost.

She closed her eyes and saw her husband-to-be walking into the kitchen of the Atlanta boarding house. She was fifteen years old, with her hair in corn rows, and the sense that something wonderful was about to happen.

Moses Marshall flashed a smile that nearly knocked her winding. She had never seen anybody who looked like this when she was growing up in Mitford, the only people of color they had in Mitford were old and white-headed.

"Who's th' one baked them good biscuits for supper?"

Louella could hardly speak. "What you want to know for?"

"Because th' one baked them good biscuits, that's th' one I'm goin' to marry."

Louella looked at old Miss Sally Lou, who had to stand on tiptoe to peer into a pot on the stove. She was so little and dried up, some said she was a hundred, but Louella knew she was only eighty-two and still the boss cook of three meals a day at the boarding house.

Louella pointed at old Miss Sally Lou, afraid to say the plain truth that she, Louella Baxter, had baked the biscuits herself, three pans full and not one left begging.

Moses Marshall looked his bright, happy look at Miss Sally Lou and walked over and picked her up and swung her around twice before he set her down. "Fine biscuits, ma'am. Will you jump th' broom with me?"

"Git out of my way 'fore I knock you in th' head," said Miss Sally Lou. "Marry that 'un yonder, she th' one do biscuits." The old woman threw back her head, looking imperious. "*I* does yeast rolls."

Hope Winchester didn't know if she believed in God. She was thinking this as she searched the James Beard bread book, making sure she had picked the right recipe.

She had thought all along that raisin bread would be perfect. Then, she had second thoughts and was convinced that salt-rising might cut through the clutter of entries and stand out more.

She sat at the table, feeling scared. She couldn't keep going back and forth, she had to decide right now and start baking.

She knew that if she believed in God, she would pray about which recipe, even if God wouldn't be interested in such petty, self-serving issues. The priest at Lord's Chapel, Father Kavanagh, had once said God wanted people to pray about everything, he told her one of the saints had said "Pray all the time," or maybe it was "Pray without ceasing."

That was alright for saints who had nothing else to do, who did not work in retail and do inventory and try to keep everyone happy, even grouchy, mean-spirited, tight-fisted people who thought they should get a discount just for living.

She pulled two straws from the broom behind the refrigerator, then shut her eyes and switched the straws around and held them in her hand. The short straw would be raisin, the long would be salt.

It was raisin.

She didn't understand why she burst into tears, as if a terrible weight had been lifted. Then she remembered, all at once and for the first time, that raisin was her mother's favorite bread.

She turned the oven on preheat, which is what the book said to do, feeling a tingle of excitement as if she'd set the stove dial while standing in a tub of water.

Whether she won or lost, she would take the bread to her mother at the hospital and show it to her through the oxygen tent, she only hoped they would let her have her bread back from the contest.

She set a jar of grape jelly on the open cookbook, to hold her place, and hurriedly pulled the ingredients from the cabinets and the refrigerator, because more than anything on earth, she wanted to start baking the bread right now, this minute, so that her mother who was dying a little every day, would be able to see it and perhaps even smell it, and find it wonderful.

Uncle Billy Watson was quiet as a mouse as he stirred about the kitchen. He had hunkered under the covers, sleeping fitfully until three A.M., then crept out of the bedroom and closed the door behind him.

He didn't know if he could do this, even with the Lord's help. What he was trying to do was re-create the sweet potato pie his mother had made in their little cabin in the valley.

Oh, they'd been a poor and ragged lot, the Watsons, but hadn't they had a fine time hunting in the woods and eating deer meat and wild turkey and even bear when they could get it?

He remembered grubbing in the sweet-smelling earth to pull those taters out, and rubbing them off on his britches and carrying them to the house by the peck and bushel.

He hadn't been able to read or write a word in those days, but he could draw. By joe, he could spot a squirrel on a log and before it could dash away, he had drawed it with his pencil, log and all.

That's when the sweet potato pies had started. Before, his mama had roasted the yams in the ashes, or sliced them up and fried them in bacon grease in a black skillet. But when he started drawing pictures of dogs and geese and partridges and all, she took to rewarding him with sweet potato pies. "Because you're special, William," she once said.

In all his seventy-eight years, or was it seventy-nine, he could not remember anything ever tasting so good. All good-tasting things had fallen short next to the faded memory of her pies.

Intoxicated by the smell of freshly-ground cinnamon and cloves, he had eagerly observed how much butter she used, and the careful way she sprinkled sugar into the orange-brown mash. But mostly, he'd watched her making the pie dough and rolling it out, her fingers working like magic to hand the soft, perfect circle off the dough board and into the old pie pans.

Through the closed door at the end of the hall came the sound of his wife snoring. He was glad his hearing hadn't gone; he could still hear a chigger in the leaves.

Everything was set out, now; he had everything he needed—everything but a recipe.

Uncle Billy closed his eyes and turned his heart back across the years to the sound of a fresh, crackling cook fire, and his mother's bare feet whispering across the wooden floor.

"Lord," he prayed in a low voice, "you're a mighty God and I'm a speck tryin' to do a foolish thing. Please help me."

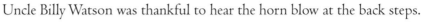

Uncle Billy Watson was thankful to hear the horn blow at the back steps.

It was Coot Hendrick in his old red truck, come to carry him to Town Hall for the judging.

"A man cain't go trottin' down th' street with a cane in one hand and a pie in th' other," said Coot.

Uncle Billy left his wife ranting and raving over the mess on the sink, the table, the counter top and the stove. "I'll clean it up soon as I git back!" he shouted above the din.

"I don't know why I done it," he said, as the truck eased onto Main Street. "Hit's th' hardest dadjing thing I ever tried t' do."

"Let me see it," said Coot, who had some expertise when it came to eating, if not baking, pies.

Uncle Billy pulled back the dish towel to reveal the pie, encased in Saran Wrap.

"That's a beauty, alright!" said Coot, who fervently hoped he'd get a piece for doing the driving.

Lew Boyd arrived early at Town Hall, and found the place already packed. People milled around like ants on a hill observing the cake, pie, loaf bread, and biscuit entries displayed on several long tables.

"How many in th' cake division?" Lew asked the Golden Band official as he filled out the entry form. As accustomed as he was to dealing with the public, he felt suddenly shy and realized he was blushing.

"Forty-seven in cake, thirty-three in pie, fourteen in loaf bread and twenty-six in biscuits!" recited the official, looking pleased with herself.

He claimed a chair toward the back and sat nervously through the slide show about making flour. As the award ceremonies began, he hammered down on biting his cuticles.

The sound system wasn't exactly borrowed from Radio City Music Hall, and during the awards part, Lew knew he misunderstood several things the judges said.

Like, when they announced the winner in the biscuit division, he could have sworn they said *Use yellow batter marshmallow.* He soon realized they said *Louella Baxter Marshall.*

Once again, he wondered why in the dickens he'd done all this, anyway. Sure, he could use the money, who couldn't, yet it seemed like the part he liked best was the baking, itself, and thinking about the good feeling he had when he won that pickle contest back in 4-H, and afterward, how Earlene Dickson had puckered up her lips and shut her eyes before she kissed him on the mouth and run off, laughing.

When the judges announced the winning cake, Lew was positive he heard wrong.

"What'd they say?" he asked Percy Mosely, who sat next to him.

"They said Dooley Barlowe."

"What about Dooley Barlowe?" asked Lew.

"Dooley won th' cake contest with a three-layer orange marmalade."

Lew felt like somebody had punched him in the stomach. He couldn't believe Granmaw Minnie's chocolate cake hadn't won; it had never occurred to him, even for a moment, that it wouldn't win. Everybody in his family, everybody in his hometown of Siler's Creek, and even the lieutenant governor who once judged it at the fair, knew her cake to be an unfailing winner.

Afraid he'd bust out crying, he got up and headed at a trot to the men's room.

Hope Winchester didn't want anyone to see how jittery she was, nor did she want anyone to think it really mattered whether she won or lost.

To further this intent, she brought a book with her and sat in the very back row of the town hall, reading Emily Eden.

"The library at St. Mary's was of a high, old-fashioned form, and within it was a small flight of steps which led to a light gallery built round . . ."

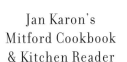

The announcement crackled over the microphone. "And now, the winning entry in the loaf bread division . . ."

"*. . . three sides of the room, giving thus an easy access to the . . .*"

". . . let's see, here's the card right here . . ."

"*. . . higher shelves of books. The room itself was full of odd, deep recesses . . .*"

". . . the very savory and delicious Beard's Raisin Bread, baked by Hope Winchester!"

Hope dropped the book on the floor and bent to pick it up, her face flaming.

"Where are you, Miss Winchester? Ah, there she is! Come right up, and we hope you have a big pocket to put all this money in!"

Hope's heart was pounding furiously as she mounted the steps to the podium. She felt an uncharacteristically large smile freeze on her face, and was concerned that it might never go away.

"Congratulations, Miss Winchester! Now, tell us, what are you going to do with your five hundred dollars?"

She hadn't expected to be asked anything at all, and was utterly stunned by the question. Without meaning to, she blurted into the microphone what she had desperately wanted to keep to herself.

"I'm going to buy my mother a wedding and engagement ring," she said. "She never had either one, really, because my father . . . because their money . . ."

She noticed that her voice was getting louder. "I mean, she had a band, but it got lost in the washing, and she never got another one because our money had to go for other things . . . and then my father was killed, and it took all she had to send me to college and buy my books and . . ."

She stopped and looked at the check handed to her and was suddenly, to her great humiliation and confusion, blinded by tears.

After filling out the form and entering his pie with thirty-two others at Town Hall, Uncle Billy realized he felt as tuckered as if he'd plowed a cornfield.

He had never seen the place so crowded, even for a town meeting. In fact, he didn't see an empty seat anywhere.

"Uncle Billy!" Winnie Ivey, who owned the Sweet Stuff Bakery, jumped up to give him her chair on the front row.

"As a professional, I can't enter th' dern contest!" she said. "So I sure don't need to sit down front! Good luck, and I hope you win."

He was mighty glad to take a load off his feet, and visit with everyone around him. And it was a treat to see Louella win the biscuit division; the whole crowd stood and cheered at the annoucement. When asked what secret she had for making such fine biscuits, Louella said, "Short'nin' is th' trick, honey, make 'em plenty short and don't hold back."

As far as the prize money was concerned, Uncle Billy figured there were lots of people who needed it more than he did. Even the oil in his tank, thanks to the good heart of the mayor, was taken care of.

Of course, winning wasn't the point, anyway, the point was to see if he could search back across the faded years and unlock the mysterious secret of his mother's pies. And in his heart, he knew he'd done it.

When he tasted the pie filling before sunrise this morning, he recognized that a wondrous thing had happened—something outside his own ken and ability, maybe a miracle.

Even the crust, which had cracked down the middle the first time, had come around to his way of thinking and slipped into the pan as perfect as you please. He had cut away the dough overhanging the pan and ate every bite of the trimmings, considering it breakfast.

"And now, ladies and gentlemen," said the Golden Band Flour spokesman, "we're going to do something we haven't done in any other of the fine towns we've visited . . .

"Our judges were so impressed by an entry called Granmaw Minnie's Chocolate Cake that we're prepared to award a very special consolation prize.

"Will Mister Lew Boyd please come forward?"

"Where is Lew?" Gene Bolick asked Percy Mosely.

"I don't know, I seen 'im go in yonder a little bit ago." Percy pointed toward the men's room.

"I'll check," said Gene.

Gene found Lew just coming out of the stall, his eyes as red as if he'd stayed up all night playing gin rummy.

"Congratulations!" said Gene, dragging him out the door and into the hall.

"On what?" asked Lew.

"The consolation prize!"

The microphone honked and squeaked. "Mr. Lew Boyd—is he *here?*"

The editor of the *Mitford Muse* pushed through the crowd with his Nikon and grabbed Lew's arm. "That's you, buddyroe. Get on up there so I can crank off a shot for Monday's front page."

As the crowd poured out of Town Hall, Gene Bolick hurried home and gave his wife a bear hug. He was proud of her and no two ways about it.

"Well, Doll, you've done it again! There were nine marmalades runnin' against you, but th' one *you* baked was . . ."

Esther ignored the joyous fibrillation of her heart. "I didn't bake it, Dooley baked it."

"It looked to me like you did most of the work."

"I didn't," said Esther. "I set it all out and told him what to do and he did it. He

earned his prize, and Hessie Mayhew called and said he gave me credit. Did you hear his speech?"

"He stood right up there and said, I baked my cake from the best cake recipe in the whole nation, compliments of Miz Esther Bolick!"

"Did he say nation? Hessie thought he said state."

"*Nation* is exactly what he said."

"Well," said Esther. A smile crept onto her face. "I declare!"

Louella Baxter Marshall asked the nurse to dial the number, and when it was busy, the nurse showed her how to push re-dial. Louella pushed re-dial two times before Miss Violet's grandson answered. He was so happy he was coming to see his granmaw that he shouted a happy shout right into the phone. "But I wouldn't wait 'til Thanksgivin'," Louella said, keeping her voice low.

Louella didn't know when she had moved so fast in a wheelchair.

She turned right into Miss Violet's room, where the crocheted ballerina slippers hung on the door. "Miss Vi'let?"

Miss Violet's paper-thin eyelids fluttered.

"Who you think is comin' t' see you nex' week?"

"I don't know. You, I guess."

"No, Miss Vi'let, this goin' t' be somebody special." Louella's large, strong hand stroked the small, frail hand.

"You're special," said Miss Violet, meaning it.

"Yes ma'm, but this be somebody han'some an' young."

"I don't know anybody handsome and young." Her chaplain at Hope House was handsome and young, but he was on vacation.

"Yes ma'm, you do," said Louella. "You try an' think, now."

Miss Violet thought hard. "Bobby Darin!" she exclaimed, lacking any earthly idea why he'd want to come all the way to Mitford from Hollywood.

"Mother?" Hope Winchester stood by the oxygen tent, the ring box in her pocket, holding the raisin bread aloft.

Her mother looked up and, for the first time in what seemed a long time, smiled at her daughter.

Hope became aware that she was saying something over and over in her mind, as the words of a song or a jingle sometimes repeat themselves and won't go away. She was saying, *Thank you, God.*

Uncle Billy asked Coot Hendrick to ride him down to the Preacher's office at the other end of Main Street.

"I'd be beholden to you for a piece of that pie," said Coot, when it appeared he wouldn't be offered any.

"I'll be bakin' another'n next day or two, I'll see to it you git a piece," said the old man.

At the church office, he put his cane over his arm and carried his pie to the door and walked in without knocking. Nobody ever knocked at the Preacher's office.

"Well, sir," he said to Father Tim, "I didn't win that fool contest up th' street." He put the pie, which was missing the judges' slice, on the rector's desk, then peeled back the tea towel to reveal his handiwork.

"Smells good!" said Father Tim, as the aroma of cinnamon and nutmeg floated out into the small room.

"I want t' give you and Miss Cynthia half of it. You'uns have been awful good to me an' Rose." Uncle Billy grinned broadly, displaying his gold tooth.

"Let's see," said Father Tim, scratching his head. "What will I carry half of it in?"

Uncle Billy pondered this. In the meantime, he thought it looked mighty tasty sitting there on the desk with the tea towel rolled back.

"Tell you what," said the old man, "let's you and me jis' set down right here and eat th' whole thing."

When Lew Boyd arrived at Golden Band Flour Company in Bishopville, just over the state line from Mitford, three people came out to the lobby to greet him, one being the vice-president of the whole shebang. A secretary aimed a point-and-shoot camera in his direction and took a picture to go in the company newsletter.

The consolation prize, which he had come to collect, was a plant tour, a night in Bishopville's finest and only hotel, a steak dinner with the marketing department, and a five-pound bag of Golden Band self-rising.

As soon as the plant tour was over, he asked what he'd wanted to ask since he hit the front door.

"Is there a phone I could use? It's a local call."

He sat in an office with his bag of flour, and carefully combed his hair. Then he looked up the number of the library where he heard she was working since her husband died.

He dialed the number with a ballpoint pen, his hand shaking.

"Earlene?" he said when she came to the phone. His throat was dry as a crumb.

"This is Lew Boyd. Remember me?"

Jan Karon's
Mitford Cookbook
& Kitchen Reader

221

Lew Boyd's Chocolate Cake

For the cake

	Unsalted butter for greasing the pans
1½ cups	cake flour, more for dusting the pans
1 cup	double strength hot coffee
4 ounces	unsweetened chocolate, chopped fine
2 cups	granulated sugar
½ teaspoon	salt
¾ teaspoon	baking soda
½ cup	vegetable oil
2 large	eggs, at room temperature, lightly beaten
½ cup	sour cream
1½ teaspoons	vanilla extract

For the frosting

1 cup	heavy cream
½ cup	unsalted butter, cut into pieces
⅓ cup	granulated sugar
¼ teaspoon	salt
1 pound	semisweet chocolate, chopped fine
¼ cup	double strength hot coffee
1 teaspoon	vanilla extract
	Chocolate shavings, for garnish

Preheat the oven to 325°F. Lightly butter two 9-inch round cake pans, line with parchment or wax paper, then butter and flour the paper, shaking out any excess. Set aside.

In a large bowl combine the hot coffee with the unsweetened chocolate and let it melt, stirring constantly. Sift the 2 cups sugar, flour, ½ teaspoon salt, and baking soda into a separate large bowl. Add the oil, eggs, sour cream, and 1½ teaspoons vanilla to the bowl with the melted chocolate, and whisk until well combined.

Stir the wet ingredients into the dry, in thirds, stirring well after each addition, until completely blended.

Divide the batter between the pans, rap each pan on the counter to expel any air pockets or bubbles, and place in the oven. Bake for 35 to 40 minutes, or until a toothpick inserted in the center comes out clean.

Place the cakes on racks to cool for 5 minutes, then invert them onto the racks to cool completely. Carefully peel off the waxed paper.

The frosting In a medium saucepan over medium heat, combine the heavy cream, butter, ⅓ cup sugar, and ¼ teaspoon salt. Slowly heat the mixture, stirring, until hot. Add the semisweet chocolate and stir until just melted. Remove the pan from the heat, pour the mixture into a large bowl, and stir in the coffee and 1 teaspoon vanilla. Let cool, stirring occasionally, for 1 hour, or until spreading consistency. Do not refrigerate or chill over ice water; harsh chilling could cause the frosting to separate and turn grainy.

To assemble the cake Arrange one cake layer on a serving platter, top side up, and frost the surface thickly. Top with the second layer, top side down, and frost the top and sides. Garnish with chocolate shavings. Let the cake sit for 3 hours or more before slicing. Store, covered, at room temperature, for up to 1 week.

Uncle Billy's
Sweet Potato Pie

½ cup	unsalted butter, more for greasing the pan
½ recipe	*Pastry for a Double Crust Pie* (see page 4) (Halve the recipe, or make the whole recipe and freeze half)
1½ cups	cooked mashed sweet potatoes
1¼ cups	granulated sugar
1 tablespoon	White Lily all-purpose flour
1 teaspoon	vanilla extract
¼ teaspoon	salt
1 teaspoon	ground cinnamon
¼ teaspoon	ground nutmeg
⅛ teaspoon	ground cloves
3 large	eggs, at room temperature
1 (5.33-ounce) can	evaporated milk

For the topping

2 tablespoons	unsalted butter
¼ cup	brown sugar
½ cup	chopped pecans
¼ teaspoon	salt
	Sweetened whipped cream, for serving

Lightly butter a 9-inch pie pan. Roll out the pastry dough and fit it into the pie pan. Refrigerate until ready to bake.

In the bowl of an electric mixer combine the sweet potatoes and ½ cup butter. Add the granulated sugar, flour, vanilla, ¼ teaspoon salt, the cinnamon, nutmeg, and cloves and mix well. Add the eggs, one at a time, mixing well after each addition. Add the evaporated milk and mix well.

Preheat the oven to 425°F. Remove the pie crust from the refrigerator and pour the sweet potato filling into the crust.

Bake the pie for 20 minutes, then reduce the heat to 325°F and continue baking for another 30 to 40 minutes, or until a knife inserted in the middle comes out clean.

The topping While the pie is baking, place 2 tablespoons butter and the brown sugar in a small skillet over low heat. Stir until the butter has melted, the brown sugar has dissolved, and the mixture is bubbling. Add the pecans and ¼ teaspoon salt.

Continue to cook, stirring, for 2 minutes. Remove from the heat and pour the mixture onto a sheet of aluminum foil. Let cool completely. Crumble the topping into small pieces and sprinkle over the pie. Let the pie cool completely before serving.

Serve pie slices topped with a dollop of whipped cream.

Louella's Buttermilk Biscuits

½ cup	lard, chilled, more for greasing the pan
4 cups	White Lily all-purpose flour, more for rolling out the dough
2 tablespoons	*Homemade Baking Powder*
1½ teaspoons	salt
1½ cups	buttermilk, chilled
2 tablespoons	unsalted butter, melted and cooled

Preheat the oven to 500°F. Lightly grease a baking sheet with lard and set aside. Sift the flour, baking powder, and salt into a large bowl. Cut in the lard with a pastry blender until it resembles coarse meal. Stir in the buttermilk and form into a ball. Gently knead on a lightly floured surface until a dough is formed. Pat or roll out the dough on a lightly floured surface into a ½-inch-thick round. Cut out biscuits with a 2½- or 3-inch round cookie cutter and arrange on the baking sheet. Gather any remaining scraps, pat into a round and continue to cut out biscuits.

Bake for 8 minutes, then brush the tops with the melted butter, and bake another 2 to 3 minutes, or until golden brown on top.

HOMEMADE BAKING POWDER

¼ cup	cream of tartar
2 tablespoons	baking soda
1 tablespoons	cornstarch

Sift all of the ingredients together, three times, into a small bowl. Transfer to a clean, tightly sealed jar. The baking powder can be stored, away from sunlight, for up to six weeks. Makes ½ cup.

Out to Canaan

Hardly anyone ever cooked for diabetes, thought the rector as they trooped out to eat cake in the shade of the pin oak. Apparently it was a disease so innocuous, so bland, and so boring to anyone other than its unwilling victims that it was blithely dismissed by the cooks of the land.

He eyed the chocolate mocha cake that Marge was slicing at the table under the tree. Wasn't that her well-known raspberry filling? From here, it certainly looked like it. . . .

Ah, well. The whole awful business of saying no, which he roundly despised, was left to him. Maybe just a thin slice, however . . . something you could see through. . . .

"He can't have any," said Cynthia.

"I can't believe I forgot!" said Marge, looking stricken. "I'm sorry, Tim! Of course, we have homemade gingersnaps, I know you like those. Rebecca Jane, please fetch the gingersnaps for Father Tim, they're on the bottom shelf."

The four-year-old toddled off, happy with her mission.

Chocolate mocha cake with raspberry filling versus gingersnaps from the bottom shelf. . . .

Clearly, the much-discussed and controversial affliction from which St. Paul had prayed thrice to be delivered had been diabetes.

—*Out to Canaan*, Chapter Four

Marge's Chocolate Raspberry Cake

For the cake

½ cup	unsalted butter, at room temperature, more for greasing the pans
2 ⅔ cups	cake flour
1½ teaspoons	baking soda
½ teaspoon	salt
⅔ cup	cocoa powder
1 teaspoon	instant espresso powder
⅔ cup	boiling water
1 cup	buttermilk
2 teaspoons	vanilla extract
2½ cups	granulated sugar
½ cup	vegetable oil
4 extra-large	eggs, at room temperature
2 extra-large	egg yolks, at room temperature

For the frosting

1 pound	semisweet chocolate, chopped
1⅓ cups	sour cream
6 tablespoons	seedless raspberry jam
¼ cup	light corn syrup
2 tablespoons	framboise eau de vie (clear raspberry brandy)
2 teaspoons	vanilla extract
3 tablespoons	unsalted butter, at room temperature

For the topping

6 tablespoons	seedless raspberry jam
6	chocolate wafer cookies, finely crushed
2 (6-ounce) baskets	fresh raspberries

The cake Preheat the oven to 350°F. Lightly butter three 9-inch cake pans, line the bottom of the pans with parchment, then grease the paper. Set aside.

Sift the flour, baking soda, and salt into a large bowl. Combine the cocoa powder and espresso powder in a medium bowl. Whisk the boiling water, then the buttermilk and 2 teaspoons vanilla, into the cocoa mixture. In the bowl of an electric mixer, beat the sugar, ½ cup butter, and the oil on medium speed until fluffy, 8 to 10 minutes. Add the eggs and egg yolks, one at a time, beating for 2 minutes after each addition. Fold in half the flour mixture with a rubber spatula. Scrape down the sides and add half of the buttermilk mixture. Fold in the remaining flour mixture, scrape down the sides, and add the remaining buttermilk mixture. Divide the batter among the pans.

Bake 25 to 30 minutes, or until a toothpick inserted into the center comes out clean. Let the cakes cool in the pans on cooling racks for 10 minutes, then run a small knife around the sides of the pans to loosen the cakes. Turn the cakes out onto the racks, peel off the paper, and cool completely before icing.

The frosting Place the chocolate in a microwave-safe bowl and microwave at medium power for 1½ minutes. Open the microwave door and stir the chocolate. Close the door and microwave again at medium power for another 1½ minutes. Stir the chocolate, and if it is not yet melted and smooth, microwave again at medium power for another minute. Pour the chocolate into a large bowl and let it cool to room temperature. Add the sour cream, 6 tablespoons jam, the corn syrup, eau de vie, and 2 teaspoons vanilla to the chocolate. Beat on medium speed with an electric mixer until the mixture is smooth, fluffy, and light in color, about 3 minutes. Beat in the butter, 1 tablespoon at a time, until well combined.

The frosting may be prepared up to 2 hours ahead. Let it stand at room temperature until ready to use.

To assemble the cake Place one cake layer on a platter. Spread 2 tablespoons of the raspberry jam over the cake. Spread ½ cup of the frosting over jam. Repeat with a second cake layer, spreading 2 tablespoons jam over it, followed by ½ cup of frosting. Top with the last cake layer. Spread the remaining 2 tablespoons of the jam on top, followed by the remaining frosting over the top and sides of the cake. Generously sprinkle the crushed wafers on top of the cake. Arrange the raspberries in concentric circles on top of the cookie crumbs.

This cake can be prepared one day in advance. Cover with a cake dome and refrigerate; let the cake stand at room temperature 1 hour before serving.

Avis Packard's booth was swamped with buyers, eager to tote home sacks of preserves, honey, pies, cakes, and bread from the valley kitchens, not to mention strawberries from California, corn from Georgia, and syrup from Vermont.

Avis stepped out of the booth for a break, while Tommy and Dooley bagged and made change. "I've about bit off more'n I can chew," said Avis, lighting up a Salem. "I've still got a load of new potatoes comin' from Georgia, and lookin' for a crate of asparagus from Florida. Thing is, I don't hardly see how a truck can get down th' street."

"I didn't know you smoked," said the rector, checking his watch.

Avis inhaled deeply. "I don't. I quit two or three years ago. I bummed this offa somebody."

The imported strawberries were selling at a pace, and Avis stepped to the booth and brought back a handful.

"Try one," he said, as proudly as if they'd come from his own patch. "You know how some taste more like straw than berry? Well, sir, these are the finest you'll ever put in your mouth. Juicy, sweet, full of sunshine. What you'd want to do is eat 'em right off th' stem, or slice 'em, marinate in a little sugar and brandy—you don't want to use

So do not worry, saying, "What shall we eat?"
or "What shall we drink?" or "What shall we wear?"
For the pagans run after all these things,
and your heavenly father knows that you need them.
But seek first his kingdom and his righteousness,
and all these things will be given to you.

—Matthew 6:31-33

th' cheap stuff—and serve with cream from the valley, whipped with a hint of fresh ginger."

Avis Packard was a regular poet laureate of grocery fare.

"Is that legal?" asked the rector.

The Strawberry: "Doubtless God could have made a better berry, doubtless God never did."

—Dr. William Butler

He watched as Dooley passed a bag over the table to a customer. "Hope you like those strawberries!"

He was thrilled to see Dooley Barlowe excited about his work. His freckles, which he and Cynthia had earlier reported missing, seemed to be back with a vengeance.

Avis laughed. "Ain't he a deal?"

—*Out to Canaan*, Chapter Eight

Avis's Strawberries with Brandy

3 (16-ounce) containers	strawberries, hulled
1 cup	brandy
¼ cup	granulated sugar
Pinch	salt
1	cinnamon stick
1 tablespoon	grated orange zest (see page 52)
¼ cup	freshly squeezed orange juice

Slice the strawberries and place them in a large bowl. In a small saucepan over medium heat combine the brandy, sugar, and a pinch of salt and simmer for 10 to 15 minutes, or until the liquid is reduced to ¼ cup. Remove from the heat and add the cinnamon stick, orange zest, and orange juice. Let the mixture sit for 5 minutes. Remove the cinnamon stick and pour the liquid over the strawberries. Cover the bowl with plastic wrap and refrigerate for up to 4 hours. Serve with *Fresh Whipped Cream with Ginger* and warm *Avis's Shortbread Cookies* (opposite).

AVIS'S FRESH WHIPPED CREAM WITH GINGER

2 cups	heavy cream, chilled
¼ cup	sour cream
5 tablespoons	confectioners' sugar
½ teaspoon	ground ginger
¼ cup	finely chopped candied ginger (in your supermarket's spice section)

Chill a mixing bowl and the beaters for 30 minutes. Whip the cream in the chilled bowl on medium speed until it holds stiff peaks. Add the sour cream, confectioners' sugar, and ground ginger and beat the mixture until it holds stiff peaks again. Refrigerate until ready to serve. Spoon the whipped cream over *Strawberries with Brandy* and garnish with the candied ginger. Makes 3 cups.

Avis's Shortbread Cookies

5½ cups	White Lily all-purpose flour
1 teaspoon	baking soda
1 teaspoon	salt
2 cups	unsalted butter, at room temperature
2 cups	granulated sugar
2 large	eggs, at room temperature
2 teaspoons	vanilla extract
	Nonstick cooking spray for the pan
	Confectioners' sugar, for sprinkling over the cookies

Sift the flour, baking soda, and salt into a large bowl and set aside. In the bowl of an electric mixer, cream the butter and granulated sugar on medium speed for 8 minutes, until light and fluffy. Add the eggs, one at a time, and continue beating. Add the vanilla, then add the flour mixture and beat until the mixture just holds together. Chill the dough for at least 1 hour before baking.

Preheat the oven to 325°F. Coat a cookie sheet with nonstick cooking spray. Use an ice cream scooper to scoop the dough out onto the pan. Bake for 12 to 15 minutes, or until the edges begin to brown. Remove the shortbreads from the pan, place on a plate, and sprinkle confectioners' sugar over the warm cookies.

Jan Karon's
Mitford Cookbook
& Kitchen Reader

Softball?" said Percy. "Are you kiddin' me?"

"I am not kidding you. August tenth, be there or be square."

"Me'n Velma will do hotdogs, but I ain't runnin' around to any bases, I got enough bases to cover in th' food business."

"Fine. You're in. Expect twenty-five from Hope House, twenty or so players . . . and who knows how many in the bleachers?"

Percy scribbled on the back of an order pad. "That's a hundred and fifty beef dogs, max, plus all th' trimmin's, includin' Velma's chili—"

"Wrong!" said Velma. "I'm not standin' over a hot stove stirrin' chili another day of my life! I've decided to go with canned from here out."

"Canned chili?" Percy was unbelieving.

"And how long has it been since you peeled spuds for french fries? Years, that's how long. They come in here frozen as a rock, like they do everywhere else that people don't want to kill theirselves workin'."

"Yeah, but frozen fries is one thing, canned chili is another."

"To you, maybe."

Velma stalked away. Percy sighed deeply.

The rector didn't say anything, but he knew darn well their conversation wasn't about chili.

It was about a cruise.

—*Out to Canaan*, Chapter Eleven

On the morning of the game at Baxter Field, Velma Mosely had a change of heart and started chopping onions.

This, she told herself, would absolutely, positively be her last pot of homemade chili.

—*Out to Canaan*, Chapter Fourteen

Velma's Chili

2 tablespoons	vegetable oil	1 tablespoon	granulated sugar
2 pounds	chopped ground round	½ teaspoon	ground cloves
2 cloves	garlic, minced	1 teaspoon	salt
1½ cups	chopped onions	½ teaspoon	freshly ground black pepper
1 cup	chopped green peppers	1 cup	red wine
1 cup	chopped celery		Grated cheddar cheese,
2 (16-ounce) cans	kidney beans, drained		for serving
2 (14½-ounce) cans	diced tomatoes in juice		Sour cream, for serving
1 (15-ounce) can	tomato sauce		Chopped green onion,
1	bay leaf		for garnish
3 tablespoons	chili powder		

Heat the oil in a large saucepan over medium heat. Add the ground round and sauté until browned, about 10 minutes. Add the garlic, onions, peppers, and celery and cook until the vegetables are soft, 8 to 10 minutes. Add the beans, tomatoes (and their juices), tomato sauce, bay leaf, chili powder, sugar, cloves, salt, and pepper, and stir well. Cover and simmer over low heat for 1½ hours. Add the red wine and cook another 30 minutes. Adjust the seasonings before serving.

Serve bowls of chili topped with grated cheese, a dollop of sour cream, and chopped green onions.

"Never trust a man who won't eat an onion."

—Jan Karon

❖ *Velma suggests that you double the recipe and freeze half for another meal. She also likes to cook her chili in a crockpot for several hours.*

❖ *The chili is also good served over rice.*

If you were to be shot at sunrise," I say to my dinner companions in an Atlanta restaurant, "what would you have for your last meal?"

"Hmmm," says then-longtime *Victoria* magazine editor Claire Whitcomb. "Good bread and some really great cheese, because I wouldn't have to worry about the cholesterol!"

Edna Lewis, the legendary mistress of Southern cooking, who has taught her art to so many Southern chefs, reflects. "Country ham," she says in her soft, elegant, old-Virginia accent, "cut up in little pieces, and simmered in red-eye gravy with cream!"

We sit bemused for a time, dreaming over such a dish, then all heads turn to Scott Peacock, an apprentice and loving friend to Miss Lewis, and the chef who created the *official* Orange Marmalade Cake recipe.

Scott doesn't hesitate. "A package of Fig Newtons!" he exclaims at once.

Astonished by this ingenuous answer, we launch into a discussion of Fig Newtons and the customary condition of the commercial variety: invariably too dry or too moist. We all agree, nonetheless, that we love Fig Newtons, as Scott did as a young child when he ate Fig Newtons with his father.

My turn. "A very crisp French champagne, with fresh lobster and drawn butter!"

We all agree we shall die happy.

Note that no one mentioned veggie burgers, tofu, or sprouts. When we're to be shot at sunrise, what we're looking for is something that uplifts the heart and enlivens the spirit, *ne c'est pas?*

Indeed their intriguing answers caused me to approach others, and here is what they said:

Jerry Burns, editor of *The Blowing Rocket,* one of the most charming small town newspapers out there: "A sandwich made with baloney (fresh-cut from a loaf) and tomato (mountain-grown, of course), with salt and plenty of pepper, literally buried in three inches of Duke's mayonnaise. Washed down with raspberry tea, and followed with my wife, Janice's, peanut-butter pinwheels."

Carolyn Carlson, my Viking Penguin editor and friend, who, early on, believed in the Mitford books: "To start, I'll order the comfort food of my Norwegian heritage—meatballs, mashed potatoes, and lingonberries, followed by the perfect Italian meal of arugula salad with shaved Parmesan, risotto with asparagus, and panna cotta with chocolate sauce."

My mother, Wanda Setzer: "I wouldn't waste my time eating, honey, I'd be trying to find a lawyer to acquit me!"

Barbara Bush, our witty and beloved former first lady: "I would have five desserts, maybe six! Otherwise, I'd have a Big Mac!"

Sam Vaughan, loveliest of gentlemen and Random House editor at large (his authors have included Wallace Stegner, Dwight D. Eisenhower, Dave Barry, Hortense Calisher, Arthur Hailey, and Stephen King), says he'll have "my wife Jo's capellini (al dente) with tomato and basil—it's to die for, and so is she."

Brenda Furman, my sister, and mother of three of my favorite people: "A cup of oyster stew, made with real cream and pure, unsalted butter; a salad of arugula, green onions, and fresh tomatoes from the garden, dressed with balsamic vinegar, olive oil, fresh garlic, and a hint of orange; a very creamy Chardonnay; fried oysters encrusted in a tempura batter, whipped potatoes, and a hot, crusty French roll that, when broken, sends crumbs flying through the air. Dessert will be a flan."

(What I notice here is that people who scarcely ever eat a *bite* want a gargantuan meal . . . but then, we *are* talking the last hurrah.)

Dr. Charles (Bunky) Davant, on whom I've often called for the diagnoses of Mitford ills and ailments: "How about champagne and lobster with Jan Karon? If this won't work, give me a fried chicken and barbecue combo plate from Bullocks in Durham, and a bottle of Zinfandel."

Nancy Lou Beard, who scares up many of the Uncle Billy jokes: "My last request would be for anything that my husband would cook for me—I *love* his cooking!"

John McDonough, possessor of the marvelous voice that enlivens many of the Mitford audiobooks: "First, I'd request enough food so that my executioners could enjoy a hearty post-mortem feast, themselves. For openers, cocktails and a tray of deviled eggs. Then, spicy meatloaf with fluffy mashed potatoes, fresh peas, pearl onions, and real lemon pie (the kind that makes you kick off your shoes), followed by a fitful sleep."

Liz Darhansoff, my literary agent, and a grand and enthusiastic hostess: "A lovely slice of foie gras, followed by a perfectly roasted organic chicken with French beans, a gorgeous salad from my own garden, and an excellent red burgundy. For dessert, a Maine wild blueberry pie with vanilla ice cream."

Susan Petersen Kennedy, President, Penguin Group USA: "Meatloaf, stewed tomatoes, mashed potatoes . . . and apple pie with vanilla ice cream. Or how about this? Heirloom tomatoes with basil and mozzarella, mushrooms, risotto, chocolate cake, and a fine red wine."

Dr. Daniel P. Jordan, President of the Thomas Jefferson Foundation, acclaimed scholar, lovely friend, and, like Father Tim, a Mississippian: "A cheeseburger from Paradise, which, as Jimmy Buffett fans know well, is a ticket straight to eternal happiness."

Theodore Roosevelt IV, great-grandson of President Teddy Roosevelt: "Wild duck, very rare, wild rice, and a good, red burgundy."

Mark, Lord Mitford, baron of the ancient village of Mitford, England: "Being British, I would . . . choose a traditional Sunday roast beef dinner, with Yorkshire pudding, roast potatoes, carrots, and really thick gravy, accompanied by a good, old Bordeaux red wine, followed by lemon meringue pie, and all washed down with a glass of vintage port."

(Really thick gravy! A man after my own heart.)

Albert Ernest, lumber man, banker, sportsman, and poet, would enjoy a fried seafood platter with a good Chablis, followed by pecan pie and a cigar of distinction.

Donna Ernest, gifted artist, eager gardener, and Albert's beautiful consort of a half-century, would content herself with "a wonderful homemade vegetable soup, crusty bread, and fresh coconut cake with peppermint ice cream." To die for!

And here's what James Beard said he'd request if in this sticky situation: "Bacon and eggs."

To conclude, I must tell you that if some poor soul troops down the hall to my barren cell and announces they're fresh out of lobster and champagne, I'll say, "So bring me what Barbara Bush is having."

—Jan Karon

When he came in from the garage, Cynthia met him in the hallway.

"It's Esther!" she said. "She had an accident, and they say it looks bad. They want you to come to the hospital at once!"

Esther! He raced to the bathroom, splashed water on his face, took his jacket off the hook in the kitchen, and once again backed the Buick out of the garage, tires screeching.

There were many ways to lose an election. He prayed to God this wasn't one of them.

"What happened?" he asked Nurse Kennedy in the hospital corridor.

"She fell off a ladder, broke her left wrist, broke the right elbow, and . . ." Nurse Kennedy shook her head.

"And what?"

"Fractured her jaw. Dr. Harper is wiring her mouth shut as we speak."

"Good Lord!"

"But she'll be fine."

THE SHOTS

"Gene's not been feelin' too good," said Esther.

"What is it?" asked Father Tim.

"Don't know exactly," Gene said, as Miss Rose strode up, "but I talked to Hoppy and went and got th' shots."

"Got the trots?" shouted Miss Rose.

Gene flushed. "No, ma'am. The shots."

"Bill had the trots last week," she said, frowning. "It could be something going around." Their hostess, who was monitoring everyone's plate to see whether her pudding had gotten its rightful reception, moved on to the next circle of guests.

—Party talk

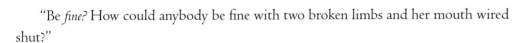

"Be *fine?* How could anybody be fine with two broken limbs and her mouth wired shut?"

"It happens, Father." Nurse Kennedy sighed and continued down the hall.

He'd just finished praying with Gene for Esther to be knit back together as good as new when Hessie Mayhew rushed into the waiting room. He looked at his watch. Eleven o'clock. Hardly anyone in this town stayed up 'til eleven o'clock.

"How is she?" asked Hessie.

"Doped up," said Gene.

"I've got to see her," insisted the Bane co-chair. Given her wide eyes and frazzled hair, Hessie looked as if she'd been plugged into an electrical outlet.

"You can't see 'er," said Gene. "Just me an' th' Father can go in."

"Do you realize that at seven in the morning, the Food Committee's gettin' together at my house to bake twelve two-layer orange marmalades, and we don't even have th' *recipe?*"

Gene slapped his forehead. "Oh, Lord help!"

"I'm sure it's written down somewhere," suggested the rector.

"Nope, it's not," said Gene.

"That's right. It's not." Hessie pursed her lips. "If I've told her once, I've told her a thousand times to write her recipes down, *especially* the orange marmalade, for heaven's sake."

"It's in her head," said Gene, defending his wife.

"Well," announced the co-chair, looking determined, "we'll have to find a way to get it out!"

When he walked into Esther's hospital room on Thursday morning, her bed was surrounded by Bane volunteers. One of them held a notepad at the ready, and he felt a definite tension in the air.

They didn't even look up as he came in.

Hessie leaned over Esther, speaking as if the patient's hearing had been severely impaired by the fall.

"Esther!" she shouted. "You've got to cooperate! The doctor said he'd give us twenty minutes and not a second more!"

"Ummaummhhhh," said Esther, desperately trying to speak through clamped jaws.

"Why couldn't she write something?" asked Vanita Bentley. "I see two fingers sticking out of her cast."

"Uhnuhhh," said Esther.

"You can't write with two fingers. Have you ever tried writing with two fingers?"

"Oh, Lord," said Vanita. "Then *you* think of something! We've got to hurry!"

"We need an alphabet board!" Hessie declared.

"Who has time to go lookin' for an alphabet board? Where would we find one, anyway?"

"Make one!" instructed the co-chair. "Write down the alphabet on your notepad and let her point 'til she spells it out."

"Ummuhuhnuh," said Esther.

"She can't move her arm to point!"

"So? We can move the notepad!"

Esther raised the forefinger of her right hand.

"One finger. *One!* Right, Esther? If it's yes, blink once, if it's no, blink twice."

"She blinked once, so that means yes. *One!* One what, Esther? Cup? Teaspoon? Tablespoon? Vanita, are you writin' this down?"

"Two blinks," said Marge Crowder. "So, it's not a cup and it's not a teaspoon."

"Butter!" said somebody. "Is it one stick of butter?"

"She blinked twice, that's no. Try again. One *tablespoon?* Oh, thank God! Vanita, one tablespoon."

"Right. But one tablespoon of *what?* Salt?"

"Oh, please, you wouldn't use a tablespoon of *salt* in a *cake!*"

"Excuse me for living," said Vanita.

"Maybe orange zest? Oh, look! *One blink!* One tablespoon of zest!"

"*Hallelujah!*" they chorused.

Esther stuck out her forefinger once, then again . . .

"One, two, three, four, . . ." someone counted.

"Four what?" asked Vanita. "Cups? No. Teaspoons? No. *Tablespoons?*"

"Three blinks, oh, Lord help us, what does *that* mean?"

"I'm glad I took my heart pill this morning," said Hessie. "Is it tablespoons of butter? I just have a feelin' it's butter. Look! Two blinks! It's butter!"

"OK, in cakes, you'd have to have baking powder. How much baking powder, Esther?"

Esther blinked and held up one finger.

"One teaspoon?"

"Uhnuhhh," said Esther, looking desperate.

"One *tablespoon?*" asked Vanita.

"You wouldn't use a *tablespoon* of baking powder in a cake!" sniffed Marge Crowder.

"Look," said Vanita, "I'm helpin' y'all just to be nice. My husband personally thinks I am a great cook, but I don't do cakes, OK, so if you'd like somebody else to take these notes, just step right up and help yourself, thank you!"

"You're doin' great, honey, keep goin'," said Hessie.

"This is a killer," said Vanita, fanning herself with the notebook. "Don't you think we could sell two-layer triple chocolates just as easy?"

"Ummunnuhhh," said Esther, her eyes burning with disapproval.

Hessie snorted. "This could take 'til kingdom come. How much time have we got left?"

> "*. . . Please tell Mrs. Bolick that I have dreamed about her marmalade cake on several occasions . . .*"
>
> —George Gaynor

Jan Karon's
Mitford Cookbook
& Kitchen Reader

"Ten minutes, maybe eleven, and we still have frostin' and fillin' to go!"

"*Eleven minutes?* Are you kidding me? We'll never finish this in eleven minutes."

"I think she told me she uses buttermilk in this recipe," said Marge Crowder. "Esther," she shouted, "how much buttermilk?"

Esther wagged her forefinger.

"One cup, right? Great! Now we're cookin'!"

"OK," commanded the co-chair, "what have we got so far?"

Vanita, being excessively near-sighted, held the notepad up for close inspection. "Three tablespoons of butter, one tablespoon of baking powder, and one cup of buttermilk."

"I've got to sit down," said the head of the Food Committee, pressing her temples.

"It looks like Esther's droppin' off to sleep, oh, Lord, Esther, honey, don't go to sleep, you can sleep tonight!"

"Could somebody ask th' nurse for a stress tab?" wondered Vanita. "Do you think they'd mind, I've written checks to th' hospital fund for nine years, goin' on ten!"

"By the way," asked Marge Crowder, "is this recipe for one layer or two?"

He decided to step into the hall for a breath of fresh air.

—*Out to Canaan*, Chapter Eighteen

THE ORANGE MARMALADE CAKE: FICTION TO FACT

When I began writing the Mitford books, it seemed clear that someone in Mitford should be a great cake baker. That's just the way things are in small towns.

As I worked through *At Home in Mitford*, it turned out that Esther Bolick was this special baker. But wouldn't any cake baker worth her salt have a specialty? Of course! And what would it be? Something chocolate, I supposed.

While this notion would pump the adrenaline of nearly anyone on the planet, chocolate has never been my favorite thing, peculiar me! Though I'd never heard of such a creation, I knew that what I would love is a cake made with orange marmalade. Thus, this fictitious cake was born, and became Esther's claim to fame.

As I wrote further into the series, readers everywhere wanted the recipe. They'd come up after I'd finish speaking and instead of asking where I get my characters or what is the gospel side, they begged for the orange marmalade cake recipe.

"But there is no recipe," I'd say. "That cake is fiction!"

Protest as I might, the cards and letters rolled in.

And so it was until 1997, when *Victoria* magazine invited me to become their writer-in-residence. During my allotted year, I wrote a Mitford story for their pages that referenced our now-legendary cake, and the ever-wise *Victoria* editor, Claire Whitcomb, decided we should have a recipe, for Pete's sake.

The recipe was created by Scott Peacock, famous chef and a devoted friend to the legendary Ms. Edna Lewis, who has written more wonderful cookbooks than Carter has liver pills.

In truth, Scott and Ms. Lewis got together in their Atlanta kitchen where, as Uncle Billy would say, they noodled their noggins, and bingo! the recipe was born.

Let me tell you, Gentle Reader, that this cake means business. If you do exactly as the recipe directs, you will end up with a cake that will make *you* famous, and no two ways about it.

So, if you'd like to taste the cake that Father Tim and Cynthia and Dooley and Uncle Billy and all the rest have enjoyed over and over again, all you have to do is make a shopping list, ask the good Lord to help you, and . . .

Start your oven!

As you may recall, Esther Bolick sent an OMC down to Whitecap for the wedding feast of Pauline Barlowe and Buck Leeper. When the islanders tasted it, they had to have the recipe, of course. On another occasion, this recipe (which was long held in absolute secrecy by Esther) slipped out to somebody who "bootlegged" it all over Mitford.

As you can imagine, several people have added their own ideas, which makes Esther furious. Someone, she heard, even adds Cointreau! The whole thing is disgusting and deceitful, of course, but that's the way it is with fame, which always, always has its dark side. —JAN KARON

Esther's Orange Marmalade Cake

For the cake

1 cup	unsalted butter, softened, more for greasing the pans
3¼ cups	cake flour, more for dusting the pans
1 tablespoon	baking powder
1 teaspoon	salt
2⅔ cups	granulated sugar
5 large	eggs, at room temperature
4 large	egg yolks, at room temperature
⅔ cup	vegetable oil
1 tablespoon	grated orange zest (see page 52)
2 teaspoons	vanilla extract
1 cup	buttermilk, at room temperature

For the orange syrup

1 cup	freshly squeezed orange juice
¼ cup	granulated sugar

For the filling

1 (12-ounce) jar	orange marmalade

For the frosting

1 cup	heavy cream, chilled
4 tablespoons	granulated sugar
1 cup	sour cream, chilled

The cake Preheat the oven to 350°F. Lightly butter three 9-inch round cake pans, line them with parchment paper, then lightly butter and flour the paper, shaking out any excess.

Sift the flour, baking powder, and salt into a large bowl. Sift a second time into another bowl. In the bowl of an electric mixer, beat the butter on medium speed until light in color, about 4 minutes. Add the 2⅔ cups sugar in a steady stream with the mixer running. Beat until light and fluffy, about 4 minutes. Add the eggs and yolks, one at a time, beating well after each addition. Be sure to stop at least once to scrape down the batter from the sides of the bowl. After all of the eggs have been added, continue to beat on medium speed for 2 more minutes. With the mixer on low speed, add the oil and beat for 1 minute. In a small bowl combine the orange zest, vanilla, and buttermilk. Using a rubber spatula, fold in half of the dry ingredients. Scrape down the sides of the bowl and add half of the buttermilk mixture. Fold in the remaining dry ingredients, scrape down the sides, and add the remaining buttermilk.

Pour the batter among the prepared pans, smooth the surface, rap each pan on the counter to expel any air pockets or bubbles, then place in the oven. Bake for 30 to 35 minutes, or until a toothpick inserted into the center comes out clean. Let the cakes cool in the pans on racks for 20 minutes.

The orange syrup In a small bowl stir together the orange juice and ¼ cup sugar until the sugar is dissolved. While the cakes are still in the cake pans, use a toothpick or skewer to poke holes at ½-inch intervals in the cake layers. Spoon the syrup over each layer, allowing the syrup to be completely absorbed before adding the remainder. Let the layers cool completely in the pans.

The filling Heat the marmalade in a small saucepan over medium heat until just melted. Let cool for 5 minutes.

The frosting In a chilled mixing bowl using the wire whisk attachment, whip the heavy cream with the 4 tablespoons sugar until stiff peaks form. Add the sour cream, a little at a time, and whisk until the mixture is a spreadable consistency.

To assemble the cake Invert one of the cake layers on a cake plate and carefully peel off the parchment. Spread one-third of the marmalade over the top, smoothing it into an even layer. Invert the second layer on top of the first, peel off the parchment, and spoon another third of the marmalade on top. Place the third cake layer on top, remove the parchment, and spoon the remaining marmalade onto the center of it, leaving a 1 ¼-inch border around the edges. Frost the sides and the top border with the frosting, leaving the marmalade on top of the cake exposed. Or, if you prefer, frost the entire cake first, adding the marmalade as a garnish on top. Chill for at least 2 hours before serving.

As a bachelor, he had wondered every year what to do on Christmas Eve. With both a five o'clock and a midnight service, he struggled to figure out when or what to eat, whether to open a few presents after he returned home at nearly one A.M. on Christmas morning, or wait and do the whole thing on Christmas afternoon while he was still exhausted from the night before.

Now it was all put into perspective and, like his bishop who loved being told what to do for a change, he listened eagerly to his wife.

"We're having a sit-down dinner at two o'clock on Christmas Eve, and we'll open one present each before we go to the midnight service. We will open our presents from Dooley on Christmas morning, because he can't wait around 'til us old people get the stiffness out of our joints, and after brunch at precisely one o'clock, we'll open the whole shebang."

She put her hands on her hips and continued to dish out the battle plan.

"For brunch, of course, we'll invite Harley upstairs. The menu will include roasted chicken and oyster pie, which I'll do while you squeeze the juice and bake the asparagus puffs."

All she needed was a few military epaulets.

"After that, Dooley will go to Pauline's and spend the night, and our Christmas dinner will be served in front of the fire, and we shall both wear our robes and slippers!"

She took a deep breath and smiled like a schoolgirl. "How's that?"

How was that? It was better than good, it was wonderful, it was fabulous. He gave her a grunting bear hug and made her laugh, which was a sound he courted these days from his overworked wife.

—*Out to Canaan*, Chapter Twenty

Jan Karon's
Mitford Cookbook
& Kitchen Reader

Cynthia's Oyster Pie

¼ cup	unsalted butter, melted, more for greasing the baking dish
1 teaspoon	salt
¼ teaspoon	cayenne pepper
2 teaspoons	Worcestershire sauce
1 tablespoon	fresh lemon juice
1 quart	shucked oysters, drained
¼ cup	finely chopped shallots
¼ cup	chopped fresh parsley
1 cup	Ritz Cracker crumbs
6 tablespoons	half-and-half
	Paprika, for sprinkling on top

Preheat the oven to 350°F. Lightly butter a 1-quart baking dish and set aside. In a small bowl combine the salt, cayenne, Worcestershire sauce, lemon juice, and melted butter. Spread half of the oysters on the bottom of the baking dish. Sprinkle with half of the shallots and half of the parsley. Pour half of the butter mixture over the oysters, then sprinkle half of the cracker crumbs on top. Make another layer, beginning with the remaining oysters, followed by the remaining shallots, parsley, butter mixture, and crackers.

Pour the half-and-half into evenly spaced holes, taking care not to moisten the cracker crumbs. Sprinkle the crumb topping lightly with paprika. Bake for 30 minutes, or until the topping is browned.

❖ *Author's note: This is among the most agreeable dishes you'll ever sit down to. One of my sworn favorites!*

Buck was shaking as they went into the study. Though the rector knew it wasn't from the cold, he asked him to sit by the fire.

There was a long silence as Buck waited for the trembling to pass; he sat with his head down, looking at the floor. The rector remembered the times of his own trembling, when his very teeth chattered as from ague.

"Does Pauline know you're back in Mitford?"

"No. I came for . . . I came for this." He looked up. "I didn't want to come back."

"I know."

"It was sucking the life out of me all the way. I was driving into Huntsville when I knew I couldn't keep going . . ."

He was shaking again, and closed his eyes. Father Tim could see a muscle flexing in his jaw.

"God a'mighty," said Buck.

What do cookbook authors eat on an ordinary day? Seared foie gras? English garden peas from their own patch? Fresh scallops sautéed in chive butter?

For lunch today, I had a sliced tomato from my brick mason's garden, and a cold salmon patty, made with salmon from a can.

For supper, I redeemed myself and dined on fresh salmon sautéed in butter, nothing more, followed by a bowl of vanilla ice cream with fresh lemon juice. Like that.

And when my farm manager brought me fresh catfish the other day, I baked it with a dash of Chardonnay (Bernardus, to be exact), and enjoyed the results with only a slice of buttered bread.

I hardly ever think of concocting the lovely dishes I read about in cookbooks. I just take what's here and make it as wonderful as I can, as fast as I can, so I can get back to the book in progress, or to a thumping good read.

My current favorite read: *Country Life*, the English magazine that lets me imagine I actually *could* buy a thatched cottage in Devonshire.

—Jan Karon

Father Tim looked at him, praying. The man who had controlled some of the biggest construction jobs in the Southeast and some of the most powerful machinery in the business couldn't, at this moment, control the shaking.

"I pulled into an Arby's parkin' lot and sat in the car and tried to pray. The only thing that came was somethin' I'd heard all those years in my grandaddy's church." Buck looked into the fire. "I said, Thy will be done."

"That's the prayer that never fails."

The clock ticked.

"He can be for your life what the foundation is for a building."

Buck met his gaze. "I want to do whatever it takes, Father."

"In the beginning, it takes only a simple prayer. Some think it's too simple, but if you pray it with your heart, it can change everything. Will you pray it with me?"

"I don't know if I can live up to . . . whatever."

"You can't, of course. No one can be completely good. The point is to surrender it all to Him, all the garbage, all the possibilities. All."

"What will happen when . . . I pray this prayer?"

"You mean what will happen now, tonight, in this room?"

"Yes."

"Something extraordinary could happen. Or it could be so subtle, so gradual, you'll never know the exact moment He comes in."

"Right," said Buck, whispering.

The rector held out his hand to a man he'd come to love, and they stood before the fire and bowed their heads.

"Thank You, God, for loving me . . ."

"Thank You, God . . ." Buck hesitated and went on, "for loving me."

". . . and for sending Your Son to die for my sins. I sincerely repent of my sins, and receive Christ as my personal savior."

> *"Cooking is like love. It should be entered into with abandon or not at all."*
>
> —HARRIET VAN HORNE

The superintendent repeated the words slowly, carefully.

"Now, as Your child, I turn my entire life over to You."

". . . as Your child," said Buck, weeping quietly, "I turn my entire life over to You."

"Amen."

"Amen."

He didn't know how long they stood before the fire, embracing as brothers—two men from Mississippi; two men who had never known the kindness of earthly fathers; two men who had determined to put their lives into the hands of yet another Father, one believing—and one hoping—that He was kindness, Itself.

—*Out to Canaan*, Chapter Twenty-One

Jan Karon's
Mitford Cookbook
& Kitchen Reader

251

A New Song

His wife went pale.

 He felt like putting his hands over his own eyes, as Uncle Billy had done.

 "I'm sorry," he said. "I didn't know how to say no. Uncle Billy is so excited. . . . They've never given a party before."

"Why in heaven's name didn't they let us *know?*"

"I think they invited everybody else and forgot to invite us."

"Lord have *mercy!*" said his overworked wife, conveniently quoting the prayer book.

They had collapsed on the study sofa for the Changing of the Light, having gone nonstop since five-thirty that morning. He had made the lemonade on this occasion, and served it with two slices of bread, each curled hastily around a filling of Puny's homemade pimiento cheese.

"I can't even *think* about a party," she said, stuffing the bread and cheese into her mouth. "My blood sugar has dropped through the soles of my tennis shoes."

Ah, the peace of this room, he thought, unbuttoning his shirt. And here they were, leaving it. They built it, and now they were leaving it. Such was life in a collar.

—A New Song, Chapter One

Jan Karon's
Mitford Cookbook
& Kitchen Reader

Two Birds with One Stone

Cooking and Writing at the Same Time

Because of the attention paid to food in the Mitford books, people often say, "I bet you're a great cook!"

I am *not* a great cook. My sister, Brenda, is a great cook. My mother, Wanda, is a great cook. I'm merely a *good* cook. In truth, I'm rather timid as a cook, unlike a friend who once described herself as "fearless in the kitchen." Also, I'm impatient. I want to be writing, not cooking.

Here's how I do both of those things at the same time.

When writing at my desk, I love to have a chicken roasting in the oven. As it roasts, it perfumes the air, encourages the writer, and gives solace in solitude.

Rinse a fresh, whole fryer. Check the cavity to see if the liver, etc., is in there. If it is, remove it and rinse the cavity. Dry with a paper towel. Rub all over with garlic cloves. Make a deep pocket in the breast skin and tuck several garlic cloves and two fat slices of lemon inside. Now pop half a lemon and several garlic cloves into the cavity. (In the automotive world, this would be called "fully loaded.")

Rub the chicken generously with a good olive oil.

Ah, dearest Jesus, holy child,
Make thee a bed, soft, undefiled,
Within my heart, that it may be
A quiet chamber kept for thee.

—Martin Luther

Sprinkle on salt, cracked pepper, and fresh rosemary leaves. Put the chicken on its back in a well-seasoned iron skillet. Roast for 30 minutes at 450°F, then turn down to 350°F for 1 hour. Let cool and carve.

Add a fresh, simple salad and a chunk of good bread. Give thanks.

My second favorite thing to cook while writing is a pot of beans.

I sauté onions in a little butter and olive oil in a Dutch oven, add water and pre-soaked beans, and let them simmer all afternoon. Oh, the perfume of a pot of beans, making magic with crushed thyme and coarse sea salt and cracked pepper and a generous dash of rosemary and lots of paprika, and a few cloves of garlic.

(After one writes the coveted 1,500 words for the day, only a couple of simple tasks remain: fry a small cake of cornbread to accompany your bowl of beans, which, upon serving, you sprinkle liberally with chopped Vidalia onions.)

And that, Gentle Readers, is how I write up a storm while my kitchen is occupied with its own pursuits!

—Jan Karon

Jan's Pot of Beans

1 pound	mixed dried beans, picked over
3 tablespoons	unsalted butter
2 tablespoons	extra-virgin olive oil
2 cups	chopped onions
3 cloves	garlic, minced
1 tablespoon	dried rosemary
1 tablespoon	dried thyme
2	bay leaves
1	ham hock
1 tablespoon	paprika
1 teaspoon	freshly ground black pepper
2 teaspoons	coarse sea salt
	Tabasco sauce to taste
	Chopped Vidalia onions, for serving

Place the beans in a large stockpot and cover with water. Bring to a rolling boil. Cover the pot, turn off the heat, and let the beans sit for 1 hour. Drain the beans. In the same stockpot, heat the butter and oil over medium heat and sauté the onions and garlic for 8 to 10 minutes, or until softened. Add the beans and enough fresh water to cover. Add the rosemary, thyme, bay leaves, ham hock, paprika, and pepper. Cover and simmer for 2 hours, checking the beans often and adding water as necessary. Remove the ham hock and add the sea salt. Simmer another hour.

Before serving, adjust the seasonings with salt, pepper, and Tabasco. Ladle into soup bowls and sprinkle each serving with chopped onions. Serve with hot cornbread.

❖ *Do not add the salt until after the beans are fully cooked, otherwise they won't be as tender.*

Cynthia's Pimiento Cheese
adapted from Puny's recipe

1 pound	Hoop cheese or extra-sharp cheddar cheese
1 (7-ounce) jar	chopped pimientos
2 tablespoons	grated Vidalia onion
¼ teaspoon	salt
½ teaspoon	freshly ground black pepper
Dash	cayenne pepper
⅔ cup	Hellmann's mayonnaise

Remove the red rind from the hoop cheese and grate the cheese into a large bowl. Stir in the pimientos, onions, salt, black pepper, cayenne, and mayonnaise. Mash everything together with a fork to desired consistency. Refrigerate for at least 2 hours before serving so the flavors can mellow.

"I've made lemonade and pimiento cheese sandwiches. We'll have afternoon tea."
"Scratch pimiento cheese?"
"Timothy! Is the pope a Catholic?"

—Cynthia and Father Tim

❖ *If making the sandwiches ahead for a party, be sure to cover them with a damp paper towel and then plastic wrap until serving time so the bread doesn't get hard.*

ou see just there?" Marion pointed toward the window. "That patch of blue between the dunes? That's the ocean!" She proclaimed this as if the ocean belonged to her personally, and she was thrilled to share it.

"Come and have your breakfast," said Sam, holding the chair for Cynthia.

On a round table laid with a neat cloth, they saw a blue vase of watermelon-colored crepe myrtle, and the result of Marion Fieldwalker's labors:

Fried perch, crisp and hot, on a platter. A pot of coffee, strong and fragrant. A pitcher of fresh orange juice. Cantaloupe, cut into thick, ripe slices. Biscuits mounded in a basket next to a golden round of cheese and a saucer of butter, with a school of jellies and preserves on the side.

"Homemade fig preserve," said Marion, pointing to the jam pots. "Raspberry jelly. Blueberry jam. And orange marmalade."

"Dearest, do you think it possible that yesterday in that brutal storm we somehow died, and are now in heaven?"

"Not only possible, but very likely!"

He'd faced it time and again in his years as a priest—how do you pour out a heart full of thanksgiving in a way that even dimly expresses your joy?

He reached for the hands of the Fieldwalkers and bowed his head.

"Father, You're so good. So good to bring us out of the storm into the light of this blessed new day, and into the company of these blessed new friends.

"Touch, Lord, the hands and heart and spirit of Marion, who prepared this food for us when she might have done something more important.

"Bless this good man for looking out for us, and waiting up for us, and gathering the workers who labored to make this a bright and shining home.

"Lord, we could be here all morning only thanking You, but we intend to press forward and enjoy the pleasures of this glorious feast which You have, by Your grace, put before us. We thank You again for Your goodness and mercy, and for tending to the needs of those less fortunate, in Jesus' name."

"Amen!"

Marion looked at the kitchen clock. "Oh, my! We'd better show you how your coffers are stocked, and get a move on!"

She took off her apron and tucked it in her handbag, then opened the refrigerator door as if raising a curtain on a stage.

"Half a low-fat ham, a baked chicken, and three loaves of Ralph Gaskell's good whole wheat . . . Lovey Hackett's bread-and-butter pickles, she's very proud of her pickles, it's her great aunt's recipe . . . then there's juice and eggs and butter, to get you started, the eggs are free-range from Marshall and Penny Duncan—he's Sam's junior warden.

"And last but not least . . ."—Marion indicated a large container on the bottom shelf—"Marjorie Lamb's apple spice cake. It's won an award at our little fair every year for ten years!"

Father Tim groaned inwardly. The endless temptations of the mortal flesh . . .

"What a generous parish you are," he said, "and God bless you for it!"

—*A New Song*, Chapter Five

I can't recall whether anyone in the Mitford series ever dons an apron. When Esther Bolick is baking the Kavanaghs' wedding cake in *A Common Life*, she's dressed in her baby doll nightgown, and wearing her favorite bunny-face slippers with plastic eyes that click when she walks. So that certainly wouldn't be an apron scene.

Perhaps Louella puts on an apron in "The Right Ingredients," when she goes to the Hope House kitchen to bake her award-winning biscuits? In any case, I'm exceedingly fond of aprons, and always, always display them in my kitchen—hanging nonchalantly on a hat rack. Specimens from the forties and fifties are easy to find at country antique fairs and roadside malls, and are typically in the five-dollar price range. Aprons are also easy to search out on the web—just type in "aprons" or my personal favorite, "vintage aprons."

A couple of years ago, I found a wonderful yellow apron with rickrack (love rickrack!), which I wore for the photo on the back cover of *Esther's Gift*. If you'd like to add a spot of real cheer (and unabashed sentiment) to your kitchen, aprons get the job done. And don't be afraid to wear one—I often wear an apron when my family comes for dinner, and am happy to tie one on the brave soul who volunteers to wash up! —JAN KARON

Jan Karon's
Mitford Cookbook
& Kitchen Reader

259

Marion's Fig Preserves

5 pounds	whole figs, stemmed
5 pounds	granulated sugar
3 large	lemons, sliced thin

Place the figs in a large pot, pour the sugar over the figs, cover, and let the figs sit overnight.

Place the pot over medium heat and cook until the sugar is dissolved. Reduce the heat to low, add the lemon slices, and cook for 2 hours, or until the syrup is thick.

Pack the figs and syrup in hot, sterilized jars and sterilize for 15 minutes according to the instructions included with the box of canning jars.

"My tongue is smiling."

—ABIGAIL TRILLIN

Marjorie Lamb's Apple Spice Cake

For the cake

	Nonstick cooking spray for the pan
1 cup	light brown sugar
1 cup	granulated sugar
1½ cups	vegetable oil
3 large	eggs, at room temperature
3 cups	White Lily all-purpose flour
1 teaspoon	baking soda
2 teaspoons	ground allspice
1 teaspoon	salt

5 medium	apples, peeled, and coarsely chopped
1 cup	chopped walnuts
2½ teaspoons	vanilla extract

For the icing

1 cup	light brown sugar
½ cup	unsalted butter
¼ cup	evaporated milk
1 teaspoon	vanilla extract
¼ teaspoon	salt

The cake Preheat the oven to 325°F. Coat a 9 x 13-inch baking pan with nonstick cooking spray and set aside. In the bowl of an electric mixer, beat the 1 cup brown sugar, granulated sugar, and vegetable oil on medium speed until light and fluffy. Add the eggs, one at a time, beating well after each addition. Sift the flour, baking soda, allspice, and 1 teaspoon salt into a separate large bowl. With the mixer going, add the dry ingredients to the wet, a little at a time. Fold in the apples, walnuts, and 2½ teaspoons vanilla. Pour the batter into the baking pan and bake for 55 to 60 minutes, or until a toothpick inserted into the center of the cake comes out clean. Remove from the oven to a cooling rack, and cool completely.

The icing Bring the 1 cup brown sugar, butter, and evaporated milk to a boil in a small saucepan over medium heat, stirring constantly. Immediately remove from the heat and stir in the 1 teaspoon vanilla and ¼ teaspoon salt. Beat the icing with a spoon until cool. Poke holes all over the top of the cake with a toothpick and pour the icing over the cake.

Cynthia's Spaghetti and Meatballs

For the meatballs		For the sauce	
	Nonstick cooking spray for the pan	3 tablespoons	extra-virgin olive oil
½ cup	breadcrumbs	½ cup	chopped onions
⅓ cup	milk	6 cloves	garlic, minced
1½ pound	ground round	2 (28-ounce) cans	chopped tomatoes in puree
1¼ cups	grated Parmesan cheese, more for serving	1 (15-ounce) can	tomato sauce
¼ cup	chopped fresh parsley	2 teaspoons	Italian seasoning
2 teaspoons	salt	1 tablespoon	granulated sugar
½ teaspoon	freshly ground black pepper	2 teaspoons	salt
1 teaspoon	Italian seasoning	½ teaspoon	freshly ground black pepper
¼ cup	chopped onions	1 pound	cooked spaghetti
2 cloves	garlic, minced		
1 large	egg, lightly beaten		

The meatballs Preheat the oven to 375°F. Coat a broiler pan with nonstick cooking spray. Toss the breadcrumbs with the milk in a small bowl. In a large bowl, combine the breadcrumbs, ground round, Parmesan, parsley, 2 teaspoons salt, ½ teaspoon pepper, 1 teaspoon Italian seasoning, chopped onions, garlic, and egg. Mix well and shape into 20 small balls. Place the meatballs on the broiler pan and bake for 20 minutes, or until browned.

The sauce Heat the oil in a large saucepan over medium heat. Add the onions and garlic and sauté 8 to 10 minutes, or until softened. Add the tomatoes, tomato sauce, Italian seasoning, sugar, 2 teaspoons salt, and ½ teaspoon pepper. Simmer for 30 minutes.

"All real men love to eat."

—MARLENE DIETRICH

Add the meatballs to the sauce and simmer for 40 to 45 minutes.

Serve the meatballs and sauce over the spaghetti, topped with Parmesan.

He cooked the requisite bowl of spaghetti while Jonathan sat in the window seat and colored a batch of Cynthia's hasty sketches. Something baking in the oven made his heart beat faster.

"Cassoulet!" said his creative wife. Though she'd never attempted such a thing, she had every confidence it would be sensational. "Fearless in the kitchen" was how she once described herself.

"It's all in the crust, the way the crust forms on top," she told him, allowing a peek into the oven. "I know it's too hot to have the oven going, but I couldn't resist."

"Where on earth did you find duck?"

"At the little market. It was lying right by the mahimahi. Isn't that wonderful?"

He certainly wouldn't mention it to Roger.

Jonathan had clambered down from the window seat. "Watch a movie!" he said, giving a tug on Father Tim's pants leg.

—*A New Song*, Chapter Eight

P'SKETTI, PLEASE

Alas, there is no spaghetti, as far as I can recall, in the Mitford books—save a single, buttered bowlful that Cynthia serves to three-year-old Jonathan Tolson in *A New Song*. "P'sketti" is absolutely the only thing this adorable, but testy, little boy would eat, and he preferred eating it with his fingers. Though I never make spaghetti anymore, I have memories of making lots and lots of it when my daughter, Candace, was a baby.

I miss spaghetti! I think I shall make some soon. After all, remember what Sophia Loren said: "Everything you see, I owe to spaghetti."

When I finally break down and make spaghetti, I'll use the sauce recipe on page 262.

—Jan Karon

Jan Karon's
Mitford Cookbook
& Kitchen Reader

Cynthia's Cassoulet

1 pound	dried Great Northern beans
8	cups water
2 tablespoons	duck fat or bacon drippings
2 medium	onions, chopped
6 cloves	garlic, minced
6 to 8 cups	*Chicken Stock* (see page 137)
2 tablespoons	chopped fresh rosemary (or 2 teaspoons dried)
2 tablespoons	chopped fresh thyme (or 2 teaspoons dried)
½ teaspoon	cayenne pepper
½ cup	brandy
2 (14½-ounce) cans	diced tomatoes in juice
3 tablespoons	tomato paste
¼ teaspoon	ground cloves
¼ teaspoon	ground nutmeg
¼ teaspoon	ground cinnamon
2 teaspoons	salt
1 teaspoon	black pepper
1½ pounds	fresh pork link sausage, cut into 2-inch pieces
3 cups	duck confit

Rinse the beans thoroughly and pick through them to remove any debris or stones. Place the beans and water in a large stockpot and bring the water to a rolling boil over high heat. Cover and boil for 2 minutes, then remove from the heat and let stand for 1 hour. Drain the beans and continue with the recipe.

Warm 1 tablespoon of the duck fat in a large Dutch oven over medium heat. Add the onions and garlic and sauté 8 to 10 minutes, or until softened. Add the beans and 6 cups of the chicken stock to the Dutch oven, raise the heat to high, and bring to a boil. Add the rosemary, thyme, cayenne, brandy, tomatoes in juice, tomato paste, cloves, nutmeg, and cinnamon, reduce the heat, and simmer for 1½ hours. Add more stock as necessary to keep the beans from drying out. Season with salt and pepper.

Heat the remaining 1 tablespoon of the duck fat in a large skillet over medium-high heat, add the sausage, and cook for 10 minutes, or until the sausage is browned.

Preheat the oven to 350°F. Layer half of the bean mixture in a 5 to 6 quart black iron, clay, or earthenware pot. Top with the sausage and duck confit. Spoon the remaining bean mixture on top, along with enough of the cooking liquid to cover the mixture, reserving the remaining bean cooking liquid. Bake, uncovered, for 1 hour. Break the top browned layer and add more liquid if the cassoulet appears dry. Reduce the heat to 250°F and bake for another 3 hours. Check the cassoulet every hour to make sure it is not too dry, adding more of the reserved stock or bean cooking liquid as needed.

Remove the cassoulet from the oven and let it cool, then cover and refrigerate overnight. Before reheating, bring the cassoulet to room temperature, add some more broth, and bake at 350°F for 40 minutes to 1 hour, or until heated through.

I possess God as tranquility in the bustle of my kitchen . . .
as if I were on my knees before the Blessed Sacrament. . . .
It is not necessary to have great things to do.
I turn my little omelet in the pan for the love of God. . . .
When I cannot do anything else, it is enough for me to have lifted
a straw from the earth for the love of God.

—BROTHER LAWRENCE (1611–1691)

M an alive! What's *this?*"

"It's my new iced tea recipe," said his wife. "Do you like it?"

He raised his glass in a salute. "It's the best I ever tasted. I didn't know you could do this."

"I didn't, either. I never knew how to make good iced tea. So, with our parish party coming up, I asked the Lord to give me the perfect recipe."

"That's the spirit!"

"Do you honestly like it?"

"I never tasted better!" he exclaimed, stealing no thunder from his mother, whose tea represented the southern ideal—heavy on sugar, and blasted with the juice of fresh lemons.

"I woke up yesterday morning and was bursting with all these new ideas about tea. It was very exciting."

"Hmm," he said, gulping draughts of the cold, fruity liquid. "Tropical. Exotic." He swigged it down to the last drop. "Two thumbs up," he said. "But I'm not sure everybody would understand where the recipe came from."

She shrugged. "If He gave William Blake those drawings, why couldn't He give me a simple tea recipe?"

"Good point. What's in it?"

"I can't tell you."

"You can't tell me?"

"No, darling, I've decided to do something very southern—which is to possess at least one secret recipe." She looked pleased with herself.

"But you can tell *me.*"

"Not on your life!"

"Why not? I'm your husband!"

"Some well-intentioned parishioner would yank it out of you just like that." She snapped her fingers.

"No!"

"Yes. And then I'd be in the same boat with poor Esther, whose once-secret orange marmalade cake recipe is circulating through Mitford like a virus."

"If that's the way you feel," he said, slightly miffed.

—*A New Song*, Chapter Nine

Jan Karon's
Mitford Cookbook
& Kitchen Reader

Cynthia's Heavenly Tea

3 Lipton family-size	teabags, tags removed
2 sprigs	fresh mint leaves, plus mint sprigs for garnish
1 cup	granulated sugar
1 (6-ounce) can	frozen lemonade, thawed
2 (11½-ounce) cans	apricot nectar
2 teaspoons	almond extract

Place the teabags and the mint in a pottery or glass pitcher and pour in 2 cups cold water. Bring a kettle with 3 cups water to a rolling boil. Pour the boiling water over the teabags and cover the pitcher with a small plate. Steep for 10 to 15 minutes, then remove the teabags and mint leaves. Add the sugar and stir until dissolved. Stir in the lemonade, apricot nectar, almond extract, and 3 more cups of cold water. Serve over ice and garnished with a fresh mint sprig.

Father Tim's Mother's Tea

2 large lemons
3 Lipton family-size teabags, tags removed
1¼ cups granulated sugar

Squeeze the lemons into a small bowl, chill the juice, and reserve the skins. Place the teabags and reserved lemon hulls in a large pottery or glass pitcher and pour in 2 cups of cold water. Bring a kettle with 4 cups water to a rolling boil. Pour the boiling water over the teabags and cover the pitcher with a small plate. Steep for 10 minutes, then remove the teabags and lemon skins. Add the sugar and lemon juice and stir until the sugar is dissolved. Add 3 more cups of cold water. Serve over ice and garnished with a fresh lemon slice.

PUNY'S SAVING GRACE #7

"Instead of usin' sugar in your tea, try dissolvin' some lemon drops or hard mint candy in it when it's good 'n hot. And instead of buyin' spice tea, make your own, it's better. Put orange peelin's, whole cloves, an' cinnamon sticks in a square piece of cheesecloth tied up with a string. Steep this little sack in hot cider or hot tea for about ten minutes. Cynthia likes this in th' wintertime when she's workin' on her little books."

Answering the loud knock, he looked through the screen door and saw Otis Bragg. Otis was carrying what appeared to be a half bushel of shrimp in a lined basket. "Cain't have a party without shrimp!" Otis said, grinning. His unlit cigar appeared to be fresh for the occasion.

"Otis! What a surprise!" Surprise, indeed. His wife would not take kindly to cooking shrimp fifteen minutes before her big tea, and he wasn't excited about it, either.

"Already cooked, ready to trot. A man over on th' Sound does these for me, all we do is peel and eat. Where you want 'em set?"

"Thanks, Otis. This is mighty generous of you." He hastily cleared one end of the table they'd brought out to the porch and draped with a blue cloth.

"Marlene'll be comin' along in a minute or two with somethin' to dip 'em in." Otis wiped his forehead with a handkerchief. "Maybe I could get a little shooter at th' bar?"

"The bar? Oh, the *bar!* We don't have a bar. But there's tea!"

"Tea." Otis chewed the cigar reflectively.

"Or sherry."

"Sherry," said Otis with a blank stare.

"Good label. Spain, I think." He recalled that Otis had sent him a bottle of something expensive, but couldn't remember where it was. . . .

"Oh, well, what th' hey, I pass. Father Morgan always set out a little bourbon, gin, scotch . . . you know."

"Aha."

Otis squinted at him. "You raised Baptist?"

"I was, actually."

"Me, too," said Otis. "But I got over it."

"Let me get you a glass of tea. Wait 'til you taste it. You'll like it, you have my word." He certainly wouldn't mention where the recipe came from.

—*A New Song*, Chapter Twelve

Otis's Peel and Eat Shrimp

2 (3-ounce) boxes	Zatarain's Crab Boil
1 large	lemon, quartered
1 large	onion, quartered
2 tablespoons	Creole seasoning
5 pounds	raw unpeeled shrimp, heads removed
	Marlene's Cocktail Sauce

Fill a large pot with water. Add the Crab Boil, lemon, onion, and Creole seasoning. Bring to a rolling boil and boil for 10 minutes. Add the shrimp and cook until evenly pink, 3 to 5 minutes. Drain the shrimp into a colander and add ice to cool the shrimp down. Peel and eat the shrimp with *Cocktail Sauce*.

MARLENE'S COCKTAIL SAUCE

1 (12-ounce) bottle	chili sauce
2 tablespoons	prepared horseradish
1 tablespoon	Worcestershire sauce
1 tablespoon	fresh lemon juice
Dash	Tabasco sauce

In a medium bowl combine the chili sauce, horseradish, Worcestershire sauce, lemon juice, and Tabasco. Add more horseradish to taste if desired. Serve with *Otis's Peel and Eat Shrimp*. Makes 1⅓ cup.

Banana bread!" crowed his wife, dumping a panful onto the counter.

"My mommy, my mommy, she makes bread," said Jonathan, nodding in the affirmative.

"One loaf for us, one loaf for the neighbors," she announced. "But wait, I forgot—we don't know the neighbors."

It was true. A couple of times, they'd waved to the people in the gray house, who seemed to come and go randomly, and the family next door hadn't shown up for the summer at all; one of the shutters on the side facing Dove Cottage had banged in the wind for a month.

Neighbors, he mused. It was an odd thought, one that made his brain feel like it had eaten a pickle.

He heard the music as he stepped off the porch into the backyard.

No idea what it might be. But one thing was certain: it was strong stuff. . . .

He listened intently as he trotted to his good deed. The steady advance of the brooding pedal tones appeared to form the basis of a harmonic progress that he found strangely disturbing. Above this, an elusive melody wove its way through a scattering of high-pitched notes that evoked images of birds agitated by an impending storm.

The effect, he thought as he heaved himself up and over the wall, was confused, almost disjointed, yet the music seemed to produce an essential unity. . . .

Clutching the banana bread in a Ziploc bag, he stood at the foot of the window from which his neighbor usually conducted his audiences, and listened as the music moved toward its climax.

He might be one crazy preacher, but he didn't think so. In fact, he'd come over the wall as if it were the most natural way in the world to go visiting. He was feeling pretty upbeat about his impetuous mission—after all, this was his neighbor for whom he was now praying, and besides, who could refuse a loaf of bread still warm from the oven?

When the music ended, he shouted, "Well done! Well done, Mr. Love!"

Floorboards creaked in the room above. "Father Kavanagh . . ."

"One and the same!"

"Your dog isn't here," snapped Morris Love.

"Yes, and what a relief! I brought you some banana bread. My wife baked it, it's still warm from the oven, I think you'll like it."

Silence.

If his neighbor didn't go for the bread, he'd just eat the whole thing on the way home.

"She said to tell you it's a token of our appreciation for your music."

Silence.

"What was that piece, anyway? It was very interesting. I don't think I've heard it before." He was a regular chatterbox.

Silence.

He began to as feel as irritable as a child. He'd come over here with a smile on his face and bread in his hand, and what did he get for his trouble? Exactly what he should have expected.

"Mr. Love, for Pete's sake, what shall I do with your *bread?*"

"Leave it in the chair," said Morris Love.

"Do what?"

"Leave it in the chair!" he roared.

—*A New Song*, Chapter Fifteen

Cynthia's Banana Bread

	Nonstick cooking spray for the pan
¾ cup	granulated sugar
⅓ cup	unsalted butter, at room temperature
2 large	eggs, at room temperature
¼ cup	plain yogurt
2 teaspoons	fresh lemon juice
3 large	very ripe bananas, mashed with a fork
2 tablespoons	grated lemon zest (see page 52)
2 cups	White Lily all-purpose flour
¾ teaspoon	baking soda
½ teaspoon	salt
1 cup	chopped walnuts

Preheat the oven to 350°F. Coat a 9 x 13-inch loaf pan with nonstick cooking spray and set aside. Place the sugar and butter in the bowl of an electric mixer and cream until light and fluffy, about 8 minutes. Add the eggs, one at a time, beating well after each addition. Add the yogurt, lemon juice, bananas, and lemon zest and beat well. Sift the flour, baking soda, and salt into a large bowl. Add the dry ingredients to the banana mixture and stir until just blended. Add the walnuts and mix again until just incorporated.

Pour the batter into the pan, smooth the top, and bake for 55 minutes, or until a toothpick inserted into the center of the bread comes out fairly clean. Do not overcook. Cool in the pan on a rack for 5 minutes, then invert onto the rack to cool completely.

Lord, in a world where many are lonely, we thank you for our friendships. In a world where many are captive, we thank you for our freedom. In a world where many are hungry, we thank you for our provisions. We pray that you will enlarge our sympathy, deepen our compassion, and give us grateful hearts. In Christ's name, amen.

—TERRY WAITE

Be thankful for the smallest blessing," Thomas à Kempis had written, "and you will deserve to receive greater. Value the least gifts no less than the greatest, and simple graces as especial favors. If you remember the dignity of the Giver, no gift will seem small or mean, for nothing can be valueless that is given by the most high God."

Father Tim remembered what the old brother had said as he ate his portion of the lasagna with gusto, and set some on the floor for Barnabas.

He thought it was the best thing he ever put in his mouth. His wife, who had always possessed a considerable appetite, was hammering down like a stevedore. Even Morris Love appeared to enjoy her handiwork, and Jonathan ate without prejudice or complaint.

Further, Ella Bridgewater had saved the day. In the packet with the sea bass, which Violet devoured, was the small jar of plum wine, which, to conserve water and washing up, they poured into their empty tea cups and drank with enthusiasm.

—A NEW SONG, CHAPTER EIGHTEEN

Cynthia's Lasagna

For the tomato sauce

6 strips	smoked bacon, cut into small pieces
1¾ pounds	ground round
1½ cups	chopped onions
1 cup	finely chopped green peppers
1 cup	finely chopped carrots
1 cup	finely chopped celery
3 cloves	garlic, minced
1 cup	white wine
2 cups	*Chicken Stock* (see recipe, page 137)
1 (14½-ounce) can	diced tomatoes in juice
2 teaspoons	salt
1 teaspoon	freshly ground black pepper

½ cup	heavy cream

For the béchamel sauce

7 tablespoons	unsalted butter
7 tablespoons	all-purpose flour
4 cups	milk
1 teaspoon	salt
1 teaspoon	Creole seasoning
½ teaspoon	ground nutmeg
	Nonstick spray for the pan
1½ cups	fresh spinach leaves, loosely packed
1 pound	cooked lasagna noodles
1 cup	grated Parmesan cheese

The tomato sauce Place the bacon in a large pot over medium heat and sauté until brown and crisp. Add the ground round, breaking it up with a fork, cooking until browned, 8 to 10 minutes. Add the onions, green peppers, carrots, celery, and garlic, and cook for 8 to 10 minutes, or until softened. Add the wine and cook until almost evaporated. Add the chicken stock and tomatoes, lower the heat, and simmer until the sauce is thick, about 2 hours. Add 2 teaspoons salt, the pepper, and the cream. Taste and adjust the seasonings. Set the sauce aside until you're ready to assemble the lasagna.

The béchamel Melt the butter in a medium saucepan over low heat. Add the flour and stir until the mixture is smooth. Gradually whisk in the milk until the mixture is smooth, adjusting the heat so the sauce is bubbling. Make sure the heat is low enough so the sauce doesn't scorch. When the béchamel has thickened, remove from the heat and add 1 teaspoon salt, the Creole seasoning, and nutmeg.

To assemble the lasagna Preheat the oven to 350°F. Coat a large rectangular baking dish with nonstick cooking spray. Spoon 1 cup of the meat sauce into the dish. Top with a single layer of fresh spinach. Cover with a layer of noodles, touching but not overlapping. Spoon a layer of béchamel over the noodles and sprinkle with Parmesan. Repeat this process until you have used all of the ingredients, saving some Parmesan. Be sure to end the layers with the béchamel. Cover with aluminum foil and bake for 45 minutes. Uncover, add the remaining Parmesan, and cook for another 15 minutes. Let stand for 10 minutes before serving.

Feeling oddly distant from one another as they sat in the chairs that flanked the fireplace, they piled onto a sofa. "You know what I'm craving?" she asked.

"I can't begin to know."

"Your mother's pork roast with those lovely angel biscuits."

"My dear Kavanagh, who was it who refused to tote the Dutch oven on our journey into the unknown?"

"I was wrong and I admit it. Can't you make her roast without it?"

"I never have."

"Does that mean you never will?"

"A pork roast in that oven is a guaranteed, hands-down success. Why should I be tempted to veer off on some reckless tangent, like wrapping it in foil or roasting it on a pizza pan or whatever?"

"You're using your pulpit voice," she remonstrated.

"A thousand pardons," he said, getting up to fiddle with the dials on the home entertainment system and trying to make something, *anything*, happen.

"Julia Child didn't require a Dutch oven to make a pork roast," she said, arching one eyebrow.

"And how did you come by this arcane knowledge?"

"I looked it up in her cookbooks in our new kitchen."

"Well," he said, not knowing what else to say.

—*A New Song*, Chapter Twenty

Jan Karon's
Mitford Cookbook
& Kitchen Reader

Father Tim's Mother's Pork Roast

2 tablespoons	vegetable oil
1 tablespoon	all-purpose flour
1 (3½ to 4 pound)	boneless Boston butt pork roast
½ cup	chopped fresh sage leaves (or 3 tablespoons dried)
½ cup	chopped fresh rosemary leaves (or 3 tablespoons dried)
¼ cup	chopped fresh thyme leaves (or 2 tablespoons dried)
10 cloves	garlic, minced
2 teaspoons	salt
3 tablespoons	bourbon
2 tablespoons	unsalted butter, softened
3 to 4 cups	*Chicken Stock* (see recipe, page 137)

Preheat the oven to 300°F. Place the oil in a heavy Dutch oven over medium-high heat. Rub the flour over the meat and place in the Dutch oven. Brown all of the sides of the meat, about 5 minutes on each side. Remove the pork from the Dutch oven and set aside.

Place the sage, rosemary, thyme, garlic, salt, bourbon, and butter in a small bowl and stir until it forms a thick paste. Rub the herb paste all over the pork roast. Return the pork to the Dutch oven. Pour 3 cups of the chicken stock around the pork, cover, and place in the oven. Cook for 5 hours, checking the meat after 3 hours and adding another cup of stock if the sauce looks too dry. Remove from the oven and let sit for 15 minutes before slicing. Serve with gravy from the pan.

❖ *Although Father Tim's mother would have never used a food processor to chop and blend the herb paste, it certainly would make this step easier!*

Father Tim's Mother's Angel Biscuits

	Nonstick cooking spray for the pan
½ cup	water
⅓ cup plus 1 teaspoon	granulated sugar
1 package	instant dry yeast
5 cups	White Lily all-purpose flour, more for rolling out the dough
1 tablespoon	baking powder
1 teaspoon	baking soda
1 teaspoon	salt
1 cup	shortening
2 cups	buttermilk

Coat a baking sheet with nonstick cooking spray and set aside. Warm the water in a small saucepan to 105° to 115°F. Stir in 1 teaspoon of the sugar. Add the yeast and stir until dissolved. Allow the yeast to proof (bubble). Sift the flour, remaining ⅓ cup of the sugar, the baking powder, baking soda, and salt into a large bowl. Cut in the shortening with a pastry blender until the mixture looks like coarse crumbs. Add the buttermilk and the yeast mixture and stir until well mixed. Turn the dough out onto a lightly floured surface and knead 3 or 4 times. Roll the dough out until it is aout ½ inch thick and cut into rounds with a 2-inch cookie cutter. Place on the cookie sheet, cover with a kitchen towel, and let rise until doubled in volume, about 45 minutes. Preheat the oven to 400°F while the biscuits are rising. Bake the biscuits for 10 to 12 minutes, or until golden brown on top.

As they drove into Mitford at eight-fifteen, he felt he was seeing it anew. Though cloaked in fog, the sights he expected to be so familiar seemed fresh and original, almost exotic to his eyes. Lights sparkled in shop windows, street lamps glowed in the heavy mist, the display window of Dora Pugh's Hardware was dressed with pumpkins and shocks of corn stalks.

"I love our town," said his wife, peering out like a kid. Barnabas had his nose flattened against the rear window; even Violet, standing in Cynthia's lap with her paws against the glass, was gazing intently at Main Street.

He realized he was grinning from ear to ear, but when he saw Fancy Skinner's pink neon sign above the Sweet Stuff Bakery, he laughed out loud.

Once they got into the yellow house and turned on the lights and Harley delivered a pan of fudge brownies, it was too late to go visiting in Mitford. Puny, warned of their homecoming, had put roast chicken, potato salad, and tomato aspic in the refrigerator. They fell upon the meal like dock hands.

—*A New Song*, Chapter Twenty-One

As he and Cynthia offered their nighttime prayers, he exhorted the Lord with something from "St. Patrick's Hymn at Evening."

"'May our sleep be deep and soft,'" he whispered, "'so our work be fresh and hard.'"

—Father Tim and Cynthia

Puny's Tomato Aspic

	Nonstick cooking spray for the mold	4 whole	cloves
2 cups	tomato juice	2	bay leaves
3 envelopes	unflavored gelatin	1 tablespoon	fresh lemon juice
2 cups	spicy tomato juice	1 teaspoon	granulated sugar
3	celery tops	½ teaspoon	salt
½ cup	chopped onions	¼ teaspoon	freshly ground black pepper
			Herb Dressing

Coat a 1-quart mold with nonstick cooking spray and set aside. Chill 1 cup of the tomato juice in a small bowl. Sprinkle in the gelatin and let it soften for 10 minutes. Place the remaining 1 cup tomato juice, the spicy tomato juice, celery tops, onions, cloves, bay leaves, lemon juice, sugar, salt, and pepper in a medium saucepan over medium heat. Bring to a boil, reduce the heat, and simmer for 30 minutes. Strain the mixture. Add 1 cup of the hot liquid to the softened gelatin. Stir the gelatin mixture into the remaining tomato juice mixture. Pour into the mold and chill until set, at least 3 hours, or overnight. Serve with *Herb Dressing*.

HERB DRESSING

1 cup	Hellmann's mayonnaise	1 tablespoon	fresh lemon juice
1 clove	garlic, minced	1 tablespoon	tarragon vinegar
6	green onions, trimmed	¼ teaspoon	salt
3	anchovy fillets	¼ teaspoon	black pepper
1 cup	fresh parsley	½ cup	sour cream

Combine all the ingredients in the bowl of a food processor fitted with the metal blade. Process until smooth. Serve over *Tomato Aspic* or fresh sliced tomatoes. Makes 2 cups.

My Spice Cabinet

My kitchen spice cabinet was made from what my grandmother, Miss Fannie, called a "goods box," or a wooden crate in which goods were shipped to mercantile stores. More than a hundred years ago, shelves were added to the box by my great-uncle, Sid Bush, who moved to California and never came back.

I have the letters Uncle Sid wrote to his mother and his beloved little sister, Fannie. They are poignant, yearning, and tender—yet there's also a bitterness that appears unconsciously between the lines. Uncle Sid had never gotten on with his father, John K. Bush, an uneducated farmer who could be a very hard man, indeed. And so, Uncle Sid was lost to the Land of Opportunity, and all we have of him is a photograph of his beautiful shingle-style home on a hill, a small portrait of himself and Aunt Luola, and, of course, his spice cabinet, which I cherish.

I realize now how much this cabinet made from a goods box meant to my grandmother. Though her brother vanished from their lives, his simple creation brought him ever to mind and made his spirit real and remembered.

Uncle Sid, however, wasn't the only brother who left the family and never returned. Uncle Clarence went away to World War I, and was sent home barely a month later in a pine box, dead of pneumonia. I look at the photo of my great-uncle Clarence sitting on a piano stool, erect and handsome and young and slender, his shoes polished, his white collar stiff and high, his eyes proud. And then he was no more.

On the top shelves of the cabinet, which was painted white over the original, rather fragile wood, reside all my cooking herbs and spices.

The bottom shelf has become the "room" of an imaginary house, peopled with a small doll family whom I consider as I cook.

The dolls, all the perfect size for this commodious bottom shelf, were found separately in dollhouse shops and, when brought together, turned out to be perfectly harmonious in familial appearance and good nature.

There is a papa, dressed in a lovely brown Edwardian-style jacket, who is lately arrived from his lumberyard, and a mama, who stands in the corner at a table, rolling out dough. (My housekeeper, after many years of dusting this tableau, recently removed the mama from her labors in the corner and set her in a chair next to the papa; I have not touched them since.)

There is also a one-legged baby in its yellow flannel nightgown, sitting on the papa's lap, and a little boy rocking happily in his rocking chair by the stone hearth.

This small world was created for me long ago by my former brother-in-law, Roger Craig, my nieces, Lisa and Jennifer, and my then-infant nephew, David, who, I am certain, had something definite even then to say about the fabric with which they covered the tiny wooden bed!

How companionable to have this small family enjoying the furniture made by loved ones!

So that is where I keep my herbs and spices, and this is a *soupçon* of what I keep:

ROSEMARY

They say that rosemary is for remembrance. I use a great deal of rosemary, and perhaps that is why I forget only a third, and not all, of the things I need to remember.

I crush it and use it on steak, chicken, lamb, and pork. In fact, I would never think of grilling, roasting, or baking any of these meats without it.

Rosemary is also pleasing in potato soup and numerous other dishes that I can't call to mind, as I haven't had any rosemary today.

THYME

My second-favorite herb, which I use as lavishly and grow in my garden. I'm especially fond of it in that pot of beans I rhapsodized over earlier.

PAPRIKA

Dressy! I use it on roast chicken, potato salad, deviled eggs, cole slaw, even in cornbread. It has a very delicate taste that is often overwhelmed by other tastes, but it always makes a dish look ready-for-company.

SEA SALT FROM BRITTANY

If you're the tireless romantic I hope you are, you'll understand why I find salt from a distant shore so appealing. I have the notion it will taste better, improve my spirits, and impart a certain *élan* to my cooking!

—Jan Karon

Harley's Brownies

	Nonstick cooking spray for the pan
4 ounces	unsweetened chocolate, coarsely chopped
¾ cup	unsalted butter, cut into small pieces
4 large	eggs, at room temperature
¼ teaspoon	salt
2 cups	granulated sugar
1 teaspoon	vanilla extract
1 cup	White Lily all-purpose flour
1½ cups	mini Hershey's Chocolate Kisses or chocolate chunks
1 cup	chopped pecans

Preheat the oven to 350°F. Coat a 9 x 13-inch pan with nonstick cooking spray and set aside. Place the unsweetened chocolate and butter in a microwave-safe bowl and microwave at medium power for 5 to 8 minutes. Stir and let cool completely. In the bowl of an electric mixer, beat the eggs, salt, sugar, and vanilla on medium speed until light and creamy, about 10 minutes. Add the cooled chocolate. Stir in the flour with a wooden spoon until just combined. Add the Kisses and pecans and stir until just combined. Pour the batter into the pan, smooth out evenly, and bake for 25 to 30 minutes, or until a toothpick inserted in the center comes out clean. Cool completely before cutting into squares.

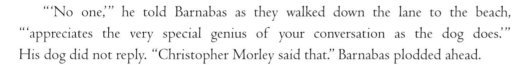

His wife set freshly made chicken salad before him, with a hot roll and steaming mug of tea. She stood holding his hand as he asked the blessing.

"What do you think of me coming home for lunch?" he asked. "I've known some who don't take kindly to husbands falling in to be fed." Might as well learn the truth, which his wife seemed generally enthusiastic to deliver.

"I love that you come home for lunch, Timothy, you're my main social contact now that I'm working so hard to finish the book." She set her own plate on the table and kissed the top of his head.

"How's it coming?"

"Peaks, valleys, highs, lows," she said, sitting down.

"Life," he said.

~

"'No one,'" he told Barnabas as they walked down the lane to the beach, "'appreciates the very special genius of your conversation as the dog does.'" His dog did not reply. "Christopher Morley said that." Barnabas plodded ahead.

—*A New Song,* Chapter Twenty-Two

"The Lord drew me up out of an horrible pit, out of the miry clay, Alleluia!
and set my feet upon a rock, Alleluia!
steadying my steps and establishing my goings, Alleluia!
And he has put a new song in my mouth, a song of praise to our God! Alleluia! Alleluia! Amen!"

—*A New Song*

Cynthia's Chicken Salad

4 cups	diced cooked chicken
½ cup	chopped toasted pecans
½ cup	chopped green onions
1 cup	chopped celery
½ cup	mayonnaise
½ cup	sour cream
2 tablespoons	fresh lemon juice
1 teaspoon	salt
½ teaspoon	freshly ground black pepper
	Tomato slices, for serving

Combine the chicken, pecans, green onions, and celery in a large bowl. In a separate small bowl, mix together the mayonnaise, sour cream, lemon juice, salt, and pepper. Stir into the chicken mixture. Refrigerate until ready to serve.

Serve with sliced garden tomatoes, *Cynthia's Crispy Green Beans with Canadian Bacon*, and *Cynthia's Vanilla Muffins*.

There is no spectacle on earth more appealing than a woman making dinner for someone she loves.

—Thomas Wolfe

Cynthia's Crispy Green Beans with Canadian Bacon

1 pound	fresh green beans
1 teaspoon	salt
1 tablespoon	unsalted butter
4 pieces	Canadian bacon, chopped
1 bunch	green onions, sliced
	Freshly ground black pepper

Remove the ends and string the green beans. Bring 2½ quarts of water to a rolling boil. Add the green beans and salt. Reduce the heat a little, cover, and cook until the green beans are crisp-tender, about 5 minutes. Drain and set aside.

Place the butter, bacon, and green onions in a large skillet over medium heat and sauté for 5 to 7 minutes, or until the bacon is crispy. Add the green beans to the skillet and toss to heat them through. Adjust the seasonings with salt and pepper and serve immediately.

Cynthia's Vanilla Muffins

	Nonstick cooking spray for the muffin tins
4 cups	White Lily all-purpose flour
1 tablespoon	baking powder
2 cups	granulated sugar
½ teaspoon	salt
2 cups	milk
2 large	eggs, lightly beaten
½ cup	unsalted butter, melted
1 tablespoon	vanilla extract

Preheat the oven to 400°F. Coat several mini-muffin tins with nonstick cooking spray and set aside. Sift the flour, baking powder, sugar, and salt into a large bowl. In a separate large bowl, whisk together the milk, eggs, butter, and vanilla. Add the wet ingredients to the dry and stir until just combined. Spoon the batter into the muffin tins and bake for 15 to 20 minutes, or until browned on top.

❖ *Editor's note: Father Tim is allowed to eat one only of these mini-muffins, due to diabetes.*

Barnabas's Dog Biscuits

1¼ cups	all-purpose flour, more for rolling out the dough
¼ cup	wheat germ
¼ cup	brewer's yeast
1 teaspoon	salt
1 clove	garlic, minced
2 tablespoons	flaxseed oil
½ cup	beef stock

Preheat the oven to 400°F. Line a baking sheet with parchment paper and set aside. In the bowl of a food processor fitted with the metal blade, combine the flour, wheat germ, yeast, salt, and garlic. Process until the mixture resembles coarse meal. With the machine running, slowly add the oil and the beef stock through the feed tube until the mixture forms a ball.

Divide the dough into 12 equal pieces. Roll out each piece of dough on a lightly floured surface until it is about ½ inch thick. Use a dog bone cookie cutter to cut out each biscuit and place on the baking sheet. Bake for 15 to 20 minutes, then turn off the oven, leaving the door closed. Let the dog biscuits remain undisturbed in the oven for 1½ hours (do not open the door to check on them).

❖ Brewer's yeast is a natural anti-flea remedy.

❖ Flaxseed oil and brewer's yeast can be found at your local health food store.

In This Mountain

They sat in the study, which was flooded with afternoon light. Father Tim thought Stuart looked surprisingly older, frayed somehow.

"Do you feel like telling me everything?" asked the bishop.

He didn't want to talk about it. Surely someone had given Stuart the details; everybody knew what had happened. He plunged ahead, however, dutiful.

"I blacked out at the wheel of my car and hit Bill Sprouse, who pastors First Baptist. He was walking his dog. His dog was killed instantly. Bill had several fractures and a mild concussion." He took a deep breath. "He's going to be all right."

That was the first time he'd given anyone a synopsis, and he had made it through. His headache was blinding.

"Yes, I heard all that, and God knows, I'm sorry. What I'd really like to hear is how you are—in your soul."

"Ah. My soul." He put his hand to his forehead, speechless.

"The Eucharist, then," said Stuart. He bolted from the chair, took his home communion kit from the kitchen island, and brought it to the coffee table.

Father Tim watched his bishop open the mahogany box to reveal the small water and wine cruets, a silver chalice and paten, a Host box, and a crisply starched fair linen.

"I was reminded the other day," said Stuart, "that when Saint John baptized Christ, he was touching God. An awesome and extraordinary thing to consider. When we receive the bread and blood, we, also, are touching God." Stuart poured the wine and drizzled a small amount of water into each glass. "I know you recognize that wondrous fact, dear brother, but sometimes it's good to be reminded."

"... Heavenly Father, Giver of life and health, comfort and hope; please visit us with such a strong sense of Your Presence that we may trust faithfully in Your mighty strength and power, in Your wisdom vastly beyond our understanding, and in Your love which surrounds us for all eternity. At this time, we ask Your grace especially upon Timothy, that he may know Your gift of a heart made joyous and strong by faith. Bless Cynthia, too, we pray, whose eager hands and heart care for him. ..."

As Father Tim knelt by the coffee table next to his wife, the tears began and he didn't try to check them.

—*In This Mountain,* Chapter Nine

The Lord's Chapel Communion Bread

½ cup	vegetable oil, more for greasing the pan
4 cups	whole wheat flour
4 teaspoons	baking powder
2 teaspoons	salt
½ cup	honey
1 cup	milk
¾ cup	water

Lightly coat a baking sheet with vegetable oil and set aside. Preheat the oven to 400°F. Sift the flour, baking powder, and salt into a large bowl. Place the honey, milk, water, and oil in a small saucepan over low heat and simmer until the ingredients are combined.

Add the wet ingredients to the dry and mix well. Turn the dough out onto a lightly floured surface and gently knead a few times. Roll out the dough until it is about ½ inch thick and roll it into a round.

Cut a cross into the surface of the dough with the blade of a sharp knife. This facilitates breaking the bread into four quarters so others can help the celebrant break into the required number of pieces. Place the bread on the baking sheet and bake for 20 to 25 minutes. Place on a cooling rack to cool completely.

"The bread which we break, is it not the communion of the body of Christ? For we, being many, are one bread and one body; for we all partake of that one bread."

—1 CORINTHIANS 10:16-17

"Father!"

Hélène Pringle darted from the side of the house and hastened up the steps to his front stoop—apparently she'd popped through the hedge—wearing blue striped oven mitts and bearing a dish covered by a tea towel.

"For you!" She thrust her offering at him with seeming joy, but how could he take it from her if oven mitts were required to handle it?

He stepped back.

Miss Pringle stepped in.

"Roast *poulet!*" she exclaimed. "With olive oil and garlic, and stuffed with currants. I so hope you—you and Cynthia—like it."

"Hélène!" His wife sailed down the hall. "What have you *done?* What smells so heavenly?"

"Roast *poulet!*" Miss Pringle exclaimed again, as if announcing royalty.

"Oh, my!" said Cynthia. "Let me just get a towel." She trotted to the bathroom at the end of the hall and was back in a flash. "Thank you very much, Hélène, I'll take it. Lovely! Won't you come in?"

"Oh, no, no indeed, I don't wish to interfere. I hope . . . that is, I heard about . . ." She paused, turning quite red. "*Merci,* Father, Cynthia, *bon appétit, au revoir!*"

She was gone down the walk, quick as a hare.

"I like her mitts," said Cynthia.

"Delicious!" He spooned the thick currant sauce over a slice of tender breast meat and nudged aside the carrots Cynthia had cooked.

"Outstanding!" He ate heartily, as if starved.

He glanced up to see his wife looking at him.

"What?" he asked.

"I haven't seen you eat like this in . . . quite a while."

"Excellent flavor! I suppose it's the currants."

"I suppose," she said.

—*In This Mountain*, Chapter Nine

Jan Karon's
Mitford Cookbook
& Kitchen Reader

Hélène's Roast Poulet with Currants

1	roasting chicken, brined (see page 145)
1 cup	currants
2 cups	boiling water
10 cloves	garlic
6 tablespoons	unsalted butter
2 teaspoons	dried thyme
	Salt and freshly ground black pepper
3 tablespoons	extra-virgin olive oil
2 cups	*Chicken Stock* (see recipe, page 137)
¼ cup	balsamic vinegar

Preheat the oven to 450°F. Drain the chicken from the brine and pat dry.

Place the currants in a small bowl and cover with the boiling water; set aside to soak for 20 minutes. In a small bowl combine 5 of the garlic cloves, 4 tablespoons of the butter, and 1 teaspoon of the thyme and place inside the cavity of the chicken. Season the outside of the chicken with salt and pepper. Heat the olive oil and the remaining 2 tablespoons of the butter in a large Dutch oven. Brown the chicken for 5 minutes on each side, finishing with the breast side down. Drain the currants and add them, with the remaining 5 cloves of garlic. With all the ingredients in the Dutch oven, roast for 30 minutes, then lower the temperature to 350°F and bake for an additional hour, or until an instant-read thermometer inserted in the breast portion registers 155°F.

Remove the chicken from the Dutch oven. Remove as much fat from the pot as you can without removing the flavored juice. Add the chicken stock and vinegar and place on the stovetop over low heat. Simmer until it has thickened, then adjust the seasonings with salt and pepper.

Slice the chicken, place it on a platter, and spoon the sauce over each piece.

His house was not a tomb nor a crypt, after all. The very light may have gone from it, but Puny Bradshaw Guthrie, his appointed guardian and watchdog, was doing her mightiest to make it shine. Dooley was coming to lunch and they were having a feast fit for royals—nay, for the heavenly hosts.

"Alleluia!" he declared to Puny, who wiped her face with her apron as she stood at the stove. Not even the air-conditioning could spare them from the furnace produced by roiling steam, sizzling grease, and the divine tumult of preparation in general. Their house help, a.k.a. his nonlegally adopted daughter, was frying chicken, making potato salad with scallions, bacon, and sour cream, cooking fresh cranberries with shavings of ginger root and orange peel, simmering a pot of creamed corn, deviling eggs with homemade mayonnaise, and rolling out biscuits on the countertop. A pitcher of sweet tea stood at the ready, covered with one end of a tea towel; his grandmother's heavy glass pitcher, filled with unsweetened tea, was covered by the other end. A three-layer coconut cake, set square in the center of the kitchen island, reigned over the room next to a small vase of early, apple-green hydrangea blossoms.

Excited as a child, he went to the downstairs powder room and tested his sugar.

The banquet being prepared for Dooley Barlowe had none of the criminal restrictions required by the diabetic. Thus, lunch would be filled with land mines that he must circumnavigate as best he could. Even so, a man could die with happiness on a day like this and have nothing at all to regret.

—*In This Mountain*, Chapter Fourteen

"A man ought to eat what's offered and be glad to get it!"

—Rose Watson

Puny's Creamed Corn

10 ears	fresh corn
1 ounce	salt pork, chopped
2 cups	milk
6 tablespoons	unsalted butter
1 tablespoon	all-purpose flour
	Salt and freshly ground black pepper

Shuck the corn and remove the silks with a stiff vegetable brush. Wash the ears. Hold each ear upright in a shallow pan, and with a sharp knife, scrape the kernels off each cob, beginning at the top. Scrape the cobs again to remove any remaining liquid.

Cook the salt pork in a large black skillet over medium heat until crisp, 8 to 10 minutes. Add the corn and its liquid, the milk, butter, and flour to the skillet. Reduce the heat to low, and cook for about 30 minutes, stirring frequently. Add salt and pepper to taste.

"Never eat more than you can lift."

—Miss Piggy

Puny's Deviled Eggs

6 large	hard-cooked eggs (see page 158), peeled
2 tablespoons	homemade or Hellmann's mayonnaise
2 tablespoons	sour cream
1 teaspoon	Dijon mustard
1	scallion, minced
1 teaspoon	fresh lemon juice
¼ teaspoon	salt
⅛ teaspoon	freshly ground black pepper
Dash	Tabasco Green Pepper Sauce
2 tablespoons	chopped fresh chives

Slice the eggs in half lengthwise and carefully remove the yolks. In a small bowl, use a fork to mash the egg yolks with the mayonnaise, sour cream, mustard, scallions, lemon juice, salt, pepper, and Tabasco. Spoon the mixture back into the egg halves. You can also spoon the egg yolk mixture into a sandwich size zip-top bag, cut a small opening in one corner of the bag, and pipe the filling into the egg white halves.

Refrigerate until ready to serve, garnish with the chopped chives, and serve on a deviled egg plate.

❖ *Author's note: My sister, Brenda, knew a dear lady who refused to acknowledge the Devil in her house, and always called these "stuffed eggs." A good idea, if you ask me!*

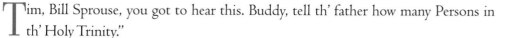

Tim, Bill Sprouse, you got to hear this. Buddy, tell th' father how many Persons in th' Holy Trinity."

Hard by the receiver, Buddy barked three times.

"Good fella! Now, how many Testaments in th' Bible?"

Two barks.

"Amen! Now tell 'im how many true Gods."

One bark.

"Brother, did you ever hear th' beat of that?"

Hooting with laughter, Father Tim snatched the receiver from the hook.

"Ask Buddy if he'd like to preach for me on Sunday."

"Sorry, but he won't be able—he's supplyin' over in Farmer."

Father Tim couldn't remember the last time he'd laughed from the heart instead of the head.

"I wanted to tell you I'm up an' hobblin' around," said Bill.

"Thanks be to God!"

"Buddy an' I'll be out on th' street first thing you know, evangelizin' the neighborhood."

All the way to the Harpers, he held on to the sound of happiness in the voice of Bill Sprouse.

Lace stood before him with the wrapped box, radiant.

"Would you like to guess? You could shake it!"

"I can't imagine . . . ," he said, feeling like a kid at Christmas. He took the deep, square box and shook it. Muffled knocking about of something heavy. "Umm . . ." He would love to make this beautiful girl laugh with a clever guess or two, but blood could not be squeezed from a turnip.

"Bellows for the fireplace?" he asked, completely pathetic.

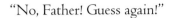

"No, Father! Guess again!"

Hoppy sat in an easy chair, one long leg crossed over the other, wearing his much-talked-about cowboy boots and grinning from ear to ear.

"Perhaps you could give him a clue!" said Olivia.

"You'll be head over heels about these!" Lace crowed. He thought it marvelous the way her amber eyes danced and shone.

He shook the box again. The pressure was on. It could be books. . . .

"Books!"

"You're warm!" she said. "Change one letter!"

In the easy chair, Hoppy couldn't seem to remove the foolish grin from his face as he conspicuously jiggled his foot.

Aha! Could it be? "No way," said Father Tim, laughing. "No way are these *boots!*"

Lace jumped up and down. "You guessed it! You did it! Now you can open the box!"

Hand-tooled. With heels. Sharp as a tack.

Boots.

"Do you like them?" Lace waited, expectant, as he trotted around the living room to a minuscule thunder of applause.

Being a loafer man for roughly the whole of his existence, he was a tad nonplussed. Boots, like capers and eggplant, might be an acquired taste. On the other hand, they seemed to fit, they definitely made him taller. . . .

"He's thinking about it," said Hoppy, "like I had to do."

"I believe I've thought it through," said their guest. "It's entirely possible that in the not-too-distant future, I may well be . . . head over heels!"

That they all gave him a congratulatory hug was a welcome bonus.

—*In This Mountain,* Chapter Fifteen

Jan Karon's
Mitford Cookbook
& Kitchen Reader

I got to do somethin' to rake in business." Percy slid into the booth, looking . . . Father Tim pondered what Percy was looking at. Percy was looking old, that's what; about like the rest of the crowd in the rear booth. He sucked up his double chin.

"Maybe I ought t' mess around with th' menu," said Percy, "an' come up with a special I could run th' same day ever' week."

"Gizzards!" said Mule.

"What about gizzards?"

"I've told you for years that gizzards is th' answer to linin' your pockets."

"Don't talk to me about gizzards, dadgummit! They're in th' same category as what goes over th' fence last. You'll never see me sellin' gizzards."

"To make it in th' restaurant business," said Mule, "you got to set your personal preferences aside. Gizzards are a big draw."

"He's right," said J. C. "You can sell gizzards in this town. This is a gizzard kind of town."

Mule swigged his coffee. "All you got to do is put out a sign and see what happens."

Percy looked skeptical. "What kind of sign?"

"Just a plain, ordinary sign. Write it up yourself an' put it in th' window, no big deal."

"When me an' Velma retire at th' end of th' year, I want to go out in th' black, maybe send 'er to Washington to see th' cherry blossoms, she's never seen th' cherry blossoms."

"That's what gizzards are about," said Mule.

"What d'you mean?"

"Gizzards'll get some cash flow in this place."

"Seem like chicken livers would draw a better crowd," said Percy.

"Livers tie up too much capital." J. C. was hammering down on country ham, eggs over easy, and a side of yogurt. "Too much cost involved with livers. You want to go where the investment's low and the profit's high."

Mule looked at J. C. with some admiration. "You been readin' th' *Wall Street Journal* again."

"What would I put on th' sign?" asked Percy.

"Here's what I'd put," said Mule. "Gizzards Today."

"That's it? *Gizzards Today?*"

"That says it all right there. Like you say, run your gizzard special once a week, maybe on . . ." Mule drummed his fingers on the table, thinking. "Let's see . . ."

"Tuesday!" said J. C. "Tuesday would be good for gizzards. You wouldn't want to start out on Monday with gizzards, that'd be too early in th' week. And Wednesday you'd want something . . ."

"More upbeat," said Mule.

Father Tim buttered the last of his toast. "Right!"

"Wednesday could be your lasagna day," said J. C. "I'd pay good money for some lasagna in this town."

There was a long, pondering silence, broken only by a belch. Everyone looked at Mule. "'scuse me," he said.

"Do y'all eat gizzards?" Percy inquired of the table.

"Not in this lifetime," said J. C.

"No way," said Mule.

"I pass," said Father Tim. "I ate a gizzard in first grade, that was enough for me."

Percy frowned. "I don't get it. You're some of my best reg'lars—why should I go to sellin' somethin' y'all won't eat?"

"We're a different demographic," said J. C.

"Oh," said Percy. "So how many gizzards would go in a servin', do you think?"

"How many chicken tenders d'you put in a serving?"

"Six," said Percy. "Which is one too many for th' price."

"So, OK, as gizzards are way less meat than tenders, I'd offer fifteen, sixteen gizzards, minimum."

J. C. sopped his egg yolk with a microwave biscuit. "Be sure you batter 'em good, fry 'em crisp, an' serve with a side of dippin' sauce."

Percy looked sober for a moment, then suddenly brightened. "Fifteen gizzards, two bucks. What d'you think?"

"I think Velma's going to D.C.," said Father Tim.

"How're the gizzards doing?" he asked Percy.

"Big," said Percy. "Really big."

"It's th' sauce," said Velma.

"I like your sign." Father Tim nodded toward the hand-lettered broadside taped to the back of the cash register.

> *Gizzards Today.*
> *Now with Velma's*
> **Homemade**
> *Dipping Sauce.*

Someone had tried to illustrate the broadside with pencil sketches of gizzards. Not a good idea.

"What we're findin,'" said Percy, "is Velma's dippin' sauce is great with a whole bunch of menu items."

"Burgers!" said Velma.

"Fries!" said Percy.

"You name it," Velma concluded. "Even turnip greens."

"Aha!"

"Th' fire chief puts it on 'is eggs, you ought to order your eggs scrambled this mornin', goes great on scrambled eggs."

"It's a little too early for dippin' sauce," said Father Tim, feeling queasy.

Velma gave him the once-over. "Variety is th' spice of life."

"Right," he said. "But not before eight o'clock."

—*In This Mountain*, Chapter Sixteen

Velma's Dipping Sauce

1 cup	Hellmann's mayonnaise
½ cup	ketchup
½ cup	chili sauce
½ cup	vegetable oil
1 medium	yellow onion, quartered
3 tablespoons	fresh lemon juice
4 cloves	garlic
1 tablespoon	paprika
1 tablespoon	water
1 tablespoon	Worcestershire sauce
1 teaspoon	black pepper
½ teaspoon	dry mustard
1 teaspoon	salt

Place all of the ingredients in the bowl of a food processor fitted with the metal blade. Process until well blended.

"Fresh salmon!" he told Avis Packard. "That's what I was hoping. But of course your seafood comes in on Thursday, and if I buy it on Thursday, I'd have to freeze it 'til Monday."

"For ten bucks I can have a couple pounds flown in fresh on Monday, right off th' boat. Should get here late afternoon."

No one in the whole of Mitford would pay hard-earned money to have salmon shipped in. But his wife loved fresh salmon, and this was no time to compromise. Not for ten bucks, anyway.

"Book it!" he said, grinning.

"You understand th' ten bucks is just for shippin'. Salmon's extra."

"Right."

"OK!" Avis rubbed his hands together with undisguised enthusiasm. "I've got just the recipe!"

Some were born to preach, others born to shop, and not a few, it seemed, born to meddle. Avis was born to advocate the culinary arts. Father Tim took a notepad and pen from his jacket pocket. "Shoot!"

"Salmon roulade!" announced Avis. "Tasty, low-fat, and good for diabetes."

"Just what the doctor ordered!" said Father Tim, feeling good about life in general.

—*In This Mountain*, Chapter Seventeen

"There is no love sincerer than the love of food."

—George Bernard Shaw

Avis's Salmon Roulade

	Nonstick cooking spray for the pan	1 cup	loosely packed fresh spinach leaves
1 pound	thin salmon fillet, skin and pin bones removed	2 tablespoons	*Chicken Stock* (see page 137)
3 tablespoons	extra-virgin olive oil	¾ teaspoon	Morton's Nature's Seasons Seasoning Blend
¼ cup	finely chopped shallots		*Avis's Shallot Sauce*
1 clove	garlic, finely chopped		

Preheat the oven to 350°F. Coat a baking dish with nonstick cooking spray and set aside.

Cut the salmon lengthwise into six 1½-inch strips. Heat the oil in a small skillet over medium heat. Add the shallots and garlic and sauté until crisp, about 8 minutes. Add the spinach, chicken stock, and seasoning blend. Cook until the spinach is wilted, then remove from the heat and let cool.

Spoon equal amounts of the filling over each piece of salmon. Roll up each piece, jelly-roll style, and secure with a toothpick. Place the salmon rolls in the baking dish and bake for 15 to 20 minutes, or until the fish is cooked through. Serve with *Avis's Shallot Sauce.*

AVIS'S SHALLOT SAUCE

2 teaspoons	unsalted butter	1 tablespoon	chopped fresh dill (or 2 teaspoons dried)
2 tablespoons	finely chopped shallots	½ teaspoon	salt
1 cup	sour cream	½ teaspoon	freshly ground black pepper
½ cup	Hellmann's mayonnaise		
1 teaspoon	fresh lemon juice		

Warm the butter in a small skillet over medium heat. Add the shallots and sauté until crisp, 5 to 8 minutes. Remove the skillet from the heat and let cool. In a medium bowl, combine the sour cream, mayonnaise, lemon juice, dill, salt, and pepper. Add the shallots, mix well, and chill until ready to serve. Makes 1¾ cups sauce.

He couldn't let the day end without talking to his boy.

"Hey," he said, when Dooley came to the phone.

"Hey, yourself!"

He heard the happiness in Dooley's voice.

"Just wanted to call and say how glad I am for today."

"Yes, sir. Me, too. I hate to go back Monday."

"I know. When you come home for Thanksgiving, maybe we can get Sammy to come, too." He felt an unexpected knot in his throat.

"He's got bad teeth."

"Yes."

"Maybe somehow we could get his teeth fixed, like Miss Sadie left money to fix mine."

"We can probably work that out." What a great idea. "Can you spare the time to swing by on Monday, on your way to Georgia? I should have Cynthia home a few minutes after twelve. You can have lunch with us, fill up on Puny's macaroni and cheese."

"OK. Great."

"Terrific."

—*In This Mountain,* Chapter Eighteen

Puny's Macaroni and Cheese

⅓ cup	unsalted butter, plus 2 tablespoons melted butter and more for greasing the baking dish
⅓ cup	all-purpose flour
3 cups	milk
½ cup	sour cream
4 ounces	cream cheese, cut into small pieces
2 teaspoons	salt
¼ teaspoon	ground nutmeg
1½ teaspoons	dry mustard
¼ teaspoon	cayenne pepper
½ teaspoon	freshly ground black pepper
4 cups	grated extra-sharp cheddar cheese
½ cup	grated Parmesan cheese
1 pound	cooked elbow macaroni
1½ cups	fresh breadcrumbs

Preheat the oven to 350°F. Butter a 3-quart baking dish and set aside.

In a large saucepan over medium heat, combine ⅓ cup of the butter and the flour and stir until smooth. Slowly add the milk and continue stirring until thickened and smooth. Add the sour cream and cream cheese, stirring to combine. Add the salt, nutmeg, mustard, cayenne, and black pepper and mix well. Stir in the cheddar and Parmesan. Add the elbows and mix well. Pour into the baking dish.

In a small bowl, combine the 2 tablespoons melted butter and the breadcrumbs and spread on top of the dish. Bake for 40 to 45 minutes, or until bubbling around the edges.

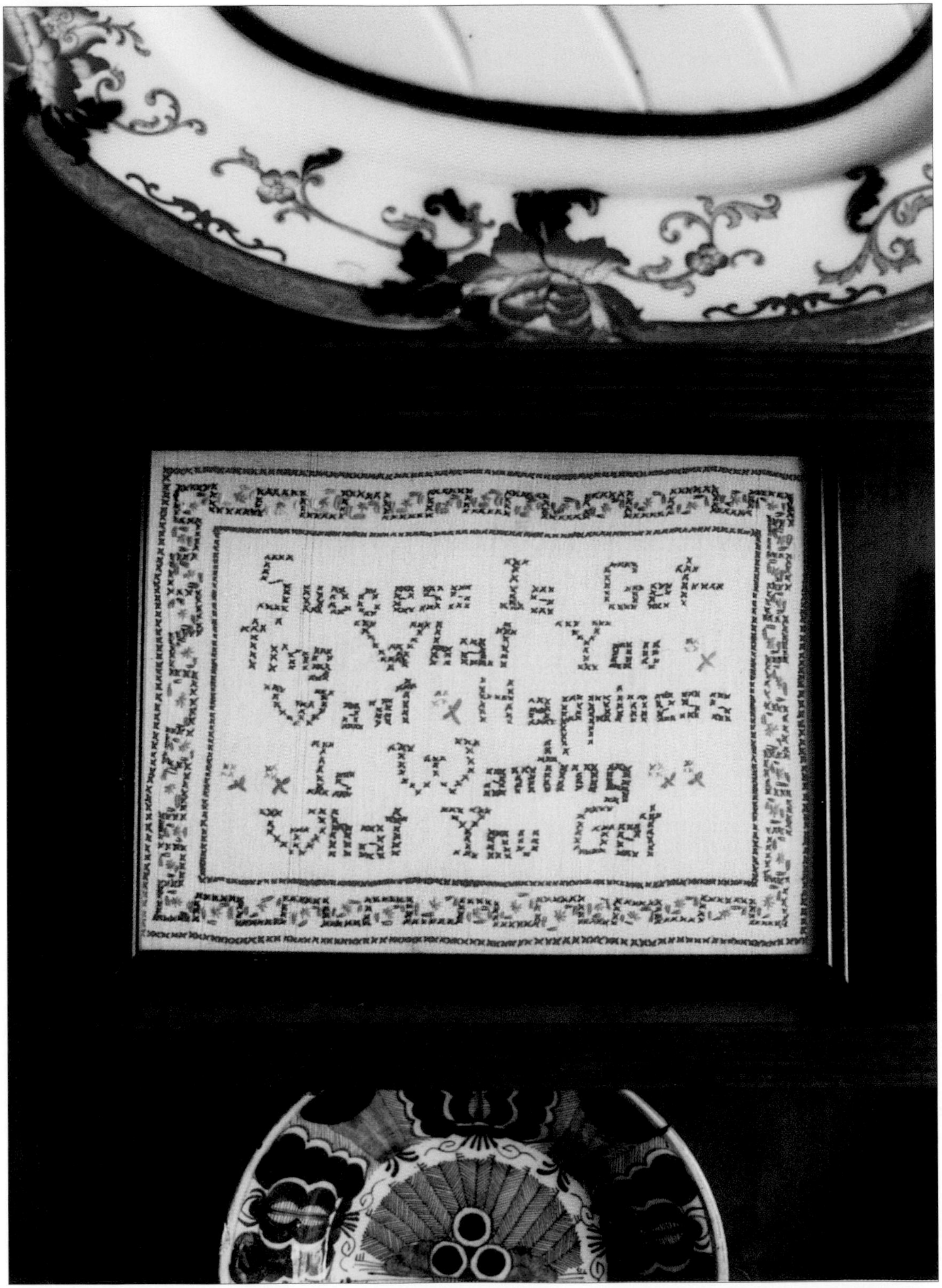
Success Is Getting What You Want Happiness Is Wanting What You Get

Shepherds Abiding

"Father!"

Andrew Gregory's head poked from the door of the Oxford Antique Shop. "Stop in for a hot cocoa."

Hot cocoa!

He hadn't tasted the delights of hot cocoa since the Boer War. In truth, the phrase was seldom heard on anyone's lips—the deal today was an oversweet and synthetic chocolate powder having nothing to do with the real thing.

"Bless my soul!" said Father Tim. He always felt a tad more eighteenth century when he visited the Oxford. He shunted his umbrella into an iron stand which stood ready at the door and strode into one of his favorite places in all of Mitford.

"Excuse the disarray," said Andrew, who, though possibly suffering some jet lag, never looked in disarray himself. In truth, Andrew's signature cashmere jacket appeared freshly-pressed if not altogether brand-new.

"The shipment from my previous trip arrived yesterday, on the heels of my own arrival. It all looks like a jumble sale at the moment, but we'll put it right, won't we, Fred?"

Fred Addison looked up from his examination of a walnut chest and grinned. "Yessir, we always do. Good mornin', Father. Wet enough for you?"

"I don't mind the rain, but my roses do. We've exchanged Japanese beetles for powdery mildew. How was your garden this year?" Fred Addison's annual vegetable garden was legendary for its large size and admirable tomatoes; Father Tim had feasted from that fertile patch on several occasions.

"Had to plow it under," said Fred, looking mournful.

"Let's look for a better go of things next year."

"Yessir, that's th' ticket."

Andrew led the way to the back room where the Oxford hot plate and coffeepot resided with such amenities as the occasional parcel of fresh scones fetched from London.

—*Shepherds Abiding*, Chapter One

Andrew's Hot Cocoa—
The Real Thing

1 (11.5-ounce) bag	Nestlé semisweet chocolate chunks
1 to 2 tablespoons	cocoa powder
1 (15-ounce) can	sweetened condensed milk
1 cup	boiling water
¾ cup	granulated sugar
4 cups	milk, scalded

In a heavy medium saucepan placed over low heat slowly melt the chocolate chunks with the cocoa, condensed milk, boiling water, and sugar, stirring to combine. When the chocolate is melted and all of the ingredients are combined, remove from the heat and let the syrup cool. The syrup can be stored in the refrigerator for up to 10 days.

To make the hot cocoa, pour 2 tablespoons of the chocolate syrup into each mug. Pour the scalded milk over the syrup and stir to combine.

❖ *To scald milk, gently heat the milk until tiny bubbles form around the edge of the pan. Be careful not to scorch it.*

During the heady days of Advent, with its special wreath and candles, and the baking done by his mother and Peggy, the house was filled with wonderful smells. These aromas, including an ever-present fragrance of chickory coffee perking on the stove, were dense and rich; he could sometimes smell them all the way to the rabbit pen, where his best friend, Tommy Noles, came to help "feed up."

—*Shepherds Abiding,* Chapter Two

Christmas Smell

1 quart	pineapple juice
1 quart	water
1 quart	apple cider
2 pieces	fresh ginger, peeled
3	cinnamon sticks
1 tablespoon	whole cloves
1 tablespoon	whole allspice
1 tablespoon	pickling spice

Place all the ingredients in a large saucepan over high heat, bring to a boil, and boil for several minutes. Lower the heat and simmer, leaving the pan on the back of the stove simmering. Add more liquid as necessary. Do not drink!

❖ *Editor's note: This Christmas smell is reminiscent of the "wonderful smells of Advent" in the Kavanagh household when Father Tim was growing up in Holly Springs, Mississippi.*

Risotto! He smelled it at once.

It was currently his favorite comfort food, though decidedly one notch below a cake of hot, golden-crusted cornbread with plenty of butter.

He could eat risotto only occasionally, and, alas, only sparingly. As diabetics had learned the hard way, rice, pasta, or potatoes turned at once to sugar when they hit the bloodstream.

Barnabas followed him along the hall to the kitchen, where Cynthia looked up in mid-stir. "Timothy!"

Seeing his blonde wife at the stove never failed to inspire him—not only was she a leading children's book author and illustrator, she was a dab hand at cookery and plenty good-looking into the bargain.

"Now, are we going to measure or are we going to cook?"

—Frances Mayes, from *Under the Tuscan Sun*

And to think that the urbane Andrew Gregory had pursued her while he, a country parson and rustic rube, had won her . . .

"Marry me!" he said, standing behind her and nuzzling her hair.

She peered into the pot and, satisfied, replaced the lid. "It's lovely of you to ask, sir, but you're entirely too late. I'm happily wed to a retired priest."

"Must be dull as dishwater living with the old so-and-so."

"Never dull," she murmured, turning to kiss him on the cheek.

"What, then?"

"Peaceful! You see, he's gone much of the time, or working away in his study. Always up to something, that fellow."

—*Shepherds Abiding*, Chapter Three

Cynthia's Risotto

2 pint containers	grape tomatoes
	Extra-virgin olive oil
	Sea salt
	Freshly ground black pepper
1 tablespoon	unsalted butter
1 tablespoon	extra-virgin olive oil
½ cup	chopped onions
2 cloves	garlic, minced
2 cups	Arborio rice
5½ to 6 cups	*Chicken Stock* (see page 137), simmering on the back burner
½ cup	grated Parmesan cheese
8 ounces	prepared pesto

Preheat the oven to 350°F. Place the tomatoes in a baking dish and drizzle oil on top. Sprinkle with sea salt and pepper. Bake the tomatoes for 30 minutes.

Make the risotto Warm the butter and olive oil in a large saucepan over medium heat. Add the onions and garlic and sauté until softened, 8 to 10 minutes.

Add the rice to the onion mixture and cook, stirring constantly, for 5 minutes. Add the hot stock, 1 cup at a time, stirring continuously until each cup of stock is absorbed, about 25 to 30 minutes total. Remove from the heat.

Stir in the Parmesan. Season to taste with sea salt.

Spoon the risotto into individual serving bowls. Top with pesto and roasted tomatoes.

Miz Kavanagh, is it alright t' give Timothy some of this candy fruit?"

"Two cherries!" he said, extending both hands. Why did Peggy have to ask his mother everything? If it was up to Peggy, he could have almost anything he wanted.

"Please," he remembered to say.

"Very well," said his mother, "but only two."

He also wanted raisins and a brazil nut, but he would ask later. He liked a lot of things that went into the fruitcake his mother and Peggy made every year, but he didn't like them *in* the cake, he liked them *out* of the cake.

—*Shepherds Abiding*, Chapter Four

Peggy's Christmas Fruitcake

1½ cups	candied fruitcake mix		½ cup	unsalted butter, softened, more for greasing the pans
1½ cups	candied pineapple wedges			
1 cup	candied whole red cherries			
1 cup	candied whole green cherries		1¾ cups	all-purpose flour, more for dusting the pans
1 cup	chopped dried apples		¾ cup	granulated sugar
1 cup	chopped pitted dates		¾ cup	light brown sugar
2 cups	raisins		5 large	eggs
1 cup	slivered almonds		2 tablespoons	dark molasses
1 cup	walnut halves		1 teaspoon	ground cinnamon
3 cups	bourbon, more for wrapping the cake		½ teaspoon	baking soda

In a large bowl, combine the fruitcake mix, pineapple wedges, red cherries, green cherries, dried apples, dates, raisins, almonds, and walnuts. Pour the bourbon over the mixture and let it soak for 3 hours, stirring occasionally.

Grease and flour two 6-cup loaf pans. Preheat the oven to 275°F. Place the flour, granulated sugar, brown sugar, butter, eggs, molasses, cinnamon, and baking soda in the bowl of an electric mixer and beat for 3 to 5 minutes on medium speed, until well combined, scraping the sides of the bowl occasionally.

Pour the batter over the fruit and nut mixture and mix well. Divide the batter into the pans and bake for 3½ hours. Cool the cakes in the pans on wire racks for 20 minutes, then invert them onto wire racks to cool completely.

Moisten 2 large pieces of cheesecloth with bourbon and wrap them around the fruitcakes, then wrap tightly in heavy-duty aluminum foil.

His mother furrowed her brow and looked at the rain lashing the windows; Peggy stirred batter in a bowl.

"What shall we serve, Peggy? Certainly, we want your wonderful yeast rolls!"

"Yes ma'am, an' Mr. Kavanagh will want his ambrosia and oyster pie."

His mother smiled, her face alight. "Always!"

"An' yo' famous *bûche de Noël!*" said Peggy. "That always get a big hand clap."

"What is boose noel?" he asked, sitting on the floor with his wooden truck.

"B*u*oosh," said Peggy. "Bu like *bu*-reau. B*u*oosh."

"Boosh."

"No, honey." Peggy bent down and stuck her face close to his. He liked Peggy's skin, it was exactly the color of gingerbread. "Look here at my lips . . . b*u* . . ."

"B*u* . . ."

"Now . . . law, how I goin' t' say this? Say shhhh, like a baby's sleepin'."

"Shhhh."

"That's right! Now, b*u*-shhh."

"B*u* . . . shhh."

"Run it all together, now. B*u*shhh."

"B*u*shhh!"

"Ain't that good, Miz Kavanagh?"

"Very good!"

Peggy stood up and began to stir again. "Listen now, honey lamb, learn t' say th' whole thing—*bûche de Noël.*"

"*Bûche de Noël!*"

"He be talkin' French, Miz Kavanagh!"

He was thrilled with their happiness; with no trouble at all, he'd gotten raisins and a Brazil nut for talking French.

"What does it mean, Mama?"

"Log of Christmas. Christmas log. A few days before Christmas, you may help us put the icing on. It's a very special job."

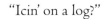

"Icin' on a log?"

"A log made from cake. We had it last year, but you probably don't remember—
you were little then." His mother smiled at him; he saw lights dancing in her eyes.

"Yes ma'am, and now I'm big."

"You ain't big," crowed Peggy, "you my *baby!*"

He hated it when Peggy said that.

—*Shepherds Abiding,* Chapter Four

Father Tim's Mother's
Bûche de Noël

For the chocolate genoise

¼ cup	unsalted butter, melted, more for greasing the pan
⅓ cup	cake flour, more for dusting the pan
⅛ teaspoon	salt
¼ cup	Dutch-processed cocoa
⅓ cup	cornstarch
3 large	eggs, at room temperature
3 large	egg yolks, at room temperature
¾ cup	granulated sugar Confectioners' sugar, for dusting the cake

For the buttercream

8 large	egg yolks, at room temperature
⅓ cup	water
1 cup plus 2 tablespoons	granulated sugar
2 cups	unsalted butter, at room temperature
1 tablespoon	espresso powder
1 tablespoon	Dutch-processed cocoa
2 tablespoons	rum

The toppings

Ground sweet chocolate
Marzipan Mushrooms and Holly (recipe follows)
Confectioners' sugar

The genoise Preheat the oven to 400°F. Lightly butter and flour a 17 x 11-inch jelly-roll pan. Line the pan with parchment and lightly butter and flour the parchment.

Sift the flour, salt, ¼ cup cocoa, and cornstarch into a large bowl and spread out onto a sheet of wax paper. In a medium saucepan over high heat, bring 2 inches of water to a boil, then reduce the heat to a simmer.

In the bowl of an electric mixer, mix the 3 eggs, 3 egg yolks, and ¾ cup granulated sugar together. Place the bowl in the simmering water and whisk gently until the mixture reaches 100°F on a candy thermometer. Return the bowl to the mixer, and using the whisk attachment whip on high speed until the egg mixture is cooled and tripled in volume, about 3 to 5 minutes.

Remove the bowl from the mixer. Using a dry measuring cup, sprinkle one-quarter of the flour mixture over the top of the egg mixture and fold the flour into the batter with a rubber spatula until just incorporated. Repeat with the remaining flour mixture, adding one-quarter of the flour each time and folding just until the flour is absorbed.

In a small bowl gently combine 1 cup of the batter with the ¼ cup melted butter, folding once again with the rubber spatula until combined. Add the butter mixture to the batter and again fold to combine.

Pour the batter into the pan, using a spatula to gently spread the batter to the edges. Bake for 5 minutes, then check to see if the cake is done by gently pressing the center of the cake with your finger. If the cake springs back, it is done. If the cake is not done, return to the oven for another 1 or 2 minutes. Be careful not to overbake the cake.

Remove the cake from the oven. Sift confectioners' sugar over a large tea towel. Run a knife around the edges of the cake to loosen it. Turn the hot cake out onto the towel and peel off the parchment. Starting at one of the long sides, gently roll the cake up in the towel, jelly-roll style. Cool completely.

The buttercream Place the 8 egg yolks in the bowl of an electric mixer. Using the whisk attachment, whip the yolks on medium speed for 4 to 7 minutes, or until light in color and fluffy in texture. Remove the bowl from the mixer and set aside.

In a small saucepan, combine the water and the 1 cup plus 2 tablespoons granulated sugar. Place over low heat, swirling the pan (not stirring) until the sugar is dissolved. Increase the heat to high and boil the sugar syrup until a candy thermometer registers 238°F (soft ball stage), using a pastry brush dipped in water to brush down any sugar crystals that appear around the sides of the saucepan. Once the syrup reaches 238°F, remove it from the heat. Quickly pour the hot syrup into the center of the egg yolk mixture. Vigorously whisk the syrup into the egg yolks by hand. Return the mixing bowl to the electric mixer base and continue to mix, using the whisk attachment, on medium speed for about 5 minutes, or until well combined. Add the 2 cups butter, one tablespoon at a time, until all of the butter has been incorporated. In a small bowl combine the espresso powder, cocoa, and rum and mix it into the buttercream.

To assemble the cake Unroll the cake and spread a layer of buttercream over the cake, leaving a 1-inch border on the sides. Roll the cake back up jelly-roll style and place it seam side down on a platter. Cover tightly with plastic and refrigerate at least 8 hours, or overnight.

Unwrap the cake and trim one end diagonally, 2 inches from the end. Place this 2-inch piece on top of the cake about two-thirds from the front end. Ice the cake with the remaining buttercream, making sure to curve around the stump on top of the cake. Run the tines of a fork down the length of the cake so it resembles bark on a log. Sprinkle the cake lightly with the ground sweet chocolate.

Decorate the cake with the *Marzipan Mushrooms and Holly.* Lightly sprinkle confectioners' sugar on the platter to resemble snow.

MARZIPAN MUSHROOMS AND HOLLY

8 ounces	almond paste
2 cups	confectioners' sugar
3 to 5 tablespoons	light corn syrup
	Cornstarch, for kneading the marzipan
	Cocoa powder, for the mushrooms
	Green food coloring paste, for the holly
	Red food coloring paste, for the holly balls

Place the almond paste and 1 cup of the confectioners' sugar in the bowl of an electric mixer and using the paddle attachment beat on low speed until the sugar is almost absorbed. Add the remaining 1 cup sugar and beat until the mixture resembles fine crumbs. Add 3 tablespoons of the corn syrup, then continue mixing until a small amount of the marzipan holds together when squeezed, adding additional corn syrup, a little at a time, as necessary. The marzipan will still appear crumbly. Transfer the marzipan to a work surface and knead until smooth. Sprinkle a small amount of cornstarch on the work surface as needed if the marzipan is sticky.

Shape one-third of the mixture into small mushrooms and smudge the tops with cocoa powder.

Divide the remaining marzipan in half. Knead green food coloring paste into one of the halves. Flatten the marzipan and cut out holly leaves out with a sharp knife.

Knead red food coloring paste into a small amount of the remaining marzipan and roll it into tiny balls for the holly.

❖ *Editor's note: If any marzipan remains, you have my permission to do what comes naturally, i.e., eat it on the spot. Life is short!*

Father Tim's Mother's Ambrosia

1½ dozen	navel oranges
2½ cups	grated fresh coconut (see page 161)
1 cup	granulated sugar
½ teaspoon	salt
	Maraschino cherries, drained

Peel the oranges with a sharp knife, removing the rind and all the outside white membrane from the sections. Separate the sections and cut into small pieces. Place the orange sections and any juice in a large bowl. Stir in the coconut, sugar, and salt. Cover tightly with plastic and refrigerate until ready to serve. Garnish with the cherries just before serving.

❖ *You can substitute packaged grated coconut for the fresh coconut.*

Oysters . . .

But how many? Chances are, his favorite thing on the menu wouldn't be so popular with this assembly.

Two pints, he wrote.

Heavy cream

10-lb ham, bone in

. . . He would bake the ham; Cynthia would trot out her unbeatable oyster pie, a vast bowl of ambrosia, and a sweet potato casserole; Hélène would bring the haricots verts, and Harley had promised a pan of his famous fudge brownies. What's more, Puny was baking a cheesecake and making cranberry relish; Louella was contributing yeast rolls from the Hope House kitchen; and rumor suggested that Esther Bolick was dropping off a two-layer orange marmalade . . .

. . . altogether a veritable minefield for the family diabetic, but he'd gotten handy at negotiating minefields.

—*Shepherds Abiding,* Chapter Seven

Puny's Cheesecake

For the crust

1 (6.75-ounce) package	Pepperidge Farm Bordeaux cookies
2 tablespoons	unsalted butter, melted, more for greasing the pan

For the filling

4 (8-ounce) containers	cream cheese, at room temperature
2 cups	granulated sugar
6 large	eggs, lightly beaten, at room temperature
2 teaspoons	vanilla extract
1 (16-ounce) container	sour cream, at room temperature

The crust In the bowl of a food processor fitted with the metal blade, crush the cookies with the melted butter. Butter the bottom and 3 inches up the sides of a 9-inch springform pan. Wrap a piece of aluminum foil around the outside bottom and sides of the springform pan. Pat the cookie crumbs into the bottom of the pan only.

The filling Preheat the oven to 375°F. Place the cream cheese and sugar in the bowl of an electric mixer and beat on medium speed until light and creamy, 8 to 10 minutes. Add the beaten eggs, one at a time, beating well after each addition. Remove the bowl from the mixer and fold in the vanilla and sour cream. Pour the filling into the pan and smooth the top. Place the cheesecake in a hot water bath (see below) and bake for 45 minutes. Turn off the oven and leave the cheesecake in the oven for 1 hour. Do not open the door to check on the cake. Remove and place on a rack to cool to room temperature. Run a knife around the edges of the pan to loosen the cake. Remove the springform pan and refrigerate the cheesecake until ready to serve.

❖ *To create a water bath, place the springform pan in a large roasting pan and pour in enough boiling-hot water to come halfway up the sides of the springform pan.*

❖ *Cheesecake is best baked the day before serving.*

Puny's Cranberry Relish

2 tablespoons	grated navel orange zest (see page 52)
2 large	navel oranges, peeled, sectioned, and coarsely chopped
1 (12-ounce) package	fresh cranberries, coarsely chopped
1 large	Granny Smith apple, coarsely chopped
1 cup	chopped celery
1 cup	coarsely chopped pineapple
1 cup	chopped pecans
1 cup	granulated sugar
¼ teaspoon	salt

In a large bowl, combine the orange zest, chopped orange sections, cranberries, apples, celery, pineapple, pecans, sugar, and salt. Cover with plastic and refrigerate. Before serving, taste and add more sugar if needed.

PUNY'S SAVING GRACE # 8

"When you're gratin' lemon or orange peel, a lot of good stuff gets stuck in th' grater holes. Instead of wastin' it, brush it off in a dish by usin' a clean toothbrush."

"You mustn't miss your nap," Cynthia reminded him.

They were slurping her Roasted Red Pepper and Tomato Soup for a fare-thee-well. He could eat a potful of this stuff.

"I'll lie on the sofa when we finish the tree, and look at the lights. I'm sure I'll nod off."

"I think you should nap for at least an hour. But do you really want to lie on *that* sofa? Ugh! It's so Victorian, you can't possibly be comfortable."

"I'll get a pillow from the bed . . ."

"I'll bring you one, and a blanket, too."

"Thanks. We've both been too blasted busy." *Slurp.* It was hard not to slurp soup. "But there's light at the end of the tunnel, my love!"

—*Shepherds Abiding,* Chapter Nine

Cynthia's Roasted Red Pepper Tomato Soup

2 tablespoons	extra-virgin olive oil
1 cup	chopped green onions or shallots
4½ cups	*Chicken Stock* (see recipe, page 137)
2 cups	chopped jarred roasted red peppers
2 (14½-ounce) cans	whole stewed tomatoes
1 teaspoon	granulated sugar
1½ teaspoons	dried basil
	Salt and freshly ground black pepper
	Sour cream, for serving

Warm the olive oil in a large heavy saucepan over medium heat. Add the green onions and sauté until soft, 8 to 10 minutes. Add the chicken stock, red peppers, tomatoes, sugar, and basil. Bring to a boil, then reduce the heat, cover, and simmer for 15 minutes.

Remove the tomatoes and peppers with a slotted spoon and transfer to a blender or food processor. Blend until smooth and then return to the liquid. Season with salt and pepper to taste. Ladle into soup bowls and garnish with a dollop of sour cream.

Light from Heaven

Dooley was coming home, and the shopping list for his favorite meal, always served on the night of his homecoming, was being hammered out.

"Steak!" exclaimed his wife, scribbling on a note pad. "Same old cut?"

"Same old, same old. New York strip."

"Russet potatoes," she said, continuing the litany.

"Always best for frying." His blood was getting up for this biannual cookathon, even if he couldn't eat much of it. While some theologians construed St. Paul's thorn to be any one of a variety of alarming dysfunctions, he'd been convinced for years that it was the same blasted affliction he'd ended up with—diabetes.

"Pie crusts," she said, still scribbling. "Oh, dear. For the life of me, I can't remember all the ingredients for his chocolate pie, and of course, I didn't bring my recipe box . . ."

"I've never liked the recipe we use," he said, suddenly confessional.

"You're not supposed to even touch chocolate pie, Timothy, so what difference does it make? Dooley loves it; it isn't half-bad, really."

"It needs something."

"Ah," she said.

"Something more . . . you know."

"Whipped cream!"

His wife loved whipped cream; with the slenderest of excuses, she would put it on anything.

"Not whipped cream. Something more like . . ." He sighed; his culinary imaginations had lately gone down the drain.

"Meringue!"

"*Meringue!*" he said, slapping his leg. "That's it!"

She bolted from her chair and trotted to the kitchen counter. "Marge's recipe box . . . I was thumbing through it the other day, and I vaguely remember . . . let's see . . . Onions in Cream Sauce, Penne Pasta with Lump Crab, that sounds good . . ."

"Keep going."

"Pie!"

"Bingo."

"Buttermilk Pie . . . Vinegar Pie . . . Coconut . . ."

"Mark that one!" he said.

"Egg Custard . . . Fresh Peach . . . Deep-Dish Apple . . ."

"Enough," he said, "I'm only human."

"Here it is. Chocolate Pie with Meringue."

"Finish the list," he said, bolting from his own chair, "and I'm out of here." Ha! He'd denied himself as sternly as one of the desert fathers these last weeks, he would have the tiniest sliver of that pie, or else . . .

"I know what you're thinking," she said, grinning.

He pulled on his jacket and foraged in the pockets for his gloves.

"You always know what I'm thinking," he said.

PUNY'S SAVING GRACE #9

"When you get a starch build-up on your iron, take it off with a little bakin' soda on a damp sponge. Make sure th' iron's unplugged and cold."

Marge's Chocolate Pie with Meringue

For the filling

2 cups	milk
1 cup	granulated sugar
¼ cup	all-purpose flour
¼ cup	cocoa powder
¼ teaspoon	salt
4 large	egg yolks, at room temperature (save the whites for the meringue)
4 tablespoons	unsalted butter
1 teaspoon	vanilla extract
½ recipe	*Pastry for a Double Crust Pie* (see page 4) (Halve the recipe, or make the whole recipe and freeze half)

For the meringue

2 teaspoons	cornstarch
¼ cup	hot water
4 large	egg whites, at room temperature
½ teaspoon	cream of tartar
½ cup	granulated sugar
½ teaspoon	vanilla extract

Preheat the oven to 350°F. Coat a 9-inch pie pan with nonstick cooking spray. Roll out the pastry dough and fit into the prepared pie pan. Line the pastry with aluminum foil and fill with pie weights or dried beans. Bake for 15 minutes. Remove the crust from the oven and discard the pie weights and aluminum foil.

The filling Gently heat the milk in a large saucepan over low heat until bubbles form around the edges. In a medium bowl combine the 1 cup sugar, flour, cocoa powder, and salt. Slowly add the dry ingredients to the heated milk, stirring constantly. In a small bowl, lightly beat the egg yolks. Add 2 tablespoons of the hot milk mixture to the eggs and mix well. Then add all of

the eggs to the milk mixture and stir over low heat until thickened. Remove from the heat and stir in the butter and vanilla. Pour the filling into the baked pie shell.

The meringue Combine the cornstarch and hot water in a small saucepan placed over low heat. Stir until dissolved, then remove from the heat and let it cool. Beat the egg whites with the cream of tartar in the bowl of an electric mixer until soft peaks form. Add the ½ cup sugar and cornstarch and continue beating until stiff peaks form again. Fold in the vanilla and spread the meringue on top of the warm chocolate filling, making sure it reaches all the way to the edges of the pie crust. Bake for 8 to 10 minutes, or until the meringue is lightly browned. Cool completely and refrigerate before serving. The pie is best served the same day it is made.

THE MAIN INGREDIENT

My first cooking experience was pure joy. No flops, no letdowns, and no leftovers.

I'm sure you had the same feeling about your own mud pies.

There they sat, baking in the sun under our rapt and marveling gaze. But these were no mere patties of rainwater and garden dirt. They were luscious puddings, deep-dish pies, three-layer cakes, and scrumptiously chewy cookies—all because the main ingredient was imagination.

I think imagination is still the main ingredient in cookery. Consider, for example, how my sister, Brenda, makes her creamy, utterly delicious mashed potatoes. She cuts up a turnip and cooks it with the potatoes, then mashes the whole caboodle using a can of evaporated milk.

"You'll never know the turnip is there," she promises. "It simply imparts a wonderful flavor." What I do know is that we clean the bowl when Brenda makes her imaginative mashed potatoes.

Another feast of imagination came when Santa Claus brought me a small tin stove for Christmas. Maybe I was six, or maybe I was seven. But that little stove was a huge hit. It had an oven door that actually opened and closed. And little pots and pans which, though light as paper, seemed serious and true—fit for anything. A veritable horde of imaginary children came to devour my pigs-in-blankets, a husband showed up on several occasions for something that would stick to his ribs, and visitors whom no one but myself could see dropped in for fried chicken.

Speaking of which, it was during this same era that I developed an undying love for this venerable dish.

Once when our grandmother, Miss Fannie, had gone off to Washington to visit a relative, my sister and I agreed we were starving. The old lady in the black dress who had come to cook was no dab hand at much of anything, as far as we could tell.

"I'd sure like to have some fried chicken," I said to my little sister.

Brenda looked at me blankly. How could we have fried chicken if Mama had gone off to Washington?

As the big sister, it seemed my duty to call a spade a spade. "But you know we'd have to kill it first."

We both pondered this disagreeable prospect. Then, as she has done so often in life, my little sister took a deep breath and summoned her courage. "I'll kill it!" she said.

And she did. But we won't tell you how.

Another early food love was Cream of Wheat, with brown sugar and lots of home-churned butter. Divine. And do you remember the lovely radio show that came on every Saturday morning, leading one's imagination down the lane, through the meadow, across the pond, and into other worlds? I can still sing the theme song:

"Cream of Wheat is so good to eat,
We have it every day . . ."

The show was called *Let's Pretend*, and I've been pretending ever since—pretending, for example, that the Mitford characters are personal friends, and the church is always open, and the hills are eternally green.

Thank you, by the way, for pretending that with me, for together, our imaginations have made Mitford real, very real—and I couldn't have done it without you.

—JAN KARON

Pansy's Pecan Pie

¼ cup	unsalted butter, at room temperature, more for greasing the pan
½ recipe	*Pastry for a Double Crust Pie* (see page 4) (Halve the recipe, or make the whole recipe and freeze half)
1 cup	granulated sugar
4 large	eggs, lightly beaten
¾ cup	light corn syrup
2 teaspoons	vanilla extract
⅛ teaspoon	salt
2 cups	chopped pecans

Preheat the oven to 350°F. Lightly butter a 9-inch pie pan. Roll out the pastry dough and fit it into the pan.

Place the sugar and butter in the bowl of an electric mixer fitted with the paddle attachment and beat until fluffy, 8 to 10 minutes. Add the eggs and beat well. Add the corn syrup, vanilla, and salt. Remove the bowl from the mixer and stir in the pecans.

Pour the filling into the unbaked pie crust and bake 40 to 45 minutes, or until the pie is nice and brown on top. Remove the pie from the oven to a cooling rack, and cool completely before serving.

I thought it would be . . . I hate to say it, Timothy, but I thought it would be romantic. You know, pick Queen Anne's lace in the meadow, sketch cows grazing in the upland pastures, picnic by the creek, gather wild sedge . . ."

"Why gather wild sedge?" When he was coming along, sedge was a blasted nuisance.

"To make a hearth broom. I always wanted to make a hearth broom."

His wife ever surprised him. "The whole thing reminds me of what we thought before going down to Whitecap."

They recited their Whitecap litany in unison. "The freedom of an island . . .

". . . the wind in our hair . . .

". . . gulls wheeling above us . . .

". . . the smell of salt air!"

He shook his head, disbelieving. "I think we walked on the beach all of three times that whole year." His stint as an interim in that idyllic spot had been filled with bolts from the blue, not to mention a hurricane that ripped the porch off their house and the roof off their church.

"What happens, Timothy?"

"Life happens."

"Who knew that running a farm would be like running General Motors? And I'm the CEO! I was never a CEO."

"And what am I, pray, sales and service?"

"Yes! Yakking it up with the neighbors, going to dinners on the grounds, zooming around on that little golf cart thing, advising the help . . ."

"What's for supper?" he asked, unable to bring any wisdom to this line of thought.

"Okra," she said, sighing. "Okra, okra, and more okra."

—*Light from Heaven*

Cynthia's Fried Okra

1 pound	fresh okra
2 to 3 cups	milk
2½ cups	White Lily self-rising cornmeal
2 tablespoons	self-rising flour
1 tablespoon	salt
1 teaspoon	freshly ground black pepper
1 teaspoon	Creole seasoning
	Vegetable oil, for frying

Cut off the tips and stem ends of the okra. Cut into ½-inch slices and place in a large bowl. Pour the milk over the okra and let the mixture sit for at least 10 minutes, or up to 30 minutes. In a separate large bowl, combine the cornmeal, flour, salt, pepper, and Creole seasoning. Use a slotted spoon to lift the okra out of the milk, allowing the excess milk to drain. Place small batches of okra in the cornmeal mixture, tossing to coat the okra well.

Heat the oil in a deep black iron skillet. Lift the okra from the bowl in batches (allowing the excess cornmeal to fall back in the bowl) and fry in the hot oil until browned. Do not overcrowd the skillet. Remove the okra from the oil with a slotted spoon and place it on paper towels to drain. Adjust the seasonings with salt and pepper while the okra is still hot.

Fresh Field Peas

3 ounces	salt pork, diced
2½ teaspoons	salt
4 cups	water
4 cups	shelled peas
	Freshly ground black pepper
	Pepper Sauce

Place the salt pork, salt, and water in a large heavy saucepan over high heat. Bring to a boil, lower the heat, and simmer for 15 minutes. Add the peas and simmer for 1 hour, or until tender. Add water if needed to keep the peas barely covered with liquid at all times. Adjust the seasonings with salt and pepper. Sprinkle each serving of peas with *Pepper Sauce* and serve with hot cornbread.

❖ *The juice from field peas or turnip greens is often called "pot likker." Spoon some pot likker over a piece of hot buttered cornbread and it will set you free.*

❖ *Lima beans or another variety of pea may be substituted for the field peas.*

PEPPER SAUCE

20 small	red and green cayenne peppers
2½ to 3 cups	white vinegar

Pack the peppers into an empty wine bottle that has been cleaned. Heat the vinegar in a small saucepan until boiling. Remove from the heat and pour the vinegar into the bottle. Let the vinegar cool and seal the bottle with the cork. Let the mixture sit for 2 weeks before using.

Add more vinegar to the same peppers as needed. The *Pepper Sauce* will last as long as you keep adding vinegar. Makes about 3 cups.

❖ Pepper Sauce *is a must on turnip greens and field peas. Most folks leave the bottle sitting out on their kitchen table with the salt and pepper shakers.*

Cucumber and Onion Salad

6 small	cucumbers, thinly sliced
1	Vidalia onion, thinly sliced
2 cups	white vinegar
1 teaspoon	salt
1 tablespoon	granulated sugar
½ teaspoon	freshly ground black pepper

In a medium bowl, combine the cucumbers, onions, vinegar, salt, sugar, and pepper. Cover with plastic and refrigerate for at least 1 hour, or up to 2 days.

Adjust the seasonings with salt and pepper and serve the salad very cold.

"Life expectancy would grow by leaps and bounds if green vegetables smelled as good as bacon."

—DOUG LARSON

With Brenda Karel, my little sister and sidekick. Our mother and father built the house behind us for $1,165 in 1937.

Already, I'm planning to teach my little sister her multiplication tables and ABCs. She learned them so well, she skipped first grade at Hudson School!

Some of the Seasoning in My Life

Hand-embroidered dresses from our father, Bob Wilson, sent to us during his European tour with the air force.

Pocketbooks sent by our father from Italy, where he was stationed in World War II.

Taken during the Shirley Temple era. Who knew Mitford was in my future?

With Brenda and my wonderful brothers: Barry Setzer on the left and Randy Setzer on the right. (The worst hair day of my life!)

Your author, age six or seven, on the front porch of my grandparents' farmhouse near Hudson, North Carolina.

With my daughter, Candace, the year we went to the dude ranch, Candace is a truly gifted photographer, and lots of fun in the kitchen. She is my treasure.

Mama's Miracles

My grandmother, Miss Fannie, had a miraculous skill: she could make something out of absolutely nothing.

Over and over, she would put a full meal on the table when it didn't appear to my little sister and me that we had anything at all to eat!

Mama's something-out-of-nothing meals might go like this:

First, she'd go out in the yard and catch a chicken. Try doing this, it is *not* easy. Then . . . do you really want to know what happened next? If not, stop reading right here and skip the following paragraph.

Okay, after she caught it, she would chop its head off. This seemed the most natural thing in the world to us, then, though I wouldn't relish seeing it done today. She would douse the chicken in a tub of boiling water to loosen the feathers, pluck it over a newspaper, and singe the fine hairs over an open flame in the kitchen wood stove.

Then she would wash the chicken, cut it up, roll the pieces in flour, add salt and pepper, and drop the whole lot into a large iron skillet sizzling with hot bacon grease. There is no high, medium, or low setting on a wood cook stove; she would have to watch that chicken like a hawk while she carried through with the rest of the dinner, which nearly always included a pan of biscuits.

Once the biscuits were cut out with the mouth of a jelly glass, and rising on her battered bake sheet, she might find a head of cabbage and set to work on a bowl of cole slaw, which became famous in our family for its unique style (short on the mayonnaise, long on the salt and vinegar). Then, since we lived in the country, she could always round up a few potatoes, which she would slice and cook, and mash into a

Facing page: My mother's very thin biscuits, hot from the oven, on my grandmother's ancient, never-fail bake sheet.

*Heavenly Father, bless us
And keep us all alive,
There's ten of us to dinner
And not enough for five.*

—Anonymous

silken cloud with milk and butter (often churned by yours truly). About this time, her hand would reach 'way back in the cabinet behind the wood stove and she would pull out a jar of jam or apple butter or pickles or succotash. And before you know it, Mama had made a meal fit for a king, out of absolutely nothing, don't you know.

In truth, that's what the upcoming *Cinnamon Stickies* recipe is all about. Let's say company shows up and you don't even have any candy or store-bought cookies in the house. You can delight a lot of kids, and even grownups, in about twenty minutes flat.

By the way, if you have a grandmother, go call her right now and tell her you love her to pieces.

Actually, if you have a mother, call her, too. Here I am with mine on an early winter's day by the fire.
Draw close. Hold hands. Life is short. God is good.

If you want to be Southern for even five minutes, you must learn how to bake biscuits. The other day, I found my grandmother's biscuit recipe, handwritten on the back of an envelope mailed to her on April 14, 1944. The recipe never varied and, like Miss Fannie herself, you can count on it.

Mama's Biscuits

2 cups	plain flour
1 teaspoon	salt
2 teaspoons	baking powder
½ teaspoon	baking soda
3 to 5 tablespoons	shortening
¾ cup	buttermilk (these biscuits won't work with 2%, nonfat, lowfat, or *any* milk but *butter*milk)

OK. Plunge your hands into this mixture and work it 'til it becomes dough. Now, let it rise a few minutes. Next, roll it out to a little less than a half-inch in thickness. Get a drinking glass out of the cabinet. Cut out the biscuits. Place them on a greased and lightly floured biscuit pan and bake at 375°F for 20 minutes.

Serve with butter and jam and strong coffee, and utter the festal shout: Hallelujah!

MAMA'S CINNAMON STICKIES

Roll biscuit dough thin. Spread with softened butter. Sprinkle on sugar, brown or white, and cinnamon (use liberally). Slice dough in long strips an inch or inch-and-a-half wide. Roll up each strip in a pinwheel. Place on a greased sheet and bake in a hot oven for 10 minutes at 350°F, or until the aroma calls you in from the porch.

That, however, is not all I have to tell you about biscuits.

My mother's biscuits are also supreme, and very different, indeed, from Miss Fannie's. Mother's are very, very thin and very, very short. They are the French pastry, if you will, of my mother's table, and most of us can eat several at one sitting. "No, Mother, I can't have another one, I promise! I've already had three." "But of course you can have another one, honey, just look how *thin* they are."

Obligingly, you look at how thin they are, and happily have another one.

Mother's Very Thin Biscuits

I typed the above recipe name into this manuscript weeks ago, and have called my mother, Wanda Setzer, again and again for her written instructions. Turns out she has tried to write it all down, but simply can't—she cooks "by ear," if you will, and has no idea how much she uses of *anything.* So, excuse me, but there is no recipe! However, I shall leave the recipe title above, simply to commemorate her fabulous biscuit recipe which, it turns out, must, for the above reasons, remain a family secret.

ONE LAST SAVING GRACE

"I hate th' way grease pops when I'm fryin' chicken, I have to clean up th' whole bloomin' stove top. So here's what I do now, I learned it out of a cookbook. Jis' sprinkle a little salt or flour in the pan before fryin,' an' it solves th' problem. I'm teachin' my girls to cook— Sassy done everybody a grilled cheese last night for supper an' Sissy baked muffins for Sunday breakfast. I'm so proud I could bust."

Cover your eyes! Plug your ears! It's confession time.

I love anything *fried!*

Potatoes, chicken, onions, cornbread, mushrooms, pork chops, et al, are all improved by frying. Using my indispensable, fully-cured black iron skillet, I cook nearly everything on the stovetop. Here, for example, is how I fry cornbread:

Get out a bowl. Pour in some yellow self-rising cornmeal. About two cups. Add whole milk or buttermilk until the batter is nice and creamy—not runny and not dry, but creamy. Chop in some onions. Add a pinch or two of thyme, salt, and pepper. Add a teaspoon of good olive oil or bacon grease. Cover the bottom of your black skillet with olive oil or bacon grease and get it hot, but not smoking. Pour in the batter.

Whatever you do, resist the temptation to turn the cornbread before it's ready. Peel up an edge and look under—is it crusty and brown? When it is, run your largest spatula under it and quick as a wink, turn it over. This will take practice. If it breaks, don't worry, keep going. Add a little more oil or bacon grease if the cornbread looks too dry. You want a crispy crust. When a small voice tells you it's ready, turn the skillet upside down over a platter.

Sprinkle with paprika, cut into wedges, and serve slathered with butter. Resist eating the whole thing yourself.

Tip: Don't add sugar or eggs—this is old-fashioned cornbread in which the meal and the milk are required to stand on their own two feet and do you proud.

—JAN KARON

"*Oddly, it is not real cooks who insist that the finest ingredients are necessary to produce a delicious something . . . Real cooks take stale bread and aging onions and make you happy.*"

—SUSAN WIEGAND, *COOKING AS COURTSHIP*

Mama's Cornbread Recipe

¼ cup	vegetable oil
1 cup	self-rising cornmeal, more for the skillet
1 cup	self-rising flour
1 cup	whole milk
1 large	egg

Preheat the oven to 400°F. Pour the oil into a black iron skillet and place the skillet in the oven to get hot.

In a large bowl, combine the cornmeal and flour. Add the milk and egg and mix well. Remove the hot skillet from the oven and pour the hot oil into the batter. Stir just until the oil is combined. Sprinkle a small amount of dry cornmeal into the bottom of the hot skillet, pour the batter in, and return the skillet to the oven. Bake until lightly browned on top, and immediately turn out onto a plate to cool.

> Great God, accept our gratitude
> For the great gifts on us bestowed—
> For raiment, shelter, and for food.
> Great God, our gratitude we bring,
> Accept our humble offering,
> For all the gifts on us bestowed,
> Thy name be evermore adored.

—Josephine Heard (1861–1921)

I Sing a Song of the Saints of God

I sing a song of the saints of God
Patient and brave and true,
Who toiled and fought and lived and died
For the Lord they loved and knew.
And one was a doctor, and one was a queen,
And one was a shepherdess on the green,
They were all of them saints of God—and I mean,
God help me to be one too.

They loved their Lord so dear, so dear,
And his love made them strong;
And they followed the right, for Jesus' sake,
The whole of their good lives long.
And one was a soldier, and one was a priest,
And one was slain by a fierce wild beast:
And there's not any reason—no, not the least—
Why I shouldn't be one too.

They live not only in ages past,
There are hundreds of thousands still,
The world is bright with joyous saints
Who love to do Jesus' will.
You can meet them in school, or in lanes, or at sea,
In church, or in trains, or in shops, or at tea,
For the saints of God are just folk like me,
And I mean to be one too.

—LESBIA SCOTT, 1929

❖ *Author's note: We stirred this into the pot simply because we love the words.*

More About Martha McIntosh

Gentle Reader,

I thought you'd like to know this Mississippi girl who appears to be completely fearless in the kitchen, so here's a bit of a chat to catch you up. If we are, indeed, what we eat, then Martha and Father Tim are not entirely unalike— though she is much cuter in an apron.

JAN: *How does being born in Mississippi influence your cooking?*

MARTHA: I was fortunate to grow up in a large, happy family in a small town in Mississippi named Mt. Olive. There were always extra people at our dinner table, in addition to my parents and four siblings, and there was always plenty of food to go around.

Summers were full of "putting up" vegetables for the winter as well as enjoying the fresh vegetables all summer long. I remember sitting in our yard, shucking fresh corn and shelling peas. I remember picking wild plums and mayhaws for jelly. My grandmother Wagner ("Gran Gran") would come to Mt. Olive and spend the whole week making batches of green tomato pickles, bread and butter pickles and chili sauce (tomato relish). *You could not walk through the kitchen without your shoes sticking to the floor during those marathon canning sessions.*

In the summer, my grandmother Blain ("Mamoo"), who lived down the street in Mt. Olive, would cook massive amounts of food for dinner (the noon meal we now call lunch) and invite seemingly everyone in town to come eat. She would serve varying combinations of fresh creamed corn, lima beans, green beans, turnip greens, fried chicken, rice and gravy, fried venison, squash, sliced fresh tomatoes, fried okra, okra and tomato stew, field peas, cornbread, peach cobbler, and very sweet iced tea. Mamoo and Papoo were happiest with their house full of family and friends enjoying their food. Years later, newly married and starving (as my husband finished law school), we would bring our ice chest home to "shop" in my parents' and grandparents' deep freeze.

My Uncle John still makes homemade molasses from cane grown on his farm. We were sad when he stopped using the mules to make it a few years ago, but it still tastes wonderful. To this day, my siblings and I fight for an extra can of the molasses. Nothing is better on a biscuit.

While my mother (who was born and raised in Memphis, Tennessee) was making pickles and blanching green beans, she was also cooking "gourmet food" for us. We had quiche made with Gruyère cheese before anyone had ever heard of quiche, much less Gruyère. Family favorites included French onion soup, seafood gumbo, Christmas English trifle, lasagna made with homemade pasta, and cheese soufflé. My mom introduced us to pâté and caviar. We grew up eating fresh herbs, asparagus, and baby lettuce grown in our yard. And while we were enjoying the "gourmet food," we loved my mom's fried quail dinner with biscuits and Uncle John's molasses.

Any party held in town announcing someone's engagement was usually given by a group of ladies at our house. My sisters and I would spend hours polishing huge silver trays, silver baskets, and biscuit boxes. We loved to help serve (much more than cleaning up). When my parents entertained with a dinner party, again my sisters and I loved to help. We also begged for the dessert to be anything flambé.

I was the child who wanted elaborate birthday parties. My mom would go out of her way to plan the most detailed party (even with five kids). My greatest memory was the birthday I requested a Croquembouche for a cake. My mom made tiny custard-filled cream puffs coated with caramel, then stacked them

Martha, and Mississippian Nancy Briggs, who introduced Martha and me. We were celebrating the end of the photo shoot with a glass of ginger ale (truly!).

into a tall pyramid and draped it with spun sugar.

JAN: What activities completely apart from cooking inspire you in the kitchen?

MARTHA: Reading Southern literature (especially Southern humor) is a favorite pastime. I love works by Harper Lee, Willie Morris, Eudora Welty, Charlotte Capers, Rick Bragg, Fannie Flagg, Olive Ann Burns, Clyde Edgerton, and, of course, my favorite, Jan Karon.

JAN: How would you describe your style of cooking?

MARTHA: As a combination of traditional Southern and what I would call "New Southern"—using typical indigenous Southern ingredients in a lighter, quicker, easier preparation.

JAN: What are some of your favorite recipes in the *Mitford Cookbook and Kitchen Reader?*

MARTHA: That's a hard question. I love Marge's Chicken Pot Pie, Company Stew, Puny's Cornbread, Louella's Fried Chicken, and Louella's Coconut Cake. My family could probably give you a completely different set of favorites!

JAN: If you were marooned on a desert island for a fortnight, what is the first dish you would ask for after being rescued?

MARTHA: Well, it's not a dish, but I would ask for sweet iced tea.

JAN: What would you request for your last meal on this mortal earth?

MARTHA: A shrimp po-boy from Pirates Cove, in Pass Christian, Mississippi, a Duck Sandwich from Bayona's Restaurant in New Orleans, Louisiana, chicken pot pie, my mother's simple green salad made with her garlic-lemon dressing, summer tomatoes with fresh basil, fresh creamed corn, Mac Mac's cranberry salad, biscuits with Uncle John's molasses, and Mama Fern's teacakes with a good strong cup of Community Coffee for dessert. Of course, sweet iced tea would be served with this meal.

JAN: Good heavens, what a way to go! Now, apart from nourishing us and keeping us alive, what do you think food is *about* anyway?

MARTHA: Food, especially in the South, is about so much more than nourishment. For any occasion, happy or sad, Southerners come together over food. For example, a new baby, a funeral, a surgery, or a new house can prompt an offering of food. When I don't know what to do for someone, I bake them a pie or make a loaf of bread. Food helps to comfort and helps to celebrate. As we make these offerings, we also offer ourselves.

Food *aromas* are also comforting. I try to have one of my son's favorite dishes cooking when he arrives home from school for the weekend.

Certain foods bring back memories and are an essential part of family traditions. We have the same Christmas Eve meal at our house every year, Crawfish Helen Mary, homemade bread, salad, and white chocolate bread pudding. I think my children would pitch a fit if I changed anything.

I've also found that in the microwave lifestyle we live today, young people really enjoy home-cooked meals. I love to cook for my children and their friends; they seem to truly appreciate it.

JAN: What makes you laugh?

MARTHA: My husband and his insane sense of humor.

Recipe Credits

APPLE JELLY WITH FRESH MINT Kevin Guice, Hattiesburg, Mississippi.

CHRISTMAS SMELL Vera Wagner, Memphis, Tennessee.

CYNTHIA'S BOUILLABAISSE, ROASTED RED PEPPER ROUILLE, and CRACKED PEPPER TOAST Adapted from recipes in *Cooks Illustrated* magazine.

CYNTHIA'S FRIED OKRA Adapted from a recipe by Susan Shuler, Central, South Carolina.

CYNTHIA'S LEG OF LAMB Kevin Guice, Hattiesburg, Mississippi.

CYNTHIA'S LEMON SQUARES Adapted from a recipe by Jill Dyer, Atlanta, Georgia.

CYNTHIA'S PUMPKIN PIE Adapted from a recipe in *The Foster's Market* by Sarah Foster.

CYNTHIA'S RASPBERRY TEA Adapted from a recipe served by the Episcopal women at Christ Church, Greenville, South Carolina.

CYNTHIA'S RISOTTO Adapted from a recipe in *Modern Classics Book I* by Donna Hay.

CYNTHIA'S ROASTED POTATOES WITH ROSEMARY Adapted from a recipe in *Come On In! Recipes from the Junior League of Jackson.*

CYNTHIA'S ROASTED RED PEPPER TOMATO SOUP Carl Briggs, Charlottesville, Virginia.

EDITH'S BEEF TENDERLOIN Kevin Guice, Hattiesburg, Mississippi.

EMMA'S COLE SLAW Vera Wagner, Memphis, Tennessee.

EMMA'S FUDGE Mrs. Ruby Allen, Jackson, Mississippi.

EMMA'S POUND CAKE Rosemary McIntosh, Jackson, Mississippi.

ESTHER'S ORANGE MARMALADE CAKE Adapted from a recipe by Scott Peacock.

FATHER TIM'S COMPANY STEW Brenda Furman, Jan's sister.

FATHER TIM'S MOTHER'S *BÛCHE DE NOËL* Adapted from recipes in *Perfect Cakes* by Nick Malgieri and *The Simple Art of Baking* by Flo Braker.

LEW BOYD'S CHOCOLATE CAKE "The Right Stuff," *Victoria* magazine.

THE LORD'S CHAPEL COMMUNION BREAD Father Francis Monastery of the Holy Spirit, Conyers, Georgia.

LOUELLA'S BREAD AND BUTTER PICKLES Beth Stevens, Mt. Olive, Mississippi.

LOUELLA'S BUTTERMILK BISCUITS and HOMEMADE BAKING POWDER "The Right Stuff," *Victoria* magazine.

LOUELLA'S COLE SLAW Adapted from a recipe from the Brookville Hotel, Brookville, Kansas.

MARION'S FIG PRESERVES Beth Stevens, Mt. Olive, Mississippi.

PEGGY NEWLAND'S SUMMER SQUASH CASSEROLE Jan's Aunt Wilma Argo, deceased, Kannapolis, North Carolina.

PUNY'S CHEESECAKE Susan Shuler, Central, South Carolina.

PUNY'S CRANBERRY SALAD Rosemary McIntosh, Jackson, Mississippi.

PUNY'S CURRIED SHRIMP Adapted from a recipe in *Southern Sideboards* by the Junior League of Jackson, Mississippi.

PUNY'S POTATO SALAD Brenda Furman, Jan's sister.

VELMA'S CHILI Joy Stevens, Jackson, Alabama.

VELMA'S DIPPING SAUCE Adapted from a recipe in *A Southern Palate* by Robert St. John.

Index

Jan Karon's
Mitford Cookbook
& Kitchen Reader

Jan Karon's
Mitford Cookbook
& Kitchen Reader

Jan Karon's
Mitford Cookbook
& Kitchen Reader

Jan Karon's
Mitford Cookbook
& Kitchen Reader

A very special doll made for me by my grandmother,
Miss Fannie, when I was quite grown. It is the best doll
I ever owned. Miss Fannie was precious to us;
we miss her each and every day.

FANNIE BELLE BUSH CLOER
1893–1993